THE PRIEST

Living Instrument and Minister of Christ, the Eternal Priest

BONAVENTURE KLOPPENBURG O.F.M.

THE PRIEST

Living Instrument and Minister of
Christ, the Eternal Priest

Translated by
Matthew J. O'Connell

FRANCISCAN HERALD PRESS
Chicago, Illinois 60609

The Priest: Living Instrument and Minister of Christ, the Eternal Priest, by Bonaventure Kloppenburg O.F.M., translated from the Portuguese by Matthew J. O'Connell. Copyright © 1974 by Franciscan Herald Press, 1434 West 51st Street, Chicago, Illinois 60609.

Library of Congress Cataloging in Publication Data:

Kloppenburg, Bonaventura, 1919-
  The priest: living instrument and minister of Christ.

  Translation of O ser do padre.
  1. Catholic Church—Clergy. 2. Pastoral theology—Catholic Church. I. Title.
BX1912.K54913   253'.2   73-23059
ISBN 0-8199-0495-3

MADE IN THE UNITED STATES OF AMERICA

Contents

Preface

These pages were written with priests' retreats in mind, and the thoughts they contain were expounded in various retreats conducted in Brazil, Argentina, Colombia, and Panama. As a matter of fact, I am not mainly a preacher of retreats but a professor of theology. Perhaps, therefore, what I write here will please neither the professional theologists nor the expert retreat-masters.

The main theme of the book is the theology of our ministerial priesthood, which is the object today of doubts and questioning. Justifiably or not, priests are in fact asking what they are, how they are to live, and what they are to do as priests of our day. At this juncture I make no pretence at teaching the parish priest his prayers. I seek only as a theologian to offer priests who are sincerely searching for their own identity some elements of that identity which I regard as "permanently valid," so that such precious pearls may not be overlooked in the current search for new forms of apostolic life.

I want my intention to be made quite clear from the very beginning. I think that in the ongoing intense work of revising the received tradition it is absolutely necessary to distinguish clearly between *being* and its *modalities*. Concretely, this means a clear distinction between the very essence of priesthood and the various possible ways of being a minister of the new covenant. These ways, or modalities, are of their nature variable and conditioned by the cultural contexts of each historical period. But the innermost being of the priest will always be the same and is to be determined by the will and decisions of the Lord and his Apostles.

In speaking of the *modalities,* the experts in pastoral matters, the sociologists, the psychologists, and the specialists in the other sciences of man all are competent; in teaching us about the *being* of the priest, the competent source is the teaching authority of the Church and the theologians. My own professional competence allows me, then, to speak more directly of the being, not the modalities, of priesthood.

It is quite true, of course, that the present "crisis among priests" is a matter primarily of such modalities or forms, but it also has repercussions in the area of the priest's very being and often calls this area into question. We speak a good deal today of the "image of the priest." Once again this image is concerned with modalities. But the widespread rejection of the traditional, inherited image of the priest leads some to reject the very essence of the priesthood as well. My concern is to save, not the inherited image, but the nature or essence of priesthood.

When the "being" or "essence" becomes concrete, it will always and inevitably develop its own "image." In the new world that is now coming into existence (desacralized and secular, exorcised and rational, demythologized and scientific, technological and objective, socialized and adult, pluralist and free, humanistic and democratic), the image of the priest will necessarily be different from the one which the past shaped for itself. In another book I have attempted to describe the characteristics of "the secularized Christian"[1];

---

[1] *O Cristao Secularizado: O Humanismo do Vaticano II* (Petrópolis: Vozes, 1971²).

the same traits will also mark "the secularized priest" or his new "image." This book, however, will not be dealing with these changeable aspects of priesthood. I am interested rather in searching out the perennial elements which constitute the essential being of the priest. For, in the turbulent waters of discussion and varied opinion, there is danger that we may lose sight of the essentials which, in fidelity to the will of the Lord, we must unqualifiedly endeavor to save, protect, and defend.

In this search for the essentials I have not turned to the psychologist or the sociologist. I have tried rather to interview, as it were, the Lord and his Apostles, as well as their successors who have spoken to us on this matter in Vatican Council II and the 1971 Synod of Bishops. In the retreats I have conducted I have tried to have the retreatants do the same: to have them, in the presence of the Lord, in prayer, meditation, and study of the Scriptures, the teachings of Vatican II, and the document of the Synod of Bishops, make the effort to grasp their own identity as living, finely tuned instruments of Christ the Priest, Prophet, and Shepherd. Once they have rediscovered the true identity of the priestly minister of the new covenant, they will experience optimism, joy, and, above all, great faith in the word of God, the immanence of the Creator, the action of the Holy Spirit, the nature of the Church as mystery, as well as in the natural values proper to man and in the positive aspects of the on-going process of secularization. Then they will inevitably see their new self-image as light of the world, salt of the earth, and leaven of mankind as it undergoes its crisis of growth.

Petrópolis, Brazil   Bonaventure Kloppenburg O.F.M.
Holy Thursday, 1972

Abbreviations

Abbott: *The Documents of Vatican II,* edited by Walter M. Abbott, S.J. (New York: Guild Press, America Press, Association Press, 1966).

The sixteen documents:

AA: *Apostolicam Actuositatem:* Decree on the Apostolate of the Laity.

AG: *Ad Gentes:* Decree on the Church's Missionary Activity.

CD: *Christus Dominus:* Decree on the Bishops' Pastoral Office in the Church.

DV: *Dei Verbum:* Dogmatic Constitution on Divine Revelation.

DH: *Dignitatis Humanae:* Declaration on Religious Freedom.

GE: *Gravissimam Educationis:* Declaration on Christian Education.

GS: *Gaudium et Spes:* Pastoral Constitution on the Church in the Modern World.

IM: *Inter Mirifica:* Decree on the Instruments of Social Communication.

LG: *Lumen Gentium:* Dogmatic Constitution on the Church.

NA: *Nostra Aetate:* Declaration on the Relationship of the Church to the Non-Christian Religions.

OE: *Orientalium Ecclesiarum:* Decree on the Eastern Catholic Churches.

OT: *Optatam Totius:* Decree on Priestly Formation.

PC: *Perfectae Caritatis:* Decree on the Appropriate Renewal of Religious Life.

PO: *Presbyterorum Ordinis:* Decree on the Ministry and Life of Priests.

SC: *Sacrosanctum Concilium:* Constitution on the Sacred Liturgy.

UR: *Unitatis Redintegratio:* Decree on Ecumenism.

TPS: *The Pope Speaks.* Washington, D.C., 1954–.

REB: *Revista Ecclesiastica Brasileira.*

Scripture is quoted from the *New American Bible,* except where otherwise indicated.

I

The Crisis in
the Priesthood

We are living in a period of crisis, crisis which Vatican
Council II with reason calls a "crisis of growth" (GS,
4c/202). With it we are entering a new era of human
history. The Council goes on to describe the crisis in a
realistic way: "Profound and rapid changes are spreading
by degrees around the whole world. Triggered by the intelligence and creative energies of man, these changes recoil upon him, upon his decisions and desires, both individual and
collective, and upon his manner of thinking and acting with
respect to things and to people. Hence we can already speak
of a true social and cultural transformation, one which has
repercussions on man's religious life as well" (GS, 4b/202).
Psychological research has made man more uncertain of
himself, more insecure; the discovery of the laws governing
the life of society has made him unsure of the direction he
ought to take. The very words he uses to define very basic

concepts may facilitate the communication of ideas, but the words also frequently acquire quite different meanings according to the varying ideologies which provide the context for their use.

In this highly complex situation many people find it increasingly difficult to decide what values are permanent and then to integrate them in a satisfactory way with the new discoveries. The scientific mind is producing a cultural system and ways of thinking which differ very much from those of earlier times. Traditional communities are daily undergoing quite radical transformations in their way of life; social conditions and outlooks on society which have centuries of experience behind them are being changed overnight. Better and more effective means of social communication are contributing to the rapid spread of new ways of thinking and acting, while the variety of human relationships is constantly increasing and new kinds of interdependence are arising. Such changes of mentality and structures inevitably raise doubts about traditional values. The institutions, laws, and ways of thinking and acting which men have inherited from the past are not readily adaptable to the new state of affairs, and this gives rise to serious disturbances in behavior and indeed in the very norms for human conduct.

Religious life cannot but be deeply influenced by this situation. The more reflective critical mind casts off any magical view of the world as well as the superstitions so widespread in popular piety, and seeks a more personal faith that will effectively shape man's life. At the same time growing masses of people are, in practice, moving away from religion. The denial of God or religion is no longer a rare and isolated event, as it was in the past; instead the denial is often seen as required by scientific progress or a new kind of humanism. In many regions the rejection of God and religion does not find expression only in philosophical circles; it also exercises a strong influence on literature, art, the interpretation of the human sciences and history, and even civil legislation. Such a situation both causes and explains the disturbance of many minds. The accelerated change, often taking a disordered form, and the growing awareness of the antinomies which fill man's world, cause or aggravate conflicts and imbalances. One of the conflicts that often arises at this juncture is the conflict between the practically oriented intelligence of contemporary man and the kind of theological knowledge which does not succeed in dominating the sum total of a man's knowledge and synthesizing it in a satisfactory way. There also arises an imbalance between practical effectiveness and the requirements of the moral conscience, as well as an imbalance between the conditions needed for community life and the exigencies of personal thought and of that contemplative wonder which alone can lead to wisdom.

It is thus that Vatican II sees the ongoing process of secularization and its repercussions on man in his behavior and his relationship to God (cf. GS, 7-8/205-6).

It is among men thus caught up in the crisis of growth that the Church realizes it must take its place, in order to be present among them as the leaven in the dough. And since "the joys and the hopes, the griefs and the anxieties of the men of this age" must be "the joys and hopes, the griefs and anxieties of the followers of Christ" (GS, 1/199-200), and since the Christian community knows itself to be inextricably bound up with mankind and its history, the Church too finds itself in the same crisis of growth. In the Apostolic Constitution *Humanae salutis* (December 25, 1961), by which Pope John XXIII convoked the Council, he said: "Today the Church is witnessing a crisis under way in society. While humanity is on the edge of a new era, tasks of immense gravity and amplitude await the Church, as in the most tragic periods of its history. It is a question in fact of bringing the modern world into contact with the vivifying and perennial energies of the gospel, a world which exalts itself with its conquests in the technical and scientific fields, but which brings also the consequences of a temporal order which some have wished to reorganize excluding God. This is why modern society is earmarked by a great material progress to which there is not a corresponding advance in the moral field" (Abbott, 703).

The crisis in society gives rise to the crisis in the Church. The reason is not that Christian life is languishing in the Church. The reason is that the Church is not prepared to meet the new needs of secularized man.

Here we have the source of the crisis in the clergy.

It would be naive and unjust to say that the whole problem began with Vatican II, or that only since the Council have we begun to see and be preoccupied with the problems of contemporary man and his world. Vatican II simply harvested a crop that had ripened before the Council. It is true, however, that the Council made official or gave authority to many preoccupations, positions, and solutions.

The Council also gave an excellent description of the deepest cause of the crisis among the clergy, when it wrote in the Decree on the Ministry and Life of Priests: "While contemplating the joys of priestly life, this most holy Synod cannot overlook the difficulties which priests experience in the circumstances of contemporary life. For it realizes how deeply economic and social conditions and even the customs of men are being transformed, and how profoundly scales of value are being changed in the estimation of man. As a result, the ministers of the Church and even, at times, the faithful themselves feel like strangers in this world, anxiously looking for appropriate ways and words with which to communicate with it. For, the modern obstacles blocking faith, the seeming sterility of their past labors, and also the bitter loneliness they experience can lead to the danger of becoming depressed in spirit" (PO, 22a-b/574-75).

Since the Council, however, the crisis in the clergy has taken on unexpected and varied forms. The symptoms of the crisis must, consequently, now be regarded as disquieting and even very serious. The main symptoms are these:

1. *The Abandonment of the Ministry.* Since 1964 about twenty thousand priests have left the ministry. During this period the requests for reduction to the lay state have increased by an average of twenty-five percent annually:

in 1964:   640 requests;
in 1965;   1,128;
in 1966:   1,418;
in 1967:   1,769;
in 1968:   2,263;
in 1969:   2,963;
in 1970:   3,800.

In Brazil alone,[1] from 1960 to 1968, 620 priests were laicized (4.6% of all the clergy) : 409 diocesan priests (6.9% of the diocesan clergy) and 211 religious priests (2.6% of the religious clergy). There are no available statistics on those who simply left without seeking authorization.

Those who leave the ministry are often the intellectual elite of the clergy; the Church is losing its "intelligentsia."

In Italy, a pilot study among former priests suggested the following hypotheses to the sociologist who conducted it:[2]

(1) The crisis in those who later left the priesthood began in a progressive weakening at the spiritual level; this led in turn to a lessening in the intensity with which they believed in and lived their specifically priestly mission. The statistics show that the abandonment of the priesthood resulted especially from two defects of a spiritual kind: the neglect of prayer (95%) and the lack of interior peace due to the spiritual and moral ambiguity which had marked the individual's life (89%). Former priests do not hesitate to admit that their decision followed logically from a state of affairs which had lasted for some time and in which they had made inadequate use of the usual means of acquiring spiritual strength. Having become interiorly empty, they saw themselves becoming bureaucrats and "functionaries";

this in turn killed their enthusiasm and zeal. The void created by an inoperative faith was filled by substitutes of various kinds: for example, affection for a woman, or drink. We are therefore confronted here with a failure to live a priestly existence with its specific calling and mission, and not with a lack of vocation.

(2) They had gradually abandoned the perennial priestly roles (ministerial and prophetic) for secondary ones (social control, administration) and had, in consequence, become immersed in an agitated activism which undermined the spiritual energies that sustain a properly priestly life. The majority of these priests were, at the moment when they left the priesthood, suffering from a neurosis. But the neurosis did not spring solely from the frustrations they felt as they lived exteriorly in the Church while being interiorly outside it. The neurosis was caused primarily by the activism into which they had immersed themselves as though trying to avoid facing their real situation. At the last, it required only some accidental happening (some scandal, etc.) to cause a confrontation and the abandonment of the priesthood.

(3) We do not find in these priests any resentment against the Church or the progressive separation from the Church which many feared. In point of fact, the priest's training is such that the fundamentals (faith, charity, etc.) remain quite strong. It may even be said that the former priest, because he is interiorly at peace, now has a better grasp of these essentials. For this very reason, the priest may be "a fish out of water," inasmuch as he lives as a layman and father of a family while retaining the instinctive outlook of a priest. From this come the contradictions he manifests, the longing, the uncertainties, the lack of interior peace. The former priest is torn between a world in which he had been very much at home and had lived a great part of his life, and a world which he does not know intimately, which is becoming insecure, and which—who knows?—he may even

find that he dislikes. Then, we find, the majority of those who leave the priesthood end up only partly, or in certain respects, satisfied with the step they had taken; the dissatisfaction increases as the years pass.

(4) If and to the extent that we can trust the data provided by the sampling, it is clear that former priests can abstract from their own experience and objectively evaluate ecclesiastical actions, judgments, and juridical norms. These men are the first to maintain that the Church should not be indulgent and allow the abandonment of ministry to be made easy. Likewise, few former priests consider it possible to unite an authentic priesthood with an authentic natural fatherhood. In the light of their experience, it is very difficult to be a married priest; for many, it is unnatural. Not a few show themselves entirely opposed to the abolition of celibacy.

(5) In general, the abandonment of the Church and the priesthood does not have happy results; on the contrary, it has perhaps even increased the former priest's already dramatic condition of uncertainty and insecurity. His experience is but a further confirmation of the fact that one cannot be a priest in an offhand way, any more than one can improvise being the father of a family or a good married man. A man trained for the celibate priesthood cannot easily move into lay life, simply by willing to do so; he is likely to fall into indifferentism or some even worse state. In general, therefore, the former priest does not have the knowledge required for the prudent choice of a companion in life, as the answers given on this point show clearly.

(6) The opinions garnered in the study confirm the Church's prudence and, even if involuntarily, amply justify her strictness in this matter. Perhaps nowhere more than when it speaks of lived celibacy as an act of love does the Church come closer to the innermost nature of pastoral ministry. The former priests who were interviewed were quite explicit on this point.

(7) Almost all of them want to be at the disposition of the Church so that the enormous and precious sum-total of anxieties, prayers, faith, and works, which they represent, may not be dispersed and lost. In numerous individuals all these elements are united into a potent whole and can be relied upon with confidence.

(8) Selection, formation, interior union with God, a prophetic role, and greater love of the hierarchy and one's brothers seem to be the elements that are essential if the temptations of solitude and idleness are not to creep into the priest's life.

The sociologist divides former priests into the following categories:

(a) Those who had no vocation. These form a small minority (perhaps 4%–5%); when they left the priesthood they disappeared, fading into anonymity, having no longer any desire to play a role which was not theirs. In their new way of life these men may perhaps find serenity and security.

(b) Those filled with longing. They were, and still are, in their hearts true priests and now suffer the consequences of their choice. If possible, they would return to the ranks. They would perhaps be prodigal sons who would not cause their good Father any further sorrow.

(c) The unsure, neurotic people who squander their energies, and who were discontented in the past and continue to be discontented. They did not know what they wanted, and still do not know what they want. They are unstable by nature and temperament. When faced with the seriousness of life they become intensely aware of their deficiencies. They are too human to be good priests; in this sense, many priests would be happy men of the world and at peace with themselves.

(d) The well-balanced individuals (perhaps 4%–5%), who could suitably be restored to particular forms of apostolate. They would be all the stronger for the agonies they had experienced and the difficulties they had overcome.

In general, when allowance is made for any facile enthusiasm and any hasty conclusions, the pilot study shows that
there continues to be a puzzling problem which is basic and
unresolved. The longings and ideals, the poorly made
choices and mistaken attitudes seem to suggest one conclusion: these men are still insecure, lack peace, and are attached to their old ideals. Have they made an illusory choice?

2. *The Phenomenon of Marginalization.* A growing number of groups, along with their priests, are moving steadily
to the periphery of the Church. The category of the "third
man" is broadening; he is the man who is indifferent to
the ecclesiastical institution, being neither a conservative
("first man") nor a progressive ("second man"), but simply
uninteresetd in any institutional "church," be it Catholic or
Protestant. Also increasing is the number of "underground
churches," "spontaneous or informal groups," "free communities," "prophetic movements," or "involved people."
These groupings are more or less spontaneous, more or less
directed, without any laws or rubrics, relying on their own
imagination and creativity, trusting solely in "charism,"
and independent of any authority or authorization. They
insist that they "are staying in the Church" and that they
want to "revise the faith," rethink and remake the Church
"from the bottom up," "disalienate the Church," strip it of
"power," "destructuralize the ecclesiastical organization,"
and join in "political involvement." There are similar
movements among priests ("protest" movements or, in the
current word, "solidarity" groups), all of which have come
into existence since 1968.[3] Some examples of these, from
various countries listed alphabetically:

Argentina: "Movement of Priests for the Third World,"
with about 400 priests.

Austria: The SOG organization, with 450 members; the
"Solidarity Group."

Belgium: The "Renewal Group," with 250 priests; the
"Presence and Witness" group; the "Conscience" group.

Canada: The "Western Priests Conference," with 370 members.

Chile: The "Young Church" movement.

Colombia: The "Golconda" group.

France: The "Exchange and Dialogue" group, whose express purpose is to "declericalize" the Church ("to kill the clergy") and which has about 850 members; the "Concerted Action" group; the "Lyons Group"; the "John XXIII Group."

Germany: The Munich group called "The Action Circle," with some 120 members; the "Frenckenhorst Circle"; the "Union of Priest Groups."

Holland: "Septuagint," with about 700 members.

Italy: The "Federation of United Priests' Associations."

United States: The "Society of Priests for a Free Ministry."

3. *The Split between Bishops and Priests.* This is believed to be the key point in the crisis of the clergy. It is a symptom which very clearly points to the deeper cause of malaise among priests. What we see, in effect, is a far-reaching split between bishops and priests. There seems to be no genuine communion embracing the whole clerical world. The bishops are certainly concerned to maintain communion with their fellow-bishops and with the pope (though in this latter instance communion often changes into servile submission or subservience). But we do not see the same concern for communion with the priests and with the faithful or the "Church" in the full and proper sense (which is the original point of "thinking with the Church"). There is a gulf between bishops and priests. On many points the thinking of the majority of priests coincides with that of only a small minority of bishops; and vice versa. "We find that those in authority are far removed from reality; they do not try to get into contact with it or even, at the very least, to engage in respectful brotherly dialogue with their priests."[4] Endless testimonies to the same effect can be easily had. Between priests and bishops there is mistrust,

distance, and monologue. In many cases contacts are rare, and, when they do occur, they are superficial, juridical, and limited to matters of business. The relationship is cold and formal, like that of diplomats. According to the statement drawn up by priests of the northeastern region of Brazil, "priests see in the bishop much more the person in authority, the man of the episcopal palace, and the executor of decisions promulgated by the Holy See, than they do the shepherd, the man of evangelical mission who assumes pastoral responsibility, along with his clergy, to meet the needs of God's People" (p. 35). As a result, the relationship of the bishop with the lower parts of the pyramid (priests, laity) becomes very difficult, even in cases where the bishop may personally be likable and where personal relationships with him may be regarded as satisfactory. In general, the bishop is the last one to find out about a priest's situation.

The priests who were studied by CERIS (Center for Religious Statistics and Social Research) and described by José Merins direct their primary criticism at the conservatism of the bishops.[5] For many of our priests the bishops "are alienated, not abreast of progress; they are not leaders, but hinder progress, and indeed are unable, due to their inadequate formation, to confront the problems of Brazil; they are old men or, simply, over-conservative." The priests also criticize the lack of unity in pastoral orientation, which arises because the bishops "do not take counsel together, thus causing perplexity among priests who look to them for some sure guidance." The criticism becomes bitter: "They are authoritarian, mere figureheads, inhuman, bent upon power, uninterested in evangelization, proud." They see the bishops as excessively preoccupied with the existing institutional Church which they head. "They are incapable of being shepherds in a pluralist world, for they were trained to be the administrative cadre of a Christendom."

One testimony is quite radical, but it forces us to reflect: "The bishops have almost always been the 'princes of the

Church' and become real persecutors of priests. They did
not come to know their priests' problems. Not infrequently
priests felt repelled by the very ordination which was to
influence their whole lives. Today bishops are a bit more
fatherly, but they continue to be very self-centered when it
comes to security. . . . I ran from the bishop, because he
has too many vested interests. Our bishops taught us to be
thieves and liars. They are not the 'servants' of the Church
but its overlords. The spirituality of the bishops centers
on chastity. A priest may be a thief, a slick operator, and
anti-social, but if he retains the outward appearance of
celibacy, everything is fine. And the bishop's purple hides
defects more serious than those of many priests."

A recent study in Spain provides evidence of a similar
situation: 53% of the priests said that their relations with
the bishop are negative or simply passive and cold; 61%
(73% among the young) said that in pastoral or disciplinary
decisions which directly affect them they are consulted
only infrequently or not at all; 76% (85% among the
young) will have little or nothing to do with authority as
exercised by the hierarchy. A similar study among priests
in the United States (a study financed by a grant from the
bishops, costing $500,000 and lasting two years) showed
identical results. In February, 1972, the well-known sociologist, Father Andrew Greeley, who directed the study, revealed that the priests were in profound disagreement with
the bishops on matters of ecclesiastical discipline, liturgy,
and moral teaching. Greeley stated emphatically that he
believed the present leadership of the Church to be morally,
intellectually, and religiously bankrupt.[6]

This whole situation, moreover, has an extremely serious
result: *a notable part of the younger clergy (who are the
future of the Church!) is moving more and more to the
periphery of the existing organization;* at best they maintain
the latter as a lesser evil or accept it with little enthusiasm
and little concern that it should function better. Of the

Spanish priests 26% said they no longer think of themselves as identified with the Church as a visible institution. Among the young as high as 49% think this way; in other words half of the young reject the ecclesiastical institution! The CERIS study reveals a similar situation in Brazil: 45% of the priests regard the institutional Church as one of the Church's major problems in Brazil; 25% judge the institutional Church to be one of the chief obstacles to the exercise of their ministry.

4. *The Decrease in Vocations.* This phenomenon is universal. On the occasion of the Fourth International Congress on Priestly Vocations, Rome, May 10-14, 1971 (sponsored by the Congregation for Catholic Education) , some statistics were presented on the present situation with regard to priestly vocations throughout the world.[7] The statistics were based on inquiries conducted in 1,297 dioceses around the world. Some results:

Minor seminarians: 111,303 in 1964; 83,360 in 1970; thus, some 32,000 fewer in six years.

Theological students: in 1970, as compared with 1964, 7,287 fewer; moreover the rate of decrease progressed notably.

New ordinations: the decline began to manifest itself in 1967 and continued thenceforth at a progressive rate:

1966-67: 416 fewer newly ordained priests than in 1965-66;
1967-68: 205 fewer newly ordained priests than in 1966-67;
1968-69: 255 fewer newly ordained priests than in 1967-68;
1969-70: 584 fewer newly ordained priests than in 1968-69;

Diocesan clergy: began to decrease from 1967:

year	newly ordained	deceased	newly ordained in relation to deceased
1964-65	5,477	4,242	+1,235;
1968-69	4,647	4,344	+ 303;
1969-70	4,063	4,352	− 289.

The decrease seen here continued in the following years

because of the decline in the number of theological students and of newly ordained priests (to say nothing of those who left the ministry).

In the report presented to the Congress we find also the following points: (a) an open refusal by many young men to *enter* the traditional institutions of ecclesiastical formation; (b) a growing tendency to *leave* such institutions after a period of stay in them; (c) a widespread uncertainty which leads young men to *stop* before major orders, even when they have finished their studies; in such cases, not a few young men either leave spontaneously or ask for a period of interruption which often ends with a voluntary departure.

The report then goes into the *causes of the decrease in vocations:* the decline of the religious spirit, in terms both of faith and of life; and the very crisis in the Church (for, the tensions in the Church, the theological controversies, the practice of subjecting everything to discussion, render it more difficult to reach a decision of a vocation). Due to the critical state of the Church parents do not encourage their sons to enter the priesthood or religious life. The image now given by ecclesiastical institutions as they struggle with the crisis of adaptation does not come through to the young as an image of ideal institutions. The various internal tensions of the Church make the young insecure concerning her and give us a "desacralized" image of her which puts greater emphasis on the layman than on the priest. A feeling of malaise concerning the Church-as-institution and ecclesiastical authority is widespread among the young, who are increasingly unwilling to accept any kind of dogmatism and Churchly authority. Such a state of mind means, of course, that relations are broken off between the young and those in authority in the Church. Also widespread among the young is a distrust of ecclesiastical structures. They will have nothing to do with stereotyped religious forms, since, to their minds, the Church-as-institution is committed to defending the religious and political status quo and to

attempting to suppress the values of contemporary civilization. Many of the young reject the outward manifestations
associated with the institutional Church and the way in
which the latter exercises authority. Many are disillusioned
by the way the authorities have dragged their feet in putting
into practice the decisions of Vatican II. Many are afraid
of becoming subject to the hierarchy and being deprived of
their own initiative, even in the area of the apostolate. All
in all, mistrust of the Church-institution is growing. Today's young people are no longer ready to submit without
question to the established authorities; they want a "trust-
worthy" authority.

The report insists that "it is impossible to separate the
present crisis in vocations from the movements which agitate
the clergy." The image of the priest is becoming so uncertain
and problematical that the young are hesistant and even repelled. In the minds of the young, the problem of priestly
ministry is connected with a deeper problem which touches
on the very nature of the Church. The young are influenced by mistaken concepts of the specific function of the
priest, as well as by the sometimes violent confrontations
within the clergy themselves; at the same time they are
aware that priestly ministry has not been adapted to the
needs of present-day man. A majority of seminarians, even
of those who decide to receive ordination, reject the priestly
ministry in its contemporary institutional form and as it
is actually carried out by the priests they see around them.
Simultaneously, the crisis in priesthood (doctrinal uncertainty on priesthood, lack of confidence in present pastoral
structures, etc.) draws young men away from the priesthood
and paralyzes efforts on behalf of vocations. Many consider
it a duty in conscience not to direct young men towards the
priesthood, inasmuch as they think the problems concerning
the priesthood are without a solution. Many young men
fear that if they become priests they will find themselves on
the periphery of society and removed from the ordinary lives

of other people. Some priests feel that they are being strangled by the structures within which they must work, and are pessimistic about the results of their efforts; young men reflect on this malaise which the clergy manifests, and ask why many priests question the priesthood itself and the meaning of their lives. There are priests who feel unable to overcome the difficulties connected with the present state of the Church: some suffer at the failure of their apostolate, others give up interiorly or exteriorly, and all of them have a negative impact on such young men as think of becoming priests.

Many priests are unhappy and feel frustrated by a lack of brotherly friendship among themselves, by economic insecurity, by isolation. Despite the efforts of bishops to draw closer to their clergy, the latter continue at times to feel that the bishops are out of contact with their personal, human problems. The young, for their part, cannot regard the simple administration of the sacraments as an ideal for their lives, and the greatest influence in favor of vocations is exercised by priests in the various apostolic movements. On the other hand, increasingly serious social problems are diverting the priest's activity into social fields; but in such a situation the young see no reason why they should become priests at all. In the minds of many of the young, the social aspect of a vocation becomes primary; they are therefore led to conclude that there is no need of becoming a priest, since a layman can do what the priest is doing. Moreover, many young men believe that they can exercise a more effective apostolate as laymen, for they want to act as responsible men. Many professional activities in the areas of social help, teaching, etc., were at one time activities proper to priests, but today laymen are assuming these responsibilities. The young people of today thus have many opportunities of sharing in the Church's mission without assuming a specifically priestly way of life. They are discovering that many apostolic activities and even the call to holiness are not the exclusive prerogative of the priest and the religious, but are possibilities open to the layman and do not require the renunciations proper to the priesthood and religious life.

The fact that many priests are leaving the ecclesiastical state also impresses the young. They are forced to ask themselves whether they are capable of meeting the requirements of celibacy, when priests of their acquaintance were not. Hesitation or even fear of committing themselves to the priesthood is thus aggravated by the fact that many other young men are leaving the seminary and many priests abandoning the ministry. Older people, too, are deeply disturbed by defections from the clergy. The young are afraid of committing themselves for life, as celibacy and the permanence of priesthood require. The numerous crises through which the clergy is moving are turning the priest into an unstable figure, and the young have no desire to enter upon a state of life in which those already committed to it are meeting with such serious problems and severe crises that they reach the point of abandoning what they had once chosen.

The report presented at Rome makes all these points on the basis of inquiries made among young men and seminarians throughout the world. We are now caught in a chain-reaction: the present crisis affecting the world at large is causing a crisis in the institutions of the Church; the crisis in the Church is causing a crisis in the image of the priest; the crisis in the priesthood is causing a crisis in the formation of seminarians; the crisis among seminarians is causing a crisis in priestly vocations.

If we are to bring healing to this situation we must investigate the relations between the Church as institution (the "institutional Church" is a phrase that is often repeated in the Roman report) and the contemporary world as it passes through its crisis of growth. For, the "Church" which is in crisis is not the Church as such or as founded by Christ, but the Church as a particular institutionalized way of being and acting. It is not priestly ministry as such that is in crisis but the "image of the priest" or the way in which the ministry is being concretely exercised at the present critical moment in mankind's history. Despite all the present distaste for scholastic distinctions, we must accept this Aristotelian distinction between being and its modalities, if we are not, in rejecting certain modalities, to eliminate the being as well. More concretely: the rejection of the contemporary image of the priest must not lead us to reject the Christian priestly ministry as such. The rejection of certain ecclesiastical institutions must not lead us to reject the Church as such, even as a social, visible institution.[8]

It was in this atmosphere of crisis that the Synod of Bishops met in 1971 in order to provide help in solving the current difficulties of priests.[9] In the final document, entitled *The Ministerial Priesthood,* the bishops give a fairly realistic description of the situation (in numbers 6-20).[10] It can be summarized as follows:

1. There are priests who feel themselves to be strangers in our contemporary world and unable to provide an answer for its problems; therefore they feel deeply frustrated and useless (7).

2. Some pastoral methods are outmoded in the present situation; this causes disquiet and a spirit of rebellion and gives rise to many questions to which no answer has thus far been given (7).

3. The process of secularization seems to require a more direct involvement in secular activities in order to sanctify them and animate them with the spirit of the Gospel. This leads priests to enter more directly into secular society in order to cooperate in the building of a more just and fraternal social order; it also leads them to enter into political life (8).

4. The present widespread religious crisis raises doubts about the meaning and value of a sacramental and cultic

ministry. These doubts in turn lead to evangelizing activity that is unenthusiastic and inattentive to sacramental practice (9).

5. The great emphasis put today on the dignity of the person makes us aware of the serious inadequacy of not a few ecclesiastical institutions which seem insufficiently appreciative of this dignity. This awareness gives rise to a lively desire to effect a radical change in the style of interpersonal relations within the Church and in the structures of authority (10).

6. The new structure of human society with its numerous specialized groupings requires greater diversification in our ministries as well as varied competences or aptitudes and varied forms of the apostolate. This requirement in turn makes relations between priests and bishops daily more difficult and raises serious problems in regard to brotherhood, cohesion, and unity in priestly ministry (11).

7. The traditional and fruitful doctrine of the common priesthood of all believers, which Vatican II has emphatically reaffirmed, seems to cast a cloud over the sacerdotal ministry of the priest. This circumstance gives rise to anxious questions about the specific reason and necessity for a presbyteral ministry and about its theological nature (12).

8. New researches in exegesis and history have brought many new problems to light. These have undermined confidence in the Church, its teaching authority, and its ability to preach the ancient Gospel in a way that is acceptable to the men of our day (13).

9. Modern culture, with its focus on science and technology is hesitant and perplexed about its own meaning and value. Many therefore, especially among the young, despair of finding any meaning in such a one-dimensional world. Some of them, therefore, take refuge in purely meditative systems and in artificial marginal paradises, while abandoning the common strivings of mankind. Others claim that without any reference to God they can reach a state of

total liberaion, and seek meaning no longer in their present personal life but in a utopian future (14-16).

Yet in this same situation of perplexed anxiety which is that of contemporary man, the Synod sees a new way for the Church to continue its mission in the present-day world; not only is its mission not obsolete, it is "of the highest relevance" (18). The bishops therefore urge all the faithful "to strive to contemplate the Lord Jesus living in his Church and to realize that he wishes to work in a special way through his ministers; they will thus be convinced that the Christian community cannot fulfill its complete mission without the ministerial priesthood" (19). The document then breaks down into two parts. In the first, the Synod Fathers intend "to set forth briefly some principles of the Church's teaching on the ministerial priesthood which are at present more urgent," and in the second to provide "some guidelines for pastoral practice" (20).

In the remaining chapters of this book we shall adopt the outline of the synodal document, starting with its doctrinal principles which we shall ground in the Scriptures and in the teaching of Vatican II, especially in the latter's Decree on the Ministry and Life of Priests (=PO).

I shall omit only a study of the section entitled "Mission: Evangelization and sacramental life" (48-61), because I have not succeeded in grasping it fully and because it seems to me rather confusing. I recognize however that what is said is nonetheless highly important in the present pastoral situation. In no. 9 the synodal document notes that contemporary thought on religion questions the value and meaning of a sacramental and cultic ministry and that therefore many priests, even those not passing through any crisis of personal identity, are asking serious questions about the methods that must be used if sacramental practice is to be the genuine expression of a faith which lays hold of the whole personal and social life of the baptized person and if Christian worship is not to be reduced, against its real nature, to pure ritualism. Such questions are frequently heard in Brazil. "Priests ask themselves whether they should go on celebrating Mass for a few hundred of the faithful who do not even know each other, baptizing children whose families they know are not practicing their religion, celebrating marriages which in practice are simply social commitments without religious content, hearing confessions without being able to provide any moral and spiritual direction, etc. In short, the activities around which the life of the parish priest is centered are being criticized today by priests themselves faced with the dilemma of either ceasing to provide the sacraments for a large number of the faithful (and thereby leaving unanswered the latter's request for those sacramental acts which society regards as necessary) or of continuing these activities while often being unconvinced of their validity."[11] The sociologist here quoted goes on to observe that in order to avoid this (possibly false) dilemma many priests try to exercise some activity regarded as professional which will occupy the time usually given to parish activities; such priests thus give themselves to the latter activities only on week-ends or for a few hours each day. Or else they look for other means of economic support, move out of parish activities, and devote themselves to some form of pastoral activity which they consider more valid, for example, evangelization and human progress, the formation of base communities, helping lay movements, etc. "But this is an individualist solution for a collective problem, inasmuch as the majority of the faithful continue to ask the priest for the same services; this solution, consequently, puts an excessive burden on those priests who continue to perform parish activities and thus proves itself a temporary solution for a few which only aggravates the problem for the group as a whole."[12]

The Synod attempts to provide an answer to this problem in the section on "Mission: Evangelization and sacramental life." No. 48 is a general introduction (but does not set up

the problem very well) ; nos. 49-53 stress the unity of evangelization and sacramental practice; nos. 54-57 provide norms
for evangelization; nos. 58-60 provide norms for sacramental
practice. In no. 60 the Synod entrusts bishops or episcopal
conferences with the task of finding ways of administering
the sacraments which are better suited to each region, and
of determining criteria for admission to the sacraments.
Faced with the current tendency to play down the administration of the sacraments, the Synod stresses "the mutual relationship between evangelization and the celebration of
the sacraments . . . in the mission of the Church" (52) and
declares that "through them [the sacraments] the word [of
God] is brought to fuller effect" (50) .

In this context the Synod also refers to the problem of
the *diversification of ministries,* which is one of the main
themes in the current theological and pastoral debate on
priestly ministry. But the Synod offers no principle or norm
for the resolution of the problem. It does, however, recognize the need for such a criterion. In no. 49 it says that
"the exercise of the priestly ministry" often needs to take
different forms; in no. 61 there is a vague allusion to "the
multiple exercise of ministries lower than the priesthood."
In point of fact, we find currently among the clergy a widespread objection to the single kind of priest who is the
result of a specific historico-cultural process. Vatican II has
already spoken of "different duties" within "one priestly
ministry on behalf of men" (PO, 8a/549) and given, as
examples, parochial or supraparochial ministry, scientific research, teaching, or manual labor shared with workers. The
work of building up Christ's Body, says the Council, is "a
work requiring manifold roles and new adjustments" (PO,
8b/550) . But the Council took no steps to implement this
insight. Nor did the Synod of Bishops, and the question
remains unanswered. In September, 1971, the general assembly of bishops and priests in Spain approved a pluralism
of forms and life-styles in the ministry, and gave the follow-

ing reasons: the impossibility of embodying in a single individual the wealth of the Church's ministry; the diversity of charisms and the freedom of the children of God which is not to be restricted without good reason; the need to seek out ways of preaching the Gospel that are more faithful to the requiremens of the Gospel itself and, at the same time, adapted to the varied conditions and needs of the human beings who are to receive it; the variety of communities and social circumstances. Such a pluralism is, then, required by the pluralist society in which we live, by the Christian community, by the priestly mission, and by the nature of the Church as a reality in space and time. There will thus be a pluralism in forms of the priesthood when the latter is considered in various ways: in terms of the fields of priestly activity (countryside, city, workmen, technologists, students, the sick, emigrants, etc.); in terms of ecclesial functions (pastors of base communities, missionaries, theologians, specialists in catechetics, liturgy, pastoral care, doctrine); in terms of life-styles (free-lance ministers, workers who also exercise a ministry, married or celibate, living alone or in community); in the more personal terms of various charisms received (or of specific professional callings which demand fidelity to a certain kind of life and community).

Here we confront the *possibility of women sharing in the exercise of the Christian priestly ministry.* During the debates at the Synod of 1971 this question was raised on two occasions: in discussing priestly ministry and in speaking of justice in the Church. The question was even formally presented to the Synod by Cardinal Flahiff, archbishop of Winnipeg, in the name of the Canadian Episcopal Conference. The Cardinal maintained that, given the radical difference in the social condition of women today as compared with Old Testament and New Testament times, certain Biblical views have proved to be sociologically determined and do not present obstacles of a dogmatic nature. He stressed the fact that Vatican II had condemned any discrimination on the basis of sex. The Council explicitly declared: "Since in our times women have an ever more active share in the whole life of society, it is very important that they participate more widely also in the various fields of the Church's apostolate" (AA, 9/500). Yet, as the Canadian cardinal observed, no move of genuine importance has as yet been made, in any concrete way, to implement the Council's demand. Now that so much is being said of diversification of ministries (the Cardinal went on to say), we must also face this problem of the participation of women, who after all make up more than half of the faifthful, either by providing new ministries that are adapted to woman's capacities and her role in the Church and society, or by adapting some existing ministries to women. The problem is indeed a delicate and difficult one, especially since the social position of women has not evolved at an equal rate everywhere in the world. But we can no longer ignore the problem and pass over it in silence. The Canadian bishops entered into lengthy consultation with the representatives of Catholic women in their country and made themselves fully aware of their aspirations and desires, which were voiced in a positive and constructive way. In the name of the Canadian Episcopal Conference, Cardinal Flahiff therefore submitted two questions to the Synod. (1) Since men and women are equals and since their equality is recognized by society and is being ever more fully reduced to practice, does the Synod think that women ought to share in our present ministries or in new ones which can be elaborated? (2) Is it already possible to discern the kind of ministry that would be best suited to the special nature of women? The Cardinal also proposed that the Synod ask the Pope to set up immediately a joint commission of bishops, priests, and religious and lay people of both sexes, in order to study the matter more thoroughly.

In subsequent speeches, some of the Synodal Fathers went

along with the Canadian bishops' proposal, including one Brazilian bishop, Bishop Valfredo Tepe. Bishop Byrne, of the United States, went so far as to say straight out that "there are no arguments for excluding women from ecclesiastical ministry, except stubborn male preconceptions, blind adherence to human traditions which originate in the particular social position of women in other ages, or a very debatable interpretation of Sacred Scripture."

In the Synodal document on justice in the world, under the heading of "The Practice of Justice: The Church's Witness," the Synod declared: "We also urge that women should have their own share of responsibility and participation in the community life of society and likewise of the Church. We propose that this matter be subjected to a serious study employing adequate means: for instance, a mixed commission of men and women, religious and lay people, of differing situations and competences."[13]

Notes

[1] On the situation in Brazil cf. Affonso Filippe Gregory, "Laicizacoes do Clero do Brasil: Estatísticas e interpretacoes," REB, 29 (1969), 924-939; and the revealing article of José Marins, "Pesquisa sobre o Clero do Brasil," REB, 29 (1969), 121-138. See, further, the study conducted by a lay group, "Inquéritos entre leigos sobre a situacao do padre," REB, 29 (1969), 636-644. Marins' report, "O Tema 'Presbíteros' na X Assembléia da CNBB," REB, 29 (1969), 622-636, makes useful reading. The volumes, *Documentos dos Presbíteros,* published in 1969 by the National Secretariat for Hierarchic Ministry of the CNBB, throws a very interesting light on the lives and anxieties of our priests; we shall be making frequent reference to these documents.

[2] Silvano Burgalassi, in *Padres Amanha?* (IDO-C, no. 2; Petrópolis: Vozes, 1970), pp. 145-170.

[3] On this subject there is a very informative, but also quite tendentious, book, *Comunidades de base y nueva Iglesia* (Madrid: Ediciones Acción Católica, 1971).

[4] Priests of the Northwest II Region, in *Documentos dos Presbíteros,* p. 19. Henceforth page references for quotations from this volume will be given in the text.

[5] Marins, "Pesquisa sobre o Clero do Brasil" (cf. note 1, above). Quotations in this and the following paragraph of the text are from this article.

[6] Andrew M. Greeley.

[7] Documentation and reports in REB, 31 (1971), 976-1002.

[8] On the Church as a social, visible institution, cf. Bonaventure Kloppenburg, *The Ecclesiology of Vatican II,* tr. by M. J. O'Connell (Chicago: Franciscan Herald Press, 1974), chapter 2.

[9] As the Synod was going on, I sent a fairly comprehensive and somewhat disappointed report from Rome, published in REB, 31 (1971), 891-936.

[10] Synod of Bishops, *The Ministerial Priesthood—Justice in the World* (Washington, D.C.: United States Catholic Conference, 1972). This publication reproduces the official English translation issued by the Vatican City Press in 1971. The two documents are printed as Appendix II and III in the present book; paragraphs have been numbered to facilitate reference to it.

[11] Gregory, *art. cit.,* pp. 935-936.

[12] *Ibid.*

[13] Synod, *op. cit.,* p. 44.

II

The Christian
Priestly Ministry

The Synod of Bishops maintained that a "crisis of identity" was the chief cause of the present crisis among the clergy. There are priests who say they do not know "what" they are or what their specific role is; therefore they leave the ministry.[1] It was in order to help resolve this crisis of identity that the bishops wrote the first part of their document on priestly ministry. The International Theological Commission had likewise studied this matter intensively and published an excellent report entitled *Priestly Ministry*.[2] Drawing inspiration from these documents I shall try to present the theology of the Christian priestly ministry in the form of six propositions.

We shall come to a true understanding of our priestly ministry only in the light of Christ's priesthood. For strictly speaking, in the new covenant under which, by God's grace, we now live, we have only one Priest and Mediator: Jesus Christ. All others who call themselves "priests" or are so named in the documents of tradition or the Church's teaching authority cannot be "priests" or "mediators" except by derivation from and in total dependence on the priesthood of Christ. For this reason, if we are to grasp the meaning of the derived priesthood, we must reflect upon it in the light of Christ the Priest. It would be absurd to dissociate the Christian priesthood from Christ in order to study it "in itself" and thus to discover its essence or nature and specific function, for such a priesthood simply does not exist. Our effort then shall be, in the first place and above all, to understand the priesthood of Christ.

1. *The priesthood of Christ realizes, or fulfills, and at the same time transcends all the priesthoods and ritual sacrifices of the Old Testament and of paganism.* The document of the 1971 Synod on ministerial priesthood makes this basic statement in no. 21. Christ did not enter the history of men while remaining isolated from his historical context. Rather, the New Covenant between God and men, of which Christ the Priest is the author, enters the history of human salvation in a context shaped by the Old Testament. This is why the New Testament cannot be understood except in constant relation to the Old Testament. Using a happy formula inspired by Augustine, Vatican II teaches: "God, the inspirer and author of both testaments, wisely arranged that the New Testament be hidden in the Old and the Old be made manifest in the New. . . . The books of the Old Testament, with all their parts, caught up into the proclamation of the gospel, acquire and show forth their full meaning in the New Testament and in turn shed light on it and explain it" (DV, 16/122). This means that the New Testament priesthood, too, is somehow hidden in the Old Testament priesthood and that the later becomes clear when realized or fulfilled in the New Testament. In other words: we must understand the priesthood of Christ as fulfilling and, at the same time, going beyond all the ancient priesthoods. Therefore the bishops of the Synod say: "All the Scriptures, especially those of the New Testa-

ment, must be interpreted as intimately inter-linked and inter-related by their single inspiration" (25).

Insistence on this relatedness to the Old Testament is of some importance at the present time. For there are those who tell us today that the Christian priestly ministry was "re-judaized" after apostolic times and that it is therefore our duty now to "de-judaize" it. There were undoubtedly excesses of "judaization," but our "dejudaization" ought not to be so radical as to forget the relations which certainly exist between Jews and Christians. We will return to this matter later on.

When we speak of Old Testament priesthood we think immediately and almost exclusively of the levitical priesthood. But the history of Israel contains other kinds of priesthood as well. The most imposing is the figure of Moses, the great mediator between God and Israel. He exercises a priestly office in receiving the word of God and communicating it to the people, and in offering sacrifices, or having them offered, to Jahweh in the name of the whole people, as we read in Exodus 24, for example.

There was also the priesthood of the heads of families and tribes. This type of priesthood later developed into the "royal priesthood." Thus there came into existence the figure of *priest-king,* who was also the advocate of the poor before God (cf. 1 Kgs 8:14-16; 2 Kgs 23:1-3) and representative of God before men (cf. Ps 2:6-9). This is the priesthood of which the Messianic psalms sing. Cf, for example, the whole of Psalm 110 with its description of the conquering Messiah as priest and king; in this psalm there occurs the words which would be taken up in the apostolic period and applied to Christ: "You are a priest forever, according to the order of Melchizedek."

Against this broader background of Jewish priesthood there arose the *levitical* priesthood which originated in a divine choice and a special calling. The levites exercised a mediation between God and the people as servants of the cultus and the law, reminding the people of Jahweh's deeds in their history, proclaiming his will, and drawing down his blessing on them. "The Lord said to Moses: 'Speak to Aaron and his sons and tell them: This is how you shall bless the Israelites. Say to them: The Lord bless you and keep you! The Lord let his face shine upon you, and be gracious to you! The Lord look upon you kindly and give you peace! So shall they invoke my name upon the Israelites, and I will bless them'" (Nm 6:22-27).

But to a few people in the Old Testament the insufficiency of this priesthood and the need for a radical change became ever more clear. The reality of *sin,* which was destructive of the Covenant, makes an *eschatological redemption* necessary. The prophets, with increasing clarity, reserve to the "last times" the perfect worship which can assure full glory to God and salvation to men; they gradually develop the idea of a new kind of priesthood, an "eschatological" priesthood. Thus Isaiah, Jeremiah, and Ezekiel look for a priesthood that will be radically new. In the conviction that these "last times," with the definitive restoration they are to bring, are still far distant, Jewish spirituality concentrates chiefly on expiation for sin through a proliferation of penitential liturgies, on the search for spiritual purity, and on a radical transformation of the heart instead of on simple ritual or cultic purifications and consecrations. The prophets even indulge in irreverent satire as they assail the uselessness of the ritual sacrifices. Thus Israel lives in hope of the eschatological event by which God himself, out of pure benevolence, will accomplish what sinful men are unable to achieve. The prophets are the great source of this deep-going development in the idea of priesthood. On the basis of the experiences of Jeremiah and Ezekiel who think of themselves as loaded down with the people's sins and making expiation for them, the image of an eschatological savior, the Servant of Jahweh, gradually emerges into clarity.

Amid a universally sinful world the *Servant of Jahweh,* of whom Second Isaiah sings (especially in 53:3-12), is the sole just and innocent man; he takes upon himself the iniquities of all in order to win full justification for all. His vocation? "It was our infirmities that he bore, our sufferings that he endured" (4); "He was pierced for our offenses, crushed for our sins; upon him was the chastisement that makes us whole, by his stripes we were healed" (5). All this, however, is the result of a mysterious divine plan which is incomprehensible to men but which the Servant fully accepts, for "he surrendered himself to death" (12). This act of obedience, in which he was "smitten for the sins of his people" (8), *has sacrificial value*: "he gives his life as an offering for sin" (10). Such a prophetic figure is unintelligible without the transposition of ritual and liturgical elements which prophetic experience makes possible, as the cultic vocabulary used here attests: the Servant wins from God precisely what the expiatory victims offered in the Temple by the Israelite priests were unable to effect: "He shall take away the sins of many, and win pardon for their offenses" (12).

The plan of God thus begins to become clear: He wants the heart of man, through a sacrificial oblation, to be entrusted entirely to him. The sacrifice God wants from his people is man himself, whole and entire. Man's life, throughout its whole extent and in all its depths, is to become an act of worship. This is the clearly expressed basic idea of the Letter to the Hebrews: "Wherefore, on coming into the world, Jesus said: Sacrifice and offering you did not desire, but a body you have prepared for me; holocausts and sin offerings you took no delight in. Then I said: As is written of me in the book, I have come to do your will, O God. First he says, 'Sacrifices and offerings, holocausts and sin offerings, you neither desired nor delighted in.' (These are offered according to the prescriptions of the law.) Then he says, 'I have come to do your will.' In other words, he takes away the first covenant to establish the second. By this 'will,' we have been sanctified through the offering of the body of Jesus Christ once for all" (Heb 10:5-10).

Then, continuing with the idea of the fulfillment and transcending of all the ancient priesthoods (which is our way of understanding Christ's priesthood), the Letter adds: "By one offering he has forever perfected those who are being sanctified" (10:14).

2. *Even when the New Testament does not apply a priestly vocabulary to Christ, it attributes priestly functions to him.* In the New Testament only the Letter to the Hebrews speaks explicitly and formally of Christ's priesthood. A "priestly" vocabulary is not used in the other books in speaking of Christ and the Apostles. This fact seems strange to us today. The early Christian community systematically avoided giving Christ, the Apostles, and the other ministers of the Church (deacons, presbyters, bishops) the name of "priest" and describing their ministry as "priestly." They certainly did not use expressions like "priestly ministry" or "ministerial priesthood" and were satisfied to speak simply of "services" or "ministries."

The fact itself is clear and undeniable. From it some conclude that a ministerial "priesthood" simply does not exist in the New Covenant. They even say that since the Church's ministry is not "priestly," it is simply a "service," something purely "functional," and therefore, when not "functioning," ceases to exist (in any ontological sense). Since it is only a function in a community, it has no meaning apart from the community; it exists only for the community and by reason of the community. Further important conclusions follow from this position, which undermine the whole traditional theology of priestly ministry in the Church. The Synod sums up these problems in a series of questions: "Does the priestly ministry have any specific nature? Is this ministry necessary? Is the priesthood incapable of being lost? What does a priest mean today? Would it not be enough to have for the service of the Christian community presidents designated for the preservation of the common good, without sacramental ordination, and exercising their office for a fixed period?" (12).

The early Christians knew the word "priest" (*hiereus* in Greek; *sacerdos* in Latin), but they applied it to the priests of the Old Testament and of paganism. Its application to Christ and the Apostles would therefore have easily led to ambiguities. Christ and the Apostles, after all, were clearly not priests in the way Old Testament and pagan priests were. From the viewpoint of the latter, Christ was—in our present vocabulary—not a priest but a layman. As the Letter to the Hebrews puts it, Christ "was of a different tribe, none of whose members ever officiated at the altar. It is clear that our Lord rose from the tribe of Judah, regarding which Moses said nothing about priests" (7:13-14).

When the New Testament books speak of the person and work of Christ, they therefore see verified in them a new kind of priesthood, one that is more effective and perfect and that has been clearly implied by the prophets, especially in the figure of the Servant of Jahweh. The Christology of the early Christians is wholly dominated by the idea that in Jesus of Nazareth the prophecy about the suffering Servant of Jahweh has been completely fulfilled. This was a basic conviction and is constantly reiterated. This same principle must become basic for us today. "For our sakes God made him who did not know sin, to be sin, so that in him we might become the very holiness of God" (2 Cor 5:21). "Christ delivered us from the power of the law's curse by himself becoming a curse for us" (Gal 3:13). Christ's death on the Cross is described in sacrificial and therefore indirectly priestly terminology. "Christ our Passover has been sacrificed" (1 Cor 5:7). The terminology is used when the texts speak of Christ's "blood" (Mk 14:24; Rm 5:9; Eph 1:17); in the repeated expression "for you" and its variants (Lk 22:19; cf. Jn 6:51b; 10:11,15; Mk 10:45); when John the

Baptist presents Christ as a lamb: "Look! There is the Lamb of God who takes away the sin of the world!" (Jn 1: 29; cf. 1:36; 19:36). The typology of the Paschal Lamb is also found in the Apocalypse: "With your blood you purchased for God men of every race and tongue, of every people and nation. You made of them a kingdom, and priests to serve our God, and they shall reign on the earth" (Rev 5:9b-10); and in the First Letter of Peter: "You were delivered . . . by Christ's blood beyond all price: the blood of a spotless, unblemished lamb" (1:18). Jesus, the Just One, is presented by St. John as a propitiatory victim (*hilasmos*: Greek) for the entire world (1 Jn 2:2), that is, as a sacrifice for sin. Christ's sacrifice for sin. Christ's sacrifice consists in his self-offering: ". . . the Lord Jesus Christ . . . gave himself for our sins" (Gal 1:4; cf. 2:20; Eph 5:25; 1 Tim 2:6; Tit 2:14). Special light is thrown on this self-oblation when we see in unity the figure of the Good Shepherd and the figure of the Servant of Jahweh (cf. Jn 10:11, 17). The love of Christ who gives himself for his Church is also expressed in sacrificial imagery in Eph 5:25: "Christ loved the Church. He gave himself up for her to make her holy"; the same letter in another passage spells out the sacrificial and therefore priestly conception more fully: "Follow the way of love, even as Christ loved you. He gave himself for us as an offering to God, a gift of pleasing fragrance" (5:2).

All these passages show that, although the title "priest" is not expressly applied to Christ, he is nonetheless the priest who offers himself as victim for sin. According to all four evangelists, Jesus himself conceived of his ministry in the light of the prophecies concerning Jahweh's suffering Servant (cf. for example, Lk 4:17-21). He is both priest and victim in the sacrifice which reconciles sinful mankind to God. "The Son of Man has not come to be served but to serve— to give his life in ransom for the many" (Mk 10:45 and parallel passages). At the Last Supper Jesus performs the ceremony of instituting a new covenant and thus establishing a new People of God. As mediator of the Sinai covenant Moses had sprinkled the people with the blood of the sacrificial victims and declared: "This is the blood of the covenant which the Lord has made with you in accordance with all these words of his" (Ex 24:8). Jesus repeats Moses' action but says: "This is my bood, the blood of the covenant, to be poured out on behalf of many" (Mk 14:24). He is the suffering Servant of Jahweh, now present and active. He is truly the one "whom the Father consecrated and sent into the world" (Jn 10:36). "God anointed him with the Holy Spirit and power" (Acts 10:38). After his baptism "Jesus, full of the Holy Spirit, . . . returned from the Jordan" (Lk 4:1; cf. 4:18-21). "The Father loves me for this: that I lay down my life to take it up again. No one takes it from me; I lay it down freely. I have power to lay it down, and I have power to take it up again. This command I received from my Father" (Jn 10:17-18). "He bore the sins of us all on the Cross; rising from the dead and being made Lord (cf. Phil 2:9-11, he reconciled us to God; and he laid the foundation of the people of the New Covenant, which is the Church" (Synod, no. 21).

"Christ Jesus, who died or rather was raised up, who is at the right hand of God and who intercedes for us" (Rom 8:34). "God is one. One also is the mediator between God and men, the man Christ Jesus, who gave himself as a ransom for all" (1 Tim 2:5-6).

It is in the Letter to the Hebrews, however, that Christ is presented to us in an explicit, formal way as sole High Priest of the new covenant, "a great high priest who has passed through the heavens" (4:14), a priest who requires no replacement but is eternal and changeless (cf. 7:24). "It was fitting that we should have such a high priest: holy, innocent, undefiled, separated from sinners, higher than the heavens. Unlike the other high priests, he has no need to offer sacrifice day after day, first for his own sins, then for those of the

people; he did that once for all when he offered himself"
(7:26-27). In him we have "a merciful and faithful high
priest before God" (2:17), a priest who "entered [the sanctu-
ary], not with the blood of goats and calves, but with his
own blood, and achieved eternal redemption. For if the
blood of goats and bulls and the sprinkling of a heifer's
ashes can sanctify those who are defiled so that their flesh
is cleansed, how much more will the blood of Christ, who
through the eternal spirit offered himself up unblemished
to God, cleanse our consciences from dead works to worship
the living God. This is why he is mediator of a new covenant: since his death has taken place for deliverance from
transgressions committed under the first covenant, those
who are called may receive the promised eternal inheritance"
(9:12-15). "Now he has appeared at the end of the ages to
take away sins once for all by his sacrifice" (9:26). "Jesus
offered one sacrifice for sins and took his seat forever at
the right hand of God; now he waits until his enemies are
placed beneath his feet. By one offering he has forever perfected those who are being sanctified" (10: 12-14).

According to the message of the New Testament, then,
Christ alone offers a perfect sacrifice by giving himself in
accordance with the Father's will. In this sense he is a
"priest," and indeed *the* priest. At the same time, however,
since this priesthood is based on his transcendent divine
sonship, it is the priesthood proper to a king, a shepherd,
and prophet. The priesthood of the New Covenant thus
embraces in the vast scope of its mediational function, the
several other mediations known in the history of Israel,
especially those of the prophet and the leader of the people.

Moses had predicted: "A prophet like me will the Lord,
your God, raise up for you from among your own kinsmen;
to him you shall listen. . . . And the Lord said to me. 'This
was well said. I will raise up for them a prophet like you
from among their kinsmen, and will put my words into his
mouth; he shall tell them all that I command him. If any

man will not listen to my words which he speaks in my name, I myself will make him answer for it' " (Deut 18:15, 17-18). When Peter spoke to the people after curing the paralytic, he declared that this prophecy of Moses had been fulfilled in Christ (Acts 3:22). Peter saw in Jesus the new Moses and realized that in him was fulfilled the prophecy, which had been so venerated in Judaism, concerning the "prophet to come," who would mean salvation or loss for the members of his people: " 'Anyone who does not listen to that prophet shall be ruthlessly cut off from the people' " (Acts 3:23). In Acts 7:37 Stephen gives voice to the same conviction, which became one of the basic certitudes of the newly-founded Church. The delegation of Jews asks John the Baptist: "Are you the Prophet?" (Jn 1:21). He had to answer No, for Jesus was the Prophet, and the voice from heaven echoed over him in the presence of Moses and Elijah: "This is my Son, my Chosen One. Listen to him" (Lk 9:35). Christ therefore applies to himself the words of the prophet concerning the Servant of Jahweh: "The spirit of the Lord is upon me; therefore he has anointed me. He has sent me to bring glad tidings to the poor, to proclaim liberty to captives, recovery of sight to the blind, and release to prisoners, to announce a year of favor from the Lord" (Lk 4:18-19; cf. Is 61:1-2). The Letter to the Hebrews, too, regards Jesus as a prophet: "In times past, God spoke in fragmentary and varied ways to our fathers through the prophets; in this, the final age, he has spoken to us through his Son" (Heb 1:1-2). According to St. John, Jesus himself insisted that "Whoever puts faith in me believes not so much in me as in him who sent me; and whoever looks on me is seeing him who sent me. I have come into the world as its light, to keep anyone who believes in me from remaining in the dark. . . . I have not spoken on my own; no, the Father who sent me has commanded me what to say and how to speak. . . . Whatever I say is spoken just as he instructed me" (Jn 12:44-50). He is the way, the truth, and the life: "No one comes to the Father but through me. If you really knew me, you would know my Father also. . . . Whoever has seen me has seen the Father. . . . The words I speak are not spoken of myself; it is the Father who lives in me accomplishing his works" (Jn 14:6-10).

Jesus, the Priest and Prophet, is also the Lord, the Kyrios: "Let the whole house of Israel know beyond any doubt that God has made both Lord and Messiah this Jesus whom you crucified" (Acts 2:36). When Paul in his letters speaks of Jesus' rank as Kyrios, he intends to express by this one word the whole mysterious power and greatness of the glorified Christ. To the Romans he writes: "If you confess with your lips that Jesus is Lord and believe in your heart that God raised him from the dead, you will be saved" (10:9). And he assures the Corinthians: "No one can say: 'Jesus is Lord,' except in the Holy Spirit" (1 Cor 12:3). Therefore: "Every tongue [must] proclaim to the glory of God the Father: Jesus Christ is Lord!" (Phil 2:11). The formula, "Jesus is Lord," is thus the briefest and most essential expression of the apostolic preaching.

Finally, these various aspects of Christ's eschatological ministry are brought together in the image of the Good Shepherd. Every part of Christ's mission is grounded in the reality of his "pastoral" love for men. We need only read Jn 10:1-18 and Is 53:3-12 in order to see how closely related the suffering Servant of Jahweh is to the "great Shepherd" (Heb 13:20), the "chief Shepherd" (1 Pet 5:4), "the Shepherd, the Guardian of your souls" (1 Pet 2:25).

All these varied dimensions, then, are part of the "ministry" or "priesthood" of Christ. And when we inquire into the nature, structure, and extension of the Christian ministerial priesthood, we must never lose sight of the amplitude of Christ's priesthood with its prophetic aspect and its pastoral or royal function. The Synod therefore says: "When . . . we speak of the priesthood of Christ, we should have before our eyes a unique, incomparable reality, which includes the prophetic and royal office of the Incarnate Word of God" (23). We shall have to bear this important principle in mind when, later on, we speak of our sharing in the priesthood of Christ, for the sharing will extend to all the functions and tasks of Christ. "As the Father has sent me, so I send you," says the risen Lord to the Apostles (Jn 20:21).

It is very much a secondary question whether or not we should continue using a terminology drawn from priesthood, either to designate the life and activity of Christ and the Apostles, or to describe the specific activity of present-day bishops and priests. Strictly speaking, it is quite legitimate and feasible to avoid such terminology, just as Christ himself and the early Church avoided it. If, for example, the contemporary process of secularization causes special hostility to the use of such terminology (because it is regarded as ambiguous in an age bent on secularization), it seems that we might well imitate Christ and the Apostles. The essential point is to be completely faithful to the ideas of power (that is, enablement and qualification) and service, which the priestly terminology expresses.

3. *Being associated with the priesthood of Christ, the Church is a priestly community.* Christ, who is Priest, Prophet, and Lord, continues his work, down the centuries, through the mediation of the Church. "Christ indeed always associates the Church with Himself in the truly great work of giving perfect praise to God and making men holy. The Church is His dearly beloved Bride who calls to her Lord, and through Him offers worship to the Eternal Father" (SC, 7b/141). The Church in its entirety is the sacrament or sign and instrument of Christ, his organ which is always visibly present among men, or "an instrument for the redemption of all" (LG, 9e/26). According to the bishops of the Synod, "The Church . . . was established to be a sacrament of the salvation which comes to us from God in Christ. In her, Christ is present and operative for the world as a

savior, so that the love offered by God to men and their response meet" (28). Through Christ, with Christ, and in Christ all the baptized have free access to God (cf. Rom 5:2; 2:18). It is in this sense that all are priests and that the People of God under the New Covenant is a priestly people. The common priesthood of the baptized thus has its exclusive source in the priesthood of Christ; it depends wholly on the latter and is determined and conditioned by it. "To him who loves us and freed us from our sins by his own blood, who has made us a royal nation of priests in the service of his God and Father—to him be glory and power forever and ever! Amen" (Rev. 1:5-6). Christians, therefore, are "priests for God," not by reason of their own sacrifices, but by reason of the one sacrifice of Christ which frees them from their sins. This is why they sing: "Worthy are you. . . , for you were slain. With your blood you purchased for God men of every race and tongue, of every people and nation. You made of them a kingdom, and priests to serve our God" (Rev 5:9-10).

The First Letter of Peter can teach, therefore, that the Church is a "priestly community." According to recent scholarship, an accurate translation of 1 Pet 2:9 would read as follows: "You are a chosen nation, a royal residence (*basileion*), a priestly community (*hierateuma*), a holy nation, a people whom God has acquired for himself."[3] *Hierateuma* is a collective term, modelled on other nouns in *-euma* and coined to designate a group of men who share a function. *Hierateuma* thus means "priestly community," and means that the Church as a whole exercises a priestly function among the peoples of the earth.

Not only does the priesthood of the people of God have its roots in the priestly service of Christ and derive the reason for its existence from it; this priesthood is also to be exercised only in him, with him, and through him. "Through him let us continually offer God a sacrifice of praise, that is, the fruit of lips which acknowledge his name"

(Heb 13:15). "Through him . . . we address our Amen to
God when we worship together" (2 Cor 1:20). Christ is
God's great Yes ("Amen"), and the Yes which the Christian community speaks through the same Christ's mediation.
Christ himself, as eternal high priest of his Church, presents
the prayers of the community to the Father (cf. Heb 7:25).
For this reason the Church, today no less than at the beginning, always prays "through our Lord Jesus Christ" (cf.
Rom 1:8; 1 Pet 4:11; Jude 25). Thus united in Christ the
faithful share in his sacrifice and proclaim the wonderful
things God does for them through Christ his Son. This
sharing and proclaiming finds its chief concrete form in
the Eucharist. St. Peter therefore urges the faithful to draw
near to Christ, "a living stone, rejected by men but approved, nonetheless, and precious in God's eyes. You too
are living stones, built as an edifice of spirit, into a holy
priesthood, offering spiritual sacrifices acceptable to God
through Jesus Christ" (1 Pet 2:4-5) — sacrifices which, as
Vatican II explains, "during the celebration of the Eucharist, . . . are most lovingly offered to the Father along with
the Lord's body" (LG, 34b/60). Only when we go to the
Father "through Jesus Christ" are our "spiritual sacrifices"
acceptable to God. (The Council tells us in what these
sacrifices consist: "all their works, prayers, and apostolic
endeavors, their ordinary married and family life, their
daily labor, their mental and physical relaxation, . . . and
even the hardships of life." If these do not pass through
Christ, they have no value in the Father's eyes. It is, therefore, by uniting itself to Christ in the Eucharist, that the
priestly people of the new covenant is enabled to "consecrate
the world itself to God" (LG, *ibid.*). Elsewhere the Council
states: "They are thereby [through the Eucharist] invited
and led to offer themselves, their labors, and all created
things together with Him. . . . So priests must instruct them
to offer to God the Father the divine Victim in the sacrifice
of the Mass, and to join to it the offering of their own

lives" (PO, 5c and e/541 and 542). Since they are priests, then "by offering the Immaculate Victim, not only through the hands of the priest, but also with him, they should learn to offer themselves too" (SC, 48/154). In this way they will be giving a concrete answer to the Apostle's request: "And now, brothers, I beg you through the mercy of God to offer your bodies as a living sacrifice holy and acceptable to God, your spiritual worship" (Rom 12:1).

Regarding this self-offering by the community, the Council once again explains: "Through the ministry of priests, the spiritual sacrifice of the faithful is made perfect in union with the sacrifice of Christ, the sole Mediator. Through the hands of priests and in the name of the whole Church, the Lord's sacrifice is offered in the Eucharist in an unbloody and sacramental manner until He Himself returns. The ministry of priests is directed toward this work and is perfected in it. For their ministry, which takes its start from the gospel message, derives its power and force from the sacrifice of Christ. Its aim is that 'the entire commonwealth of the redeemed, that is, the community and society of the saints, be offered as a universal sacrifice to God through the High Priest who in His Passion offered His very Self for us that we might be the body of so exalted a Head' " (PO, 2f/535-536).[4] In this statement the Council is anticipating one of the essential and specific functions of the priest: The Christian community exercises its common priesthood through the mediation of the special priesthood of presbyters. Without a priest the baptized are not in a position to exercise their priesthood in that way which is the center and high point of their Christian life.[5] Here we can see the essential difference (not a difference simply of degree) between the two ways of sharing in Christ's priesthood, and how the one is ordered to the other. Here too light is shed upon the teaching of Vatican II concerning the common priesthood of the faithful:

"Christ the Lord, High Priest taken from among men

(cf. Heb 5:1-5), 'made a kingdom and priests to God his Father' (Apoc 1:6; cf. 5:9-10) out of this new people. The baptized, by regeneration and the anointing of the Holy Spirit, are consecrated into a spiritual house and a holy priesthood. Thus through all those works befitting Christian men they can offer spiritual sacrifices and proclaim the power of Him who has called them out of darkness into His marvelous light (cf. 1 Pet 2:4-10). Therefore all the disciples of Christ, persevering in prayer and praising God (cf. Acts 2:42-47), should present themselves as living sacrifices, holy and pleasing to God (cf. Rom 12:1). Everywhere on earth they must bear witness to Christ and give an answer to those who seek an account of that hope of eternal life which is in them (cf. 1 Pet 3:15).

"Though they differ from one another in essence and not only in degree, the common priesthood of the faithful and the ministerial or hierarchic priesthood are nonetheless interrelated. Each of them in its own special way is a participation in the one priesthood of Christ. The ministerial priest, by the sacred power he enjoys, molds and rules the priestly people. Acting in the person of Christ, he brings about the Eucharistic Sacrifice, and offers it to God in the name of all the people. For their part, the faithful join in the offering of the Eucharist by virtue of their royal priesthood. They likewise exercise that priesthood by receiving the sacraments, by prayer and thanksgiving, by the witness of a holy life, and by self-denial and active charity" (LG, 10/26-27).

But the priestly people also exercises its common priesthood when it suffers with Christ. As the Apostle sees in his sufferings a sharing in the sufferings of Christ (cf. Phil 3:10; 2 Cor 4:10), so when the priestly community undergoes tribulations for Christ, it renders his passion present for itself: "It is your special privilege to take Christ's part—not only to believe in him but also to suffer for him. Yours is the same struggle as mine, the one in which you formerly saw me engaged and now hear that I am caught up" (Phil 1:29). St. Peter, too, maintains: "If you put up with suffering for doing what is right, this is acceptable in God's eyes. It was for this that you were called, since Christ suffered for you in just this way and left you an example, to have you follow in his footsteps" (1 Pet 2:21). The principle is hard to accept but it is nonetheless permanently valid. Vatican II expresses it thus: "Prompted by the Holy Spirit, the Church must walk the same road which Christ walked: a road of poverty and obedience, of service and self-sacrifice to the death, from which death He came forth a victor by His resurrection. For thus did all the Apostles walk in hope. On behalf of Christ's body, which is the Church, they supplied what was wanting of the sufferings of Christ by their own many trials and sufferings (cf. Col. 1:24). Often, too, the blood of Christians was like a seed" (AG, 5e/590). Again: "Still in pilgrimage upon the earth, we trace in trial and under oppression the paths He trod. Made one with His sufferings as the body is one with the head, we endure with Him, that with Him we may be glorified" (LG, 7f/21). Thus the Christians of the priestly Church "follow the poor Christ, the humble and cross-bearing Christ, in order to be made worthy of being partakers in His glory" (LG, 41a/67-68).

Vatican II makes it clear, moreover, that the priestly community has an "organic structure" (LG, 11a/27). Or, as the Synod of Bishops puts it: "The Church, which through the gift of the Spirit is made up organically, participates in different ways in the functions of Christ as Priest, Prophet, and King, in order to carry out her mission of salvation in his name and by his power, as a priestly people" (29). The following pages will clarify the meaning and scope of this statement.

4. *Christ associated the Twelve in a special way with his priestly, eschatological ministry.* According to contemporary Biblical studies, ecclesial ministry is an institution explicitly

intended by Christ. It is not, then, simply the result of a purely sociological growth-process. Both in the first Christian community at Jerusalem and in the earthly activity of Jesus of Nazareth before his resurrection, the Twelve have a privileged place. The authority in which they are clad derives from their being chosen and invested by Christ. He called them, picked them out, and gave them a special role to play in the founding of the Church. More than this, the analysis of the exegetes invites us to see in the college of Twelve a "function" instituted by Christ for the service of the New Israel. The bishops of the Synod state: "It is clear from the New Testament writings that an Apostle and a community of faithful united with one another by a mutual link under Christ as head and the influence of his Spirit belong to the original inalienable structure of the Church" (30).

This question is especially important today because of the movement for "declericalization" of the ministry. It is clear that "ministers" gradually came to form a special social class in the Church (the "clergy"), with an acknowledged structure and image. It may be strightway admitted that the "clergy," thus understood, is not of divine institution; consequently it is legitimate to speak of a "declericalization" on the sociological level. But such a process will necessarily have its limits and cannot fail to influence the sphere of theology, inasmuch as it touches on the very foundations of ministry and on the very structure of the ecclesial organization with its dimensions of both community and hierarchy. It is evident that at this theological level the extent of declericalization is determined by the will or institution of Christ and not by sociological laws.

Clearly, then, from the very first decade of the Church on, the Twelve, with Peter, were by no means a mere collection of individuals but a specific group, formally acknowledged as such. There are plenty of testimonies to back up this claim.[6]

(a)   The testimony of St. Paul in 1 Cor 15:5-7 (where we have, perhaps, the oldest confession of faith by the Palestinian Church). According to the tradition which St. Paul here passes on, the risen Christ appeared first to Peter, then to the Twelve, then to a large number of believers. The passage makes it clear that the early Church, in the oldest confession of faith that has been preserved for us, attributes a very special place to Peter and the Twelve. These men are the first witnesses to the risen Lord. We are here carried back to the early, post-Easter, community, in which, beyond doubt, the Twelve formed a distinct group within the body of believers and exercised a predominant function.

(b)   The testimony of St. Mark (3:13-19) takes us back to the time before the resurrection. "He named [*epoiesen*: literally, "made or constituted"] twelve as his companions whom he would send to preach the good news; they were likewise to have authority to expel demons" (3:14). The evangelist here tells of the choice and establishment of the Twelve by Jesus. They are, as a group, the object of a special vocation: being called and set apart from among the other disciples, the Twelve are "established" by Christ "in order to be with him" and at his disposition. In this passage the verb "to make" (constitute, establish) with the name of a person or group of persons as its direct object recalls Old Testament usage in regard to the establishing of priests (cf. 1 Kgs 13:33; 2 Chron 2:18). The Lord "appointed [literally: "made"] Moses and Aaron" (1 Sam 12:6). "To make" is here equivalent to "to institute" (cf. also Heb 3:2; Acts 2:36). Thus the Twelve are "made" and form a single group, for a specific function, with special powers, in bringing to pass the new world which Jesus has begun. The group will be closely associated with Christ's own power and activity in the service of the community of believers. The group is a creation of Jesus, and has specific powers and functions. We find similar language used in Acts: "the apostles he had chosen" (1:2). It was therefore not by their

own decision nor by the community's choice that they acquired their ministry. Jesus himself "chose them" in the
period before his Resurrection (cf. also Lk 6:12-16). Election to the apostolate was connected with the person of the
earthly and the glorified Christ, with his word, his power,
and his instructions.

(c) The testimony of St. Matthew (19:28) and St. Luke
(22:28-30) : "You who have followed me shall likewise take
your places on twelve thrones to judge the twelve tribes of
Israel." The Twelve as a group will be associated with the
authority of the Son of Man, for in communion with Christ
they will govern the New Israel. It is precisely with a view
to the establishment of this New Israel that Jesus forms for
himself a group of twelve disciples. They are to be the
guides or, to use a Biblical term, the "judges" of the community of believers: their mission among the latter will be
to direct them in the Lord's name.

The Twelve are thus at the very heart of Jesus' "project,"
for they are appointed in order to rule the New Israel and
thereby charged with an eschatological mission, which is
identical with Christ's own. The Twelve do not exist for
their own sake, but "in function of" something else, namely,
the service of Christ and the realities of which the Gospel
speaks. They are to help in the moving of God's kingdom
into the lives of men.

The Acts of the Apostles show us the close relationship
of the post-Resurrectional exercise of the apostolate with
the institution of the latter by Jesus as well as with the
coming of the Holy Spirit as the Savior's gift (Acts 1:8;
4:29; 10:42). According to St. Luke, in this book, the Twelve
are the witnesses (Acts 1:21-22) not only of the risen Christ,
now exalted to the heavens, but also of the Christ who
entered into our history. Their testimony is presented as
being a responsibility, an office (*episkope*: 1:2), the ministry of apostolate (*diakonia apostoles*: 1:25). The title
"Apostle" (reserved to the Twelve in Lk 6:13; 9:10; 17:5;

22:14; 24:10) is a title which refers essentially to mandate and authority: "He who hears you, hears me. He who rejects you, rejects me. And he who rejects me, rejects him who sent me" (Lk 10:16). The early Church became ever more clearly aware that the ministry and powers of Jesus had been communicated to the Apostles, that is, to the group of Twelve.

In order to enable them to carry out such important functions, the event of Pentecost took place, wherein "you will receive power when the Holy Spirit comes down on you" (Acts 1:8).

The Gospel of St. John enables us to penetrate still more deeply into the formulas used in Mk 3:13-19. In the Priestly Prayer of the fourth gospel Christ presents himself as the high priest. Just as on the feast of the Great Forgiveness (Yom Kippur) the Jewish high priest pronounced God's name and prayed for himself, the other priests, and all the people, so Christ here reveals God's name and prays for himself, the Apostles, and all the people. He prays for the Apostles that they may be "consecrated" by means of the truth (Jn 17:17): "Consecrate them by means of the truth — 'Your word is truth.'" Thus, after the fashion of him whom the Father consecrated and sent into the world (Jn 10:36), the Apostles too are consecrated and sent into the world (Jn 17:18; 20:21). For this reason they share in the power of eschatological judgment which belongs to Jesus, the Son of Man (Jn 20:22-23).

In the likeness of Jesus, the Servant-Shepherd, the Apostles are the servant-shepherds of the eschatological flock (cf. Jn 13:12-20; 21:15-17); they share in his eschatological ministry and are thereby committed to share his eschatological suffering and death. In both the Synoptic gospels and that of St. John the call to the apostolate and the apostolic mandate involve following Christ and sharing in the mystery of his suffering (Mk 8:34; 9:43-48; 10:35-45; Jn 13:1-11, 36-38; 21:15-23).

In this context we must pay special attention to the apostolate of *St. Paul* inasmuch as we have rather specific, detailed information about it. In the Letter to the Romans he understands his dedication to the Gospel as a priestly ministry and describes it in priestly terms: "Yet I have written to you rather boldly in parts of this letter by way of reminder. I take this liberty because God has given me the grace to be a minister (*leiturgos*) of Christ Jesus among the Gentiles, with the priestly duty (*hierurgein*) of preaching the gospel of God so that the Gentiles may be offered up as a pleasing sacrifice, consecrated by the Holy Spirit" (15:15-16). The text merits a careful, meditative reading, and Vatican II calls attention to the Greek original of it (cf. PO, 2f/535-36).

In another letter Paul speaks of himself as one of the "administrators (*oikonomos*) of the mysteries of God" (1 Cor 4:1). He and the other Apostles act as "ambassadors for Christ, God as it were appealing through us" (2 Cor 5:20; cf. Eph 6:2). And since he has authority he asks obedience and is ready to require it (cf. Phil 2:12; 1 Cor 7:17; 11:34; 16:1) and to punish disobedience (2 Cor 10:6). He does not derive the authority from his own personality or from his talents and spiritual gifts but from his apostolic office, for he is aware of being "an apostle sent, not by men or by any man, but by Jesus Christ and God his Father" (Gal 1:1). But he is also aware that his authority is vicarious. That is why he issues orders "in the name of the Lord Jesus Christ" (2 Thess 3:6), admonishes "in the name of our Lord Jesus Christ" (1 Cor 1:10), and gives commands "in the Lord Jesus" (1 Thess 4:2). Since his authority is Christ's authority, "I will not dare to speak of anything except what Christ has done through me" (Rom 15:18). Furthermore, he knows that his authority is an authority for service: "Domineering over your faith is not my purpose. I prefer to work with you toward your happiness" (2 Cor 1:23).

He regards himself as "set apart" by God for the exercise

of his ministry (Gal 1:15; Rom 1:1), as "called" (Rom 1:1; Cor 1:1; Gal 1:15), as "sent" (1 Cor 1:17; Gal 2:8). "If I do it willingly, I have my recompense; if unwillingly, I am nontheless entrusted with a charge" (1 Cor 9:17). Therefore, "preaching the gospel is not the subject of a boast; I am under compulsion and have no choice. I am ruined if I do not preach it!" (1 Cor 9:16). "Having met the test imposed on us by God, as men entrusted with the good tidings, we speak like those who strive to please God" (1 Thess 2:4). "Before God I tell you, in Christ, I have done everything to build you up" (2 Cor 12:19). "Christ speaks in me," Paul declares, and this is why "we thank God constantly that in receiving the message from us you took it, not as the word of men, but as it truly is, the word of God at work within you who believe" (1 Thess 2:13). Paul is aware, therefore, that he has received the grace of apostleship in order to "bring to obedient faith all the Gentiles" (Rom 1:5; cf. 15:18). He is fully aware that his ministry was entrusted to him, even imposed on him, by God and not by the community, much less by his own initiative and self-esteem. It is God who, through Christ, "has given us the ministry of reconciliation. . . . This makes us ambassadors for Christ, God as it were appealing through us" (2 Cor 5:18, 20). God not only sends Paul but also gives him the necessary qualifications for the task: "This great confidence in God is ours, through Christ. It is not that we are entitled of ourselves to take credit for anything. Our sole credit is from God, who has made us qualified ministers of a new covenant" (2 Cor 3:4-6).

Set apart, chosen, called, sent, authorized, and qualified by God, the bearer of apostolic ministry must be totally dedicated to his way of life: "Those things I used to consider gain I have now reappraised as loss in the light of Christ. I have come to rate all as loss in the light of the surpassing knowledge of my Lord Jesus Christ. . . . I have accounted all else rubbish so that Christ may be my wealth"

(Phil 3:7-8). Christ uses the apostle as he wishes, and the Apostle puts himself wholly at the disposition of the Lord. He even renounces the right he has of being supported by the community (1 Cor 9:12-18; 2 Cor 11:7-10; Phil 4:10-11). For love of the Gospel, "what I do, is discipline my own body and master it" (1 Cor 9:27). That his service may be undivided, he even renounces marriage (1 Cor 7:7), for "the unmarried man is busy with the Lord's affairs, concerned with pleasing the Lord; but the married man is busy with this world's demands and occupied with pleasing his wife. This means he is divided" (1 Cor 7:33-34). For the sake of the Gospel he welcomes all tribulations, interior and exterior, thereby imitating Christ (cf. Cor 11:17-33) and sharing in his sufferings (cf. Phil 3:10). His life thus becomes a reflection of the Gospel: "Continually we carry about in our bodies the dying of Jesus, so that in our bodies the life of Jesus may also be revealed" (2 Cor 4:10).

On the other hand, St. Paul never regards his own ministry as being different from the ministry of "those who were apostles before me" (Gal 1:17). His constant preoccupation—it is almost an obsession—is simply to base his rights as an Apostle on a mandate from the Lord. Here we see that the apostolic Church, to which Paul must explain himself, neither knows nor admits any apostolate but the one which derives from the clearly expressed will of Jesus and is wholly dependent on him. The ministry of the Twelve, like that of Paul, is established by a choice and calling from Christ, and is a mission for Christ, in the Holy Spirit. The ministry does not have its basis in a charism, even though it is greatly helped by the gifts of the Spirit; the basis for, or roots of, the apostolate are always in the mandate of Christ himself. The apostolate is an *apostle* (a being sent), a *diakonia* (a service), an *oikonomia* (a task of administration); it is a public ministerial function, carried out under authorization from God and with divine empowerment. The *exousia* (power) of Jesus is continued and perpetuated in the community by means of the apostolate of the Twelve and Paul. Because Christ's power is priestly and eschatological, the apostolate of the Twelve is also priestly and eschatological.

5. *Participation in the apostolate or priestly ministry of the Twelve takes the form of various ministries instituted or sanctioned by the apostolic Church.* The apostolic Church is interpreter of the Lord's will. Such interpretation, however, requires time and experience and was therefore dependent on the pastoral experiences and circumstances of the early communities. The Twelve have been commissioned to establish the Church, bring their witness to the ends of the earth, and guide the community of believers. They could not carry out such an immense task all by themselves. Others therefore helped them, but with close and constant reference to the Twelve and their witness. In this sense we can speak of a succession to or, better, an association with the mission of the apostles. Vatican II sums up as follows the way in which the Apostles proceeded:

"That divine mission, entrusted by Christ to the Apostles, will last until the end of the world (Mt. 28:20), since the gospel which was to be handed down by them is for all time the source of all life for the Church. For this reason the Apostles took care to appoint successors in this hierarchically structured society. For they not only had helpers in their ministry, but also, in order that the mission assigned to them might continue after their death, they passed on to their immediate cooperators, as a kind of testament, the duty of perfecting and consolidating the work begun by themselves, charging them to attend to the whole flock in which the Holy Spirit placed them to shepherd the Church of God (cf. Acts 20:28). They therefore appointed such men, and authorized the arrangement that, when these men should have died, other approved men would take up their ministry" (LG, 20a-b/39; cf. Synod, 30).

A careful reading of some characteristic New Testament

passages will help us better to understand the new situations which the early Church had to meet and the new solutions that were applied. We may take as an example the following passage from Acts, since it is rather crowded with interesting details and is concerned with the first essay by the Apostles at a diversification of ministries:

"In those days, as the number of disciples grew, the ones who spoke Greek complained that their widows were being neglected in the daily distribution of food, as compared with the widows of those who spoke Hebrew. The Twelve assembled the community of the disciples and said: 'It is not right for us to neglect the word of God in order to wait on tables. Look around among your own number, brothers, for seven men acknowledged to be deeply spiritual and prudent, and we shall appoint them to this task. This will permit us to concentrate on prayer and the ministry of the word.' The proposal was unanimously accepted by the community. Following this they selected Stephen, a man filled with faith and the Holy Spirit; Philip, Prochorus, Nicanor, Timon, Parmenas, and Nicolaus of Antioch, who had been a convert to Judaism. They presented these men to the apostles, who first prayed over them and then imposed hands on them" (6:1-6).

Some observations on this passage:

(1) A new fact, the growth of the Church, confronted the early Christian community with an unexpected situation, to which some adaptation had to be made. The Apostles could not do everything by themselves, and saw the need for new kinds of service within the growing community. The Church felt itself quite able to make such a structural adaptation.

(2) The special position of the Twelve is evident. They are the ones who, as leaders, give the community a new orientation; they take the initiative when they see that the new services needed are incompatible with the carrying out of their own essential functions.

(3) The specific ministry of the Apostles is here clearly defined and delimited: "to concentrate on prayer and the ministry of the word." These two essential occupations are to fill the life of the apostles. First of all, prayer: not only personal prayer, of which Jesus had given a vivid example and which he had stressed to his disciples (cf. Lk 11:1-13; 18:1-8), but also, and above all, the liturgical celebration amid, and with, the community. Secondly, the preaching of God's word: this was for them a sacred charge and a serious responsibility. "I am ruined if I do not preach it!" (1 Cor 9:16). Prayer and the preaching of God's word are, in the apostles' eyes, the absolutely essential tasks: anything that might prevent the fulfillment of this calling must be removed.

(4) Yet social service to the poor and helpless is also an obligation of the young Church. Without neglecting the essential requirements of their own calling and ministry and while respecting carefully the scale of values ("It is not right for us to neglect the word of God in order to wait on tables"), the Apostles cannot but provide some way of carrying out tasks of charity for the community. To meet this need they seek out collaborators and helpers. *Here is the beginning of the diversification of ministries in the Church,* as a response to new and different situations and to the needs of the community.

(5) To solve the new problem, the Apostles "assembled the community of the disciples." They have a clear conception of their own obligations and of their rights as leaders to make decisions. But they also recognize the dignity and co-responsibility of the faithful, who are here, for the first time, called "disciples."

(6) The Apostles require special qualities in those to be chosen: they must be men of good reputation, filled with the spirit and with wisdom. We find the same preoccupation in the Pastoral Letters to Timothy and Titus. Those selected must have certain human qualities (men of prestige and

good repute) and certain spiritual gifts (spirituality and prudence).

(7) It is up to the community to select the candidates. Those elected seem all to be Greek-speaking Jews, since their names are Greek. The Apostles were Hebrew-speaking or native Palestinian Jews. The Greek-speaking Jews had the reputation of being less devoted to Jewish traditions and were therefore more open to new and different ways of looking at things. With men from two different sociological groups thus in positions of authority, it would be easier to reconcile inevitable differences and to preserve the unity of the Church amid the diversity of its members.

(8) Those selected are presented to the Apostles who "prayed over them and then imposed hands on them." Thus the Apostles lay hands on the men chosen by the community: "Look around among your own number, brothers, for seven men . . . and we shall appoint them to this task." Selection by the community is not enough. The Apostles have received from Christ the Lord a mission and power; they in turn are to commission and empower others. Here we have the clear beginnings of an internal organization of the Church "which rise on the foundations of the apostles and prophets, with Christ Jesus himself as the capstone. Through him the whole structure is fitted together and takes shape as a holy temple in the Lord" (Eph 2:20).

(9) The communication of office and authority is done by prayer and the imposition of hands. Here a "sacrament" makes its appearance in the Church. The imposition of hands itself had already been known to the Jews. Thus Moses was to impose hands on Joshua: "Invest him with some of your own dignity, that the whole Israelite community may obey him" (Nm 27:20). Deuteronomy tells us of the effects of this laying on of hands: "Now Joshua, son of Nun, was filled with the spirit of wisdom, since Moses had laid his hands on him" (34:9).

(10) We may note that the text does not call the seven

"deacons," althought it does make use of the noun "service" (*diakonia*) and the verb "to serve" (*diakonein*). Stephen will become a zealous minister of the word. Philip will baptize (Acts 8:12-13, 38) and will be called an "evangelist" (Acts 21:8). The seven seem in fact to have been the first "bishops" or "presbyters" of the Church (the two terms were synonyms at this period).

Let us turn to another example of a new situation and a new solution; it is taken, once again, from the Acts of the Apostles:

"Paul sent word from Miletus to Ephesus, summoning the presbyters of that Church. When they came to him, he delivered this address: . . . 'Keep watch over yourselves, and over the whole flock the Holy Spirit has given you to guard. Shepherd the church of God, which he has acquired at the price of his own blood. I know that when I am gone, savage wolves will come among you who will not spare the flock. From your own number, men will present themselves distorting the truth and leading astray any who follow them. Be on guard, therefore' " (20:17-18, 28-31).

Some observations on the passage:

(1) Each Christian community was to have its own presbyter. We are told in Acts 14:21-28 of the missionary methods of Barnabas and Paul as they advanced through Asia Minor. "In each church they installed presbyters and, with prayer and fasting, commended them to the Lord in whom they had put their faith" (Acts 14:23). Here we have a clear communication of commission and authority. In Paul's recommendations to Titus we find the same preoccupation with providing presbyters: "My purpose in leaving you in Crete was that you might accomplish what had been left undone, especially the appointment of presbyters in every town" (Tit 1:5). Paul left Titus in Crete with powers for continuing his own work; thus he gave him the responsibility for completing the internal organization of the communities, regulating the situation in each, and thus "ac-

complishing what had been left undone." Titus' main task, however, was the "appointment (*kathistanai* = to establish, constitute, dispose) of presbyters" wherever Christian communities existed. He was to make strict demands for their qualification; above all, they were to hold fast to the teaching of sound doctrine (1:9). For even at this early date, "irresponsible teachers, . . . empty talkers and deceivers" were to be found who "are upsetting whole families by teaching things they have no right to teach" (1:10-11). "These must be silenced" (1:11), and forbidden to preach in public.

(2) The terminology, here as in other New Testament texts, is not yet clear and unambiguous. The "presbyters" of Acts 20:17 are called "bishops" in 20:28. (So too, the presbyters" of Tit 1:5 are "bishops" in 1:7). The primary stress is on the image and vocabulary of the "shepherd," which had been used by Christ and occurs frequently in the New Testament writings with their background of contemporary rural culture.

(3) Ministers are "presbyters" or "bishops," not by their own decision or the will of the community. Rather, the Holy Spirit establishes them so that they may shepherd the Church of God. This happens at the moment of the imposition of hands. This is why the Apostle urges Timothy "to stir into flame the gift of God bestowed when my hands were laid on you" (2 Tim 1:6). For the same reason we are dealing here with a highly important ministry. Paul tells Timothy: "You can depend on this: whoever wants to be a bishop aspires to a noble task" (1 Tim 3:1). It is on this account that Paul requires presbyters to give good example and to fulfill their duties in the proper way: "Those who serve well . . . gain a worthy place for themselves and much assurance in their faith in Christ Jesus" (1 Tim 3:11). "Presbyters who do well as leaders deserve to be paid double, especially those whose work is preaching and teaching" (1 Tim 5:17). To justify this view Paul appeals to words of Christ which are also preserved by Matthew (10:10)

and Luke (10:7): "The worker deserves his wages" (1 Tim 5:18). In similar fashion he writes to the Corinthians: "If we have sown for you in the spirit, is it too much to expect a material harvest from you? . . . Do you not realize that those who work in the temple are supported by the temple, and those who minister at the altar share the offerings of the altar? Likewise the Lord himself ordered that those who preach the gospel should live by the gospel" (1 Cor 9:11-14). And he asks the Thessalonians: "We beg you, brothers, respect those among you whose task it is to exercise authority in the Lord and admonish you; esteem them with the greatest love because of their work" (1 Thess 5:12-13).

We notice, too, that according to these early texts, the servants or ministers of the new covenant are beginning to enjoy a special social status in the apostolic Christian community. Those who today urge the "declericalization" of the Church should not overlook this fact as they read their Bibles. They can, of course, appeal to the example of St. Paul but they should not overlook the fact that, even as he spontaneously renounces certain rights he has as minister of the Gospel or the altar, he stresses the existence of these rights.

(4) The Church is a "community of God" which was not brought together simply by the agreement of men but was "acquired by God" at a divine price: "the price of his own blood." Paul tells his readers: "All men are now undeservedly justified by the gift of God, through the redemption wrought in Christ Jesus. Through his blood, God made him the means of expiation for all who believe" (Rom. 3: 24-25). It is for the well-being of this "community of God," which God has acquired for himself in such a fashion, that the presbyters must labor.

(5) There are also dangers confronting the Church: "Savage wolves will come among you who will not spare the flock." The image is related, of course, to the image of

the shepherd. Jesus himself had warned: "Be on your guard against false prophets, who come to you in sheep's clothing but underneath are wolves on the prowl" (Mt 7:15). The danger, however, does not come only from without: "From your own number, men will present themselves distorting the truth and leading astray any who follow them." Concern regarding these men who "distort the truth" within the Church itself was one of the abiding preoccupations of the "bishops."

(6) Paul issues a serious warning and reminds the "presbyters" of a serious duty: "Be on guard, therefore!" St. Peter is no less urgent: "To the elders among you I, a fellow elder, a witness of Christ's sufferings and sharer in the glory that is to be revealed, make this appeal. God's flock is in your midst; give it a shepherd's care. Watch over it willingly as God would have you do, not under constraint; and not for shameful profit either, but generously. Be examples to the flock, not lording it over those assigned to you so that when the chief Shepherd appears you will win for yourselves the unfading crown of glory" (1 Pet 5:1-4).

It is not difficult to see that the Acts of the Apostles and the apostolic Letters provide us with rather explicit and detailed data which enable us to recreate for ourselves the broad lines of the constitution of the hierarchy within the "organic structure of the priestly community" (LG, 11a/27-28). The fifth proposition presented by the International Theological Commission to the Synod of Bishops in 1971 is, therefore, true and happily expressed: "Even while we recognize that there was a period in which ecclesial structures only gradually reached their full development, we may not set up an opposition between a purely charismatic constitution of the Pauline churches and a ministerial constitution in the other churches."[7]

This point is important today, in view of the studies by Käsemann and other Bultmannians, with which Hans Küng agrees in his book *The Church*. These scholars maintain that the church of Corinth was unacquainted with presbyters, bishops, and ordination, and that their life-style was based solely on the spontaneous utterances of charismatics; they maintain, further, that despite this fact the church of Corinth was a complete Christian community and even had the celebration of the Eucharist. Hence they contrast the purely charismatic churches whose inspiration Paul was, and the institutionalized churches deriving from the organized community of Jerusalem. Hans Küng writes: "Our examination of the Pauline constitution of the Church showed that a charismatic ordering of the community without any special appointing of ministries (such as ordination) is perfectly possible; in Corinth there were neither *episkopoi* nor presbyters, nor ordination, but, apart from the Apostle, only freely expressed charisms. Despite this, the church at Corinth was a community provided with everything that was necessary, equipped with the preaching of the word, baptism, the Lord's Supper, and all kinds of ministries."[8]

The report of the Internationl Theological Commission justly remarks that this position of Küng "does not stand up to criticism."[9] But it does oblige us to look more closely at the place of the Spirit in the early Church. It is clear, to begin with, that the charisms, especially that of prophecy, were closely connected with the apostolic ministry. It may even be said that the apostolate had a prophetic and charismatic character. The Apostles are presented as the prophets of the new covenant: "For this reason I shall send you prophets and wise men and scribes" (Mt 23:34). They are superior to the prophets of the old covenant because to them are revealed the mysteries of the kingdom (Mt 13:11). In the Acts of the Apostles we read that the Twelve were specially equipped by the Holy Spirit for their prophetic function: "We testify to this. So too does the Holy Spirit" (Acts 5:32).

On the other hand, these men were Apostles not because of the charisms they had but because of an earlier appointment by Christ before his resurrection. They were not Apostles for the sake of being charismatics but charismatics for the sake of their apostolate. "For the discharging of such great duties, the Apostles were enriched by Christ with a special outpouring of the Holy Spirit, who came upon them. This spiritual gift they passed on to their helpers by the imposition of hands" (LG, 21c/41). Thus there is no opposition in principle between charism and apostolic ministry. It is also true, however, that in addition to the Apostles, prophets and other charismatics were to be found in the early community. Despite this fact, there was no incompatibility between the prophetic charism and the institutional organization of the Church. The Apostles and "elders" of Jerusalem sent Judas and Silas, prophets both (cf. Acts 15:32), to Antioch to communicate to the Christians of that place the decree which asserted their freedom from the Mosaic Law.

However, St. Paul shows no awareness that he is organizing communities of a different type than that of Jerusalem, despite the fact that he also proclaims his emancipation from the Law. On the contrary, his constant preoccupation is with the unity that should exist between the communities he establishes among the gentiles and the mother community at Jerusalem. He refers to the tradition of the latter church in order to correct abuses at Corinth or to restore purity of doctrine (1 Cor 11:16-23; 15:1-11; 1 Thess 2:14). He addresses his First Letter to the Corinthians (written at Ephesus) to "all the saints," because the leaders of the Corinthian community had arrived and were with him (1 Cor 16:15-18). His invitation to the Corinthians to honor such men (16:16) recalls 1 Thess 5:12-13: "We beg you, brothers, respect those among you whose task it is to exercise authority in the Lord and admonish you; esteem them with the greatest love because of their work."

The existence of charisms, therefore, does not prevent leaders or local presiding officers from having a place. On the contrary, there is even some indication that there were presiding officers at Corinth itself. This evidence emerges in the discussions about the importance of Apollos who is put on equal footing with Paul and Cephas (1 Cor 1:12; 3:4-5) and is called, with Paul, "co-workers of God" (3:9) and an "administrator of the mysteries of God" (4:1). It is clear that Apollos was not at Corinth when Paul wrote his letter, but he was to arrive immediately, and there is nothing to suggest that in his absence the city had no "shepherd."

A comparison between the church of Corinth and the church of Philippi (Paul's favorite community) throws even more light on the situation. In the Letter to the Philippians, Paul and Timothy address themselves "to all the holy ones at Philippi, *with their bishops and deacons* in Christ Jesus" (Phil 1:1; italics added). Clearly, Paul did not rely simply on the wealth of charisms to keep his communities pure in their faith and fervent in love. This passage also allows us to connect the prescriptions given in the Pastoral Letters with Paul's activity as described in Acts 14:23 where he is said during his *first* journey to have appointed presbyters in every city.

The function of the ministries set up by the Apostles to help them in their work is defined, first of all, by the proclamation of the Gospel: to spread the good news (*euaggelizesthai*), to preach (*kerussein*), to *teach* (*didaskein*), to speak (*lalein*), to exhort (*parakalein*), to proclaim (*paraggelein*) (cf. 2 Tim 1:8; 2:2; 4:2,5; 1 Tim 4:11, 13; 6:20; 2 Tim 1:13). Furthermore, however, their work included the direction of the liturgical services (1 Tim 3:9) and the guidance of the community (1 Tim 3:15; 5:17-19).

These ministries (of the *presbyteroi* or *episkopoi*) are connected with the Apostles and, as can be seen from the Pastoral Letters, are both grounded in apostolic tradition and regulated by it (cf. 1 Tim 4:6,11-16; 6:17; 2 Tim 1:13-14; 2:2,7; 3:11-14; 1 Tim 3:15; 3:7; Tit 1:5). As early as 1

Cor. 4:17 this dependence on the Apostles is already explicit. Those responsible for the churches, the "shepherds," do not exercise their functions properly if they do not assure the fidelity of the communities to their initial apostolic structure. What the Apostles did is and continues to be a norm for all later times (cf. Synod, no. 32). Only forty years after Paul's First Letter to the Corinthians, St. Clement of Rome wrote a well-known letter to the same community in which he states, as a universally acknowledged and unchallenged fact, that ever since the days of the Apostles there had always been official shepherds set over the churches and that this was true of Corinth in particular. He recalls that Apollos was one of those to whom the Christians of Corinth owed obedience as a man established and approved by the Apostles (47:4), like the bishops who are also approved and established (42:4), and like the successors of the latter (44: 2). Clement is not satisfied to speak of authority and obedience in general terms; he refers specifically to the function of bishops, presbyters, and deacons in the liturgy, in the offering of gifts, and in priestly service (41:2; 43:1; 44:4).

Patristic tradition remained faithful in this matter. In the Letters of St. Ignatius of Antioch (first decade of second century) there is no room for a community without an established hierarchy. But we must note that in 107, when he wrote his letters, Ignatius was already an old man and had lived his life, therefore during the age of the Apostles themselves. In his brief letters he speaks sixty times of bishops, and mentions presbyters twenty-two times and deacons fifteen times. It has been justly said that we need only read these letters to be convinced that this hierarchy was not invented in Ignatius' old age or shortly before. It derived from the Apostles themselves. To the Ephesians Ignatius writes that "one should look upon the bishop as upon the Lord Himself" (6:1).[10] To the Magnesians he says that "the bishop is to preside in the place of God" (6:1),[11] while to the Trallians he roundly declares that "apart from these [bishops, presbyters, and deacons], no church deserves the name" (3:1).[12] He teaches the Philadelphians that the bishop holds" the supreme office in the community not by his own efforts, or by men's doing, or for personal glory. No, he holds it by the love of God the Father and the Lord Jesus Christ" (1:1).[13] And he warns the Smyrnaeans: "Let no one do anything touching the Church, apart from the bishop. Let that celebration of the Eucharist be considered valid which is held under the bishop or anyone to whom he has committed it. Where the bishop appears, let the people be, just as where Jesus Christ is, there is the Catholic Church. It is not permitted without authorization from the bishop either to baptize or to hold an agape" (8:1-2).[14] Finally, he reminds young Bishop Polycarp of the "garment of grace" he has received (1:2).[15]

In his struggle with the Gnostic heresies, St. Irenaeus stresses the teaching function of the bishops who have received "the charism of truth" (*Against Heresies* IV, 26:2). Hippolytus of Rome depicts the bishops as successors to the Apostles in the three areas of teaching, priestly activity, and pastoral activity; presbyters are their coworkers.

In the light of these testimonies, we may allow for an important development of ministries but we may not set up an opposition between the "charismatic constitution" of the Pauline churches and the "episcopal-presbyteral constitution" of the other churches. For the Christians of the early Church there was no opposition between the freedom of the Spirit and the existence of a basic Church structure. To find in the early Church a conflict between charismatics and institutionalists is undobutedly to project our contemporary problems back upon the apostolic age.

How then are we to explain the surprising absence of a "priestly" terminology in the New Testament in speaking of the activity of the Apostles? The explanation possibly lies in the ambiguity which would have characterized such terminology in the minds of early Christians and in the originality or radical newness of Christ's "priesthood." The vocabulary which the New Testament prefers is certainly the vocabulary of service: service that is authorized or based on an authorization from God. Apostolic service is understood as service of God (2 Cor 6:4; 1 Tim 3:2), service of Christ (2 Cor 11:23; Col 1:7), service of the Gospel (Eph 2:7; Col 1:23; 2 Thess 3:2), service of the new covenant (2 Cor 3:6), service of the faithful and their salvation (1 Cor 3:5), service in the Lord (Eph 6:21; 2 Cor 4:17). All this at least implies a priestly outlook. Furthermore, the terms "shepherd" and "servant," as taken in the sense in which Christ applied them to himself and as seen in the light of the prophecy about the suffering Servant of Jahweh, also suggest a "priestly" outlook, with priesthood understood in the same sense in which it applies to Christ: the fulfillment and the transcending of all the priesthoods of the Old Testament. The Apostles, after all, thought of their mission and activity as a continuation of the mission and activity of Christ who, as we have seen, was a "priest."

Nonetheless, we must recognize that the New Testament very rarely uses priestly terminology to describe the ministerial activity of the Apostles and their co-workers. It was only later that there came a "sacerdotalization" and "sacralization" of the apostolic and ecclesial ministry. But even this fact must be properly understood. We have already noted that the terminology of priesthood would have been ambiguous for the early Christians. Neither Christ nor the Apostles were "priests" in the Old Testament sense, that is, in the sense that Aaron and the levites were priests; much less were they priests in the sense of the contemporary pagan priesthoods. On the contrary: with Christ an entirely original, different, new, complete, definitive, and unparalleled priesthood made its appearance. Christ's priesthood, as we have seen, brought to fulfillment and at the same time wholly transcended all the priesthoods of the Old Testament. The early Christians had to be made fully aware of this point:

the ministry of the new covenant originates not in Moses or Aaron but in Christ and the Apostles. Once this was clearly grasped, Christians adopted terms and institutions from the Old Testament but they viewed them in a typological perspective which, without destroying continuity between the two covenants, made it possible to remain clearly aware of the distance between image and reality, shadow and substance. At the same time, however, we must admit that even given this typological approach, the use of Old Testament terminology and institutions tended to make men lose sight of the essential transcendence of the new covenant, that is, of the radically new thing which had come on the scene in and with Christ. The transparently clear Christian concept of ministry could be obscured under the influence of considerations based on Old Testament institutions. Thus there was the real danger of an undue, even an extreme, "sacerdotalization" and "sacralization" or "culticization" of the apostolic and ecclesiastical ministry. In this sense we may speak of a legitimate and perhaps even necessary "desacerdotalization" and "desacralization" or "deculticization" of the Christian ministry. This would represent a good and legitimate process of purification of concepts and would help us better understand the radical newness of Christ's "priesthood" and of its continuation in the ministerial activity of the Apostles and their successors and collaborators in the priestly community (or *hierateuma*) of the new covenant.

6. *The New Testament minister is specially called by God and enabled to act publicly in the person of Christ on behalf of men.* Here we have, in my opinion, the most accurate definition of the Christian ministerial priesthood in general (applying to the Apostle, the bishop, and the presbyter).[16] And it follows from what we have seen in the previous five propositions. This ministry began with Jesus Christ when "the time of fulfillment came" (Mk 1:15), and is, for that reason, eschatological. It can therefore be understood and exercised only in a constant and total relationship to

Christ. In this respect the ministry is not comparable with any other public office; it is unique and by its nature can be understood only by theological reflection in the light of revelation, not by sociology. It forms part of the nature of the Church as "mystery" and is a theological, not a pyschological or sociological, datum.

We have also seen that in the Apostles ministry is not to be confused or identified with charism; that is, charism is not the reason or ground for someone being an "Apostle." The apostolate is rather a ministry of the Spirit, for which a person must be chosen, called, sent, authorized, and qualified by God. It thus supposes an *exousia,* a power or authority or special competence in virtue of which the Apostle acts publicly as Christ's minister and comes forward as his ambassador to speak and act in his name. In a similar way, the ministry of bishops and presbyters is not a pure and simple charism of service; it is also a ministry or office for which one must be called ("vocation"), sent ("mission"), and qualified ("ordination") by God. When Paul bids Timothy "to stir into flame the gift of God bestowed when my hands were laid on you" (2 Tim 1:6), he is implying that through the imposition of hands Timothy's very *being* became that of a minister. "Do not neglect the gift you received when, as a result of prophecy, the presbyters laid their hands on you" (1 Tim 4:14). Through the imposition of hands in the sacrament of orders the ordinand receives something new, something which he did not have before and which distinguishes him "in essence and not only in degree" (LG, 10b/27) from the other baptized. This "something" is a genuinely ontological reality: "In consecration is given an ontological participation in sacred functions," says the Prefatory Note of Explanation for Chapter Three of *Lumen Gentium* (Abbott, p. 99). It is irremovable and affects the very root of a man's ministerial being, so configuring him to Christ the Priest that he is now able to speak and act publicly for men in the person of Christ the Head (cf. PO,

2b/534) and to share in the authority by which Christ himself builds up, sanctifies, and rules his body. This ontological
reality or radical qualification conferred by the sacrament
of orders is also called an "indelible character" in the theological tradition (cf. Synod, nos. 37-40). It is what transforms a man into a ministerial priest of the new covenant
and distinguishes him from lay people. Here we have his
nature or essence. Here we have the very being of the priest.
With the Apostle he can say: "Our sole credit is from God,
who has made us qualified ministers of a new covenant"
(2 Cor 3:6). With the Apostle he can speak of "the authority
the Lord has given me" (2 Cor 13:10; cf. 10:8).

The document of the Synod says: "Among the various
charisms and services, the priestly ministry of the New Testament, which continues Christ's function as mediator, and
which in essence and not merely in degree is distinct from
the common priesthood of all the faithful (cf. LG, 10), alone
perpetuates the essential work of the Apostles: by effectively
proclaiming the Gospel, by gathering together and leading
the community, by remitting sins, and especially by celebrating the Eucharist, it makes Christ, the head of the community, present in the exercise of his work of redeeming
mankind and glorifying God perfectly" (33). A little
further on: "He [the minister] is a guarantor both of the
first proclamation of the Gospel for the gathering together
of the Church and of the ceaseless renewal of the Church
which has already been gathered together. If the Church
lacks the presence and activity of the ministry which is received by the laying on of hands with prayer, she cannot
have full certainty of her fidelity and of her visible continuity" (36). There is therefore no authentic ("fully
realized") Church of Christ without the sacerdotal ministry.
This is why, in the introductory section of the document,
the bishops offer a basic consideration: "We fraternally
urge all the faithful to strive to contemplate the Lord Jesus
living in his Church and to realize that he wishes to work

in a special way through his ministers; they will thus be convinced that the Christian community cannot fulfill its complete mission without the ministerial priesthood" (19).

In view of certain contemporary tendencies in Catholic theology we must recall these words of the Council of Trent (Session 22, July 15, 1563): "Moreover, in the sacrament of orders, just as in baptism and confirmation, a character is imprinted which can neither be blotted out nor taken away. Therefore, this holy council rightly condemns the opinion of those who say that the priests of the New Testament have merely temporary power, and that once they have been duly ordained they can become laymen again if they do not exercise the ministry of the word of God. But if anyone says that all Christians without exception are priests of the New Testament or are endowed with equal spiritual power, it is apparent that he upsets the ecclesiastical hierarchy, which is like an army in battle array (*see Cant. 6:3*), as much as if, contrary to Paul's teaching, all were apostles, all prophets, all evangelists, all pastors and teachers (*see 1 Cor. 12:29; Eph. 4:11*). Therefore the holy council declares that, besides the other ecclesiastical grades, the bishops, who have succeeded the Apostles, belong in a special way to the hierarchical order; and placed as the Apostle says by the Holy Spirit to rule the Church of God (*see Acts 20:28*), they are superior to priests, and can confer the sacrament of confirmation, can ordain ministers for the Church, and they have the power to perform many other functions that those of an inferior grade cannot. Moreover, the holy council declares that in the ordination of bishops, of priests, and of other grades, the consent, call, or authority, neither of the people nor of any secular power or public authority is necessary to the extent that without it the ordination is invalid. Rather it decrees that all those who have been called and appointed merely by the people or by the secular power or ruler, and thus undertake to exercise these ministries, and that all those who arrogate these ministries to themselves on their own authority, are not minsters of the Church but should be considered as thieves and robbers who have not entered through the door *(see John 10:1)*."[17] There is a good deal in this text that would call for comment. For the moment, however, we need note only one point: the main point of this text, and thus its chief direct intention, is to contradict those who would maintain that the priests of the New Testament are simply functionaries of the community and that everyone in the Christian community enjoys identical priestly prerogatives, requiring for the exercise of these only a simple appointment by the community. In the classical language of theology, these affirmations are heresy pure and simple. It is still possible today to have heretical positions in this matter. Thus the fourth proposition formulated by the International Theological Commission for the Synod of Bishops reads: "The Christian who is called to the priestly ministry receives in his ordination not a purely external function but a new and unique share in the priesthhood of Christ. In virtue of this sharing he represents Christ at the head of the community and, as it were, over against the community. The ministry is thus a specific way of living a life of Christian service in the Church. Its specific character appears most clearly in the minister's role of presiding at the Eucharist (a presidency that is required if Christian worship is to have its full reality). The preaching of the word and pastoral care are ordered to the Eucharist, for the latter consecrates the whole of the Christian's existence in the world."

The qualification the minister receives for his work ought therefore leave him open for the reception of charisms, that is, for the special gifts of the Holy Spirit which will enable him better to carry out his ministry. To this end, the minister must create the proper existential context, that is, he must live a spiritual life or a life "in the Spirit" (the theme of the following chapter).

What a splendid thing the ministry of the new covenant

is! "God, who alone is holy and bestows holiness, willed to raise up for Himself as companions and helpers men who would humbly dedicate themselves to the work of sanctification. Hence, through the ministry of the bishop, God consecrates priests so that they can share by a special title in the priesthood of Christ. Thus, in performing sacred functions they can act as the ministers of Him who in the liturgy continually exercises his priestly office on our behalf by the action of His Spirit" (PO, 5a/541). "They [priests] have been consecrated to God in a new way by the reception of orders. They have become living instruments of Christ the eternal priest" (PO, 12b/558). In the present situation of crisis among the clergy we do well to reflect upon the Apostle's words: "You can depend on this: whoever aspires to be a bishop [or a presbyter, for the two are identical in Paul] aspires to a noble task" (1 Tim 3:1). Let us not be afraid to speak, even today, of "the excellence . . . of the priesthood" (PO, 11b/556) and "the excellence of the priestly ministry" (PO, 11f/557). For, as the bishops of the Synod declare, "in the midst of the Christian community which, in spite of its defects, lives by the Spirit, he [the priest] is a pledge of the salvific presence of Christ" (39).

Notes

[1] A recent study in Brazil (Marins, "Pesquisa sobre o Clero do Brasil"; this study, already cited above, should be read in the light of the 1971 Synod) showed that 20% of the priests interviewed were puzzled about how to define their mission; the remaining 80% were divided among six different positions, no one of which was defended by a large number of priests. The views expressed were varied and independent of one another. The priests recognized that there was plenty to do in the Church, but many of them saw no necessity of being a priest: in the measure that the Church was officially acknowledging the importance of the laity and assigning them a number of missions which had previously been reserved to the clergy, the latter were losing their grasp on their own specific role. Priests there-

fore are seriously asking themselves: "Why should I be a priest, if laymen can do what I do?" or "What is so exclusively the priest's mission in the Church that it can require a total dedication?" If 80% of the priests interviewed could give varying, individual responses to those questions, then the clergy as a whole is in a state of confusion. That is the main conclusion reached by the study: there is no general agreement on the definition of the priest's specific mission. Such a lack means that ends are not defined with sufficient clarity that the most suitable means can be sought; or else the ends are defined in varying ways. The clergy as a whole does not know which of its missions is specific to it (cf. especially the last part of Marins' study, pp. 135-138).

Another study (Gregory, *art. cit.*) reached the same conclusions (cf. especially pp. 435-438): while the Church, during the Council and later, was rethinking its mission in the world, priests were raising the question of the meaning of priesthood, and many could not say what it means to be a priest today. What years ago seemed crystal-clear is now obscure. Among the views expressed, some offered reflections of the following kind: The only actions exclusively reserved to the priest are the Eucharistic consecration and the absolution from sins; but, if that is what is specific to the priest, why should the latter live the same kind of life now as he did in an earlier time when the layman's role in the Church was predominantly a passive one? That is, why should the priest be a celibate, put his whole day at the disposition of the faithful, direct charitable and other parochial works, build, visit homes, etc.? All these activities, after all, can be carried on by people who do not receive the sacrament of orders, yet are not exceeding the limits assigned them in the life of the Church. Gregory's study is concerned chiefly with laicizations of clergymen and is climaxed by the statement that "the priest does not really 'leave' the priestly ministry; rather, he never finds it" (p. 937). The evidence shows that a search for priestly activity is going on and that the search is never rewarded by any vital experience. The priest who seeks laicization does so because he does not know — or, in the case of those who at one time did have a satisfying priestly experience, no longer knows — how to carry out his mission concretely. He therefore seeks personal fulfillment in the activities of lay life.

[2] The full title is: *Rapport de la Commission Internationale de Théologie: Le ministère sacerdotal* (Paris: Editions du Cerf, 1971). The report was drawn up by a sub-commission: Hans Urs von Balthasar, Carlo Colombo, González de Cardedal, M.-J. Le Guillou (chairman), F. Lescrauwaet (secretary), and J. Medina-Estevez. The text was discussed in a plenary session of the Commission in October, 1970, and approved as a working document to be forwarded to the Synod of Bishops. It contains eight chapters. Its chief purpose is to show the foundations, in Scripture and Tradition, of the priestly ministry, and it stresses primarily the Christological and Apostolic bases of this ministry and its character as eschatological service. With certain already widespread views in mind, the report emphasizes the "priestly" nature of the life and work of Christ and the ministry of the

Apostles; it goes rather fully into the problem of the absence of any "priestly" terminology in the early Church and the question of the "sacerdotalization" of ecclesiastical ministry under the influence chiefly of the Old Testament and secondarily of pagan "priesthood" (the "sacralization" of the ministry). With direct reference to Hans Küng and the Bultmannians, the document shows the non-existence of the supposed opposition between the "charismatic" outlook of the Pauline church (especially Corinth) and the "institutional" outlook of the church of Jerusalem which, in this view, later on won out in Asia Minor, especially because of St. Ignatius of Antioch. The document ends with a list of six propositions which were formally voted on and approved by the Commission. The reader of the Commission's report will see that its main concerns recur in the present book and enrich it. An English translation is printed as Appendix I.

[3] Cf. *Le ministère sacerdotal*, p. 36, with the bibliography in note 2. For information on these groups, which may or may not contain lay-people as well, cf., e.g., Ruud J. Bunnik, "Common-Purpose Groups in Western Europe," in *Contestation in the Church* (*Concilium*, 68, ed. by Teodoro Jiménez Urresti; New York: Herder and Herder, 1971), pp. 22-31; Frans Haarsma, "A Critical Community in Beverwijk," in *The Unifying Role of the Bishop* (*Concilium*, 71, ed. by Edward Schillebeeckx; New York: Herder and Herder, 1972), pp. 145-53; Walter Hollenweger, "The Quest for Authenticity in Solidarity Groups," in *Man in a New Society* (*Concilium*, 75, ed. by Franz Böckle; New York: Herder and Herder, 1972), pp. 68-79.

[4] The quotation in this passage is from St. Augustine, *The City of God*, Book X, chapter 6 (PL, 41:284).

[5] Here we have the chief theological reason why the Church has the duty of supplying priests so that under normal circumstances each community may have its priest and be able to exercise its common priesthood. To baptize people and then not supply them with the needed priests (but there are not enough celibates?—But that is a matter of purely ecclesiastical law!) is to give men the common priesthood and at the same time deny them its exercise.

[6] Cf. Jean Giblet, "Les Douze: Histoire et théologie," in *Le Prêtre: Foi et contestation* (Paris: Lethielleux, 1970).

[7] The six propositions drawn up by the International Theological Commission (in *Le ministère sacerdotal*, pp. 125-126; cf. end of note 2, above) are given below in Appendix I.

[8] Hans Küng, *The Church*, tr. by Ray and Rosaleen Ockenden (New York: Sheed & Ward, 1967), p. 442.

[9] *Le ministère sacerdotal*, p. 62.

[10] *The Epistles of St. Clement of Rome and St. Ignatius of Antioch*, tr. by James A. Kleist, S.J. (*Ancient Christian Writers*, 1; Westminster, Md.: Newman, 1946), p. 62.

[11] *Op. cit.*, pp. 70-71.

[12] *Op. cit.*, p. 76.

[13] *Op. cit.*, p. 85.

[14] *Op. cit.*, p. 93.

[15] *Op. cit.*, p. 96.

[16] This is the position of Vatican II, especially in its Decree on the Ministry and Life of Priests, no. 2. On this subject, cf. my book, *The Ecclesiology of Vatican II*, especially chapter 9: "The Theology of the Priesthood." According to repeated, explicit statements of the Theological Commission, it was the express intention of Vatican II to go beyond the Scholastic definition of priesthood (presupposed by the Council of Trent), according to which the essence of the priesthood was seen only in terms of relationship to the Eucharist. Vatican II intended to define the priesthood rather in terms of apostolic ministry in general; the nature and mission of the presbyter was to be derived from the nature and mission of the bishop, the nature and mission of bishops from the nature and mission of the Apostles, and the nature and mission of the Apostles from the nature and mission of Christ. As the Father consecrated and sent Christ, so Christ consecrated and sent the Apostles, and the Apostles consecrated and sent the bishops. It is in this consecration and mission of the bishop that we are to look for the nature of the ministerial priesthood of presbyters. Such was the perspective and intention of Vatican II.

[17] Latin text in Denzinger-Schönmetzer, *Enchiridion symbolorum, definitionum, et declarationum de rebus fidei et morum*, 32nd ed. (Freiburg: Herder, 1963, nos. 1767-1769; older editions, no. 960. Tr. from *The Church Teaches: Documents of the Church in English translation*, selected and translated by John F. Clarkson, S.J., *et al.* (St. Louis: B. Herder, 1955), no. 843, pp. 330-331.

III

The Spiritual Life
of the Priest

Priests are fairly unanimous in agreeing that a personal spiritual life is a necessity. A priest without a spiritual life is a contradiction. At the moment, however, the clergy is passing through a serious "crisis of spirituality." But the crisis, if correctly grasped, is not a crisis of substance (that is, there is no lack of personal Christian life) but a crisis of forms, inasmuch as the traditional models of spirituality and asceticism seem to be of no use to many priests in their efforts to live a personal Christian and priestly life. There is a clear reaction against ritualism and formalism, and this often leads to the abandonment of traditional spiritual practices, such as the breviary, personal prayer, some devotions (Rosary, visits to the Blessed Sacrament), frequent confession, voluntary self-denial, spiritual reading, spiritual direction, retreats. Such are the chief symptoms of the problem, and they come in for mention in almost all meetings of priests where the crisis of spirituality is discussed.

When the question of causes is raised, priests usually point

75

to the following: a spiritual formation that has no connection with pastoral action; the application of monastic spirituality to priests who live in the world; predetermined and stereotyped forms, which are given preference or even juridically imposed; a dichotomy between spirituality (thought of as "the interior life") and pastoral activity (thought of as "activism") ; spirituality defined as a set of individualistic acts of piety, unrelated to the community and empty of meaning for contemporary man; disorientation through a false opposition between horizontalism (service to the community or the individual person) and verticalism (service of God) ; devaluation of the human and the temporal ("flight from the world") .

On all sides there is a great desire for and sincere concern with discovering forms of spiritual life which will square better with contemporary life-styles. People are looking for new forms of self-expression and new modes of behavior which will do justice to the aspirations of modern man and make it possible for him to live out the requirements of the Gospel in a more incarnate and authentic way in our secularized world. The broad outlines of such a new spirituality are already perceptible: it will have to be more incarnate and more closely linked to pastoral action; more Biblical and liturgical; more community-oriented; more alive, creative, dynamic, and spontaneous; more free of formalism; more pluralistic or diversified according to mentality, period, education, and personality; more directed to human values and to creation in its entirety, with an asceticism that flows from the effort to build up the world. The spiritual life needs to be stripped of the juridicism, with its "obligations in conscience," which creates false, useless, and prejudicial guilt complexes. A new Church discipline must foster freedom, conviction, and personal responsibility in the realm of spirituality. Many people have, furthermore, the desire to recapture the best values of the past and, with a view to creating a basic synthesis for the contemporary priest, to integrate these with the new dimensions of spirituality indicated by the signs of the times. Some new practices are already making their way; revision of life; communal penance services; meditative reading of the word of God; small groups of priests living a common life; a new liturgical life. Everywhere we see an attitude of attentiveness and openness to God who speaks to us in his word and addresses his calls to us through events and through all aspects and circumstances of our daily life.

The new spirituality of the priest, which is now taking shape, will always have to be based on certain permanently valid principles. In our effort to determine these principles the Synod of Bishops offers little or no help, for what it has to say about the spiritual life of the priest (nos. 70-75) is weak, confused, and lacking in courage. We shall therefore follow the principles and norms provided by Vatican II in its Decree on the Ministry and Life of Priests, for here we have a document that is positive, clear, and courageous in pointing out new ways to ground and direct our search for a priestly spirituality.

1. *The priest should live in the light of what he is.* His spirituality is the living out of what he is as a priest. An authentic priestly spirituality, therefore, must find its point of departure in the theology of Christian ministerial priesthood. What does this theology have to say to us? It teaches us that the priest is so configured to Christ the Priest that he is able to act and speak publicly for men in the person of Christ the Head and that he shares in the authority by which Christ himself builds up, sanctifies, and rules his body (cf. PO, 2/533-36). Thus, as the Church is a "mystery," that is, is the sign and instrument of the glorified Lord and his Spirit, so too, we may say, the priest is by his nature a "mystery": he is the sign and instrument of Christ the Priest. "By the sacrament of orders priests are configured to Christ the Priest so that as ministers of the Head and co-workers of the episcopal order they can build up and

establish His whole Body which is the Church. Already indeed, in the consecration of baptism, like all Christians, they received the sign and gift of so lofty a vocation and grace that even despite human weakness they can and must pursue perfection according to the Lord's words: 'You therefore are to be perfect, even as your heavenly Father is perfect' (Mt 5:48). To the acquisition of this perfection priests are bound by a special claim, since they have been consecrated to God in a new way by the reception of orders. They have become living instruments of Christ the eternal priest, so that through the ages they can accomplish His wonderful work of reuniting the whole society of men with heavenly power" (PO, 12a-b/557-58).

Here we have an extraordinarily fruitful principle for the spiritual life of the priest. In the new covenant we have in fact but one eternal changeless priest (cf. Heb 7:24) who "by one offering . . . has forever perfected those who are being sanctified" (Heb 10:14). But Christ, though invisible since the Ascension, continues to be present and active in the world. To give himself a visible form and to make his sacrifice and his word ever present anew to men, he chooses some of the baptized and transforms them by means of a special sacrament into his living instruments. Henceforth it is he, the Priest and Mediator, who sanctifies men through these living instruments. It is he, the Teacher and Prophet, who teaches through them. It is he, the Shepherd and Lord, who uses these instruments in order to guide his faithful followers. As a sign and instrument the priest has but a purely relative and secondary value, but a value that is also necessary, sublime, and indispensable. We would have no sacraments without the sensible elements that go into them. There would be no Eucharist without bread and wine. So too the priest is necessary, and between Christ and his instrument there is a union comparable to the Hypostatic Union itself (cf. LG, 8a/22). "God, who alone is holy and bestows holiness, willed to raise up for Himself as com-

panions and helpers men who would humbly dedicate themselves to the work of sanctification. Hence, through the
ministry of the bishop, God consecrates priests so that they
can share by a special title in the priesthood of Christ. Thus,
in performing sacred functions they can act as the ministers
of Him who in the liturgy continually exercises his priestly
office on our behalf by the action of His Spirit" (PO,
5a/541). The nature of the liturgy will, in fact, help us to
understand the nature of Christian priestly action.

In its Constitution on the Sacred Liturgy, Vatican II
teaches that in order to carry on the work of saving and redeeming the world "Christ is always present in His Church,
especially in her liturgical celebrations" (SC, 7a/140-41);
that in this activity of glorifying God and sanctifying men
"Christ indeed always associates the Church with Himself"
(SC, 7b/141); that "rightly, then, the liturgy is considered
as an exercise of the priestly office of Jesus Christ" (7c/141);
and that "from this it follows that every liturgical celebration, because it is an action of Christ the Priest and of His
Body the Church, is a sacred action surpassing all others"
(7d/141). The important point at every step is that Christ
is the principal agent in every liturgical action while the
priest is only an instrumental agent. This "only" is the
priest's great motive for humility, even while it is also the
reason for his authentic greatness and excellence. Above
all, however, it is here that we find the basis for his specifically priestly spirituality. It is not he who offers sacrifice,
but Christ who offers through him. It is not he who baptizes,
but Christ who baptizes through him. It is not he who
absolves from sin, but Christ who absolves through him. It
is not he who blesses, but Christ who blesses through him.
It is not he who speaks the word of God, but Christ who
speaks it through him. It is not he who teaches the truths
of faith, but Christ who teaches them through him. "The
life I live now is not my own; Christ is living in me" (Gal
2:20). This objective identification with Christ must day

by day become a more conscious, subjectively verified reality. It will effect in the priest a profound inner transformation of mentality and outlook. If he stands at the altar or approaches the microphone with the conviction that "it is not I who am to speak; the divine Master wants to teach through me," then Father So-and-So will disappear, with his pet ideas, his private principles, his eccentric enthusiasms, and his personal political leanings. In his place we will find a man whom the faithful will immediately perceive to be radically identified with his Lord and Master. Then Jesus will speak to his disciples.

2. *The priest should live out what he does as a priest.* Before Vatican II spiritual writers used to speak with some reserve about a priest's pastoral functions. They warned against the danger of "works" and the "heresy of action," and failed to recognize the true value of action. They thought it difficult, in their words, "to unite an apostolate to an interior life." Now Vatican II has forcefully insisted on the sanctifying power of the ministry. In the Dogmatic Constitution on the Church it is said of bishops that they should make their ministry "the principal means of their own sanctification" (LG, 41b/68). To the priest the Council then says: "Let him not be undone by his apostolic cares, dangers, and toils, but rather led by them to higher sanctity" (LG, 41d/68).

It is, however, chiefly in the Decree on the Ministry and Life of Priests that the Council expounds this principle. When nos. 12-13 of this document were being drawn up, the Fathers made it clear that their intent was to make a clear statement on the intrinsic relation between sanctity and pastoral action: the ministry is not simply an occasion but a means of sanctification; it is not just one means among others but the specific (though not sole) means available to a priest. The priest does not achieve his own sanctification prior to or independently of his mission, but in and through the exercise of his ministry.

In no. 12 of the Decree, the Council presents the principle; in no. 13 it applies the principle. In 12a-b there is a general statement of the obligation or, better, the need the priest has of becoming holy. The text refers to his special identification with Christ the Priest and adds that "Therefore . . . he is also enriched with special grace. Thus, serving the people committed to him and the entire People of God, he can more properly imitate the perfection of Him whose part he takes. Thus, too, the weakness of human flesh can be healed by the holiness of Him who has become for our sake a high priest 'holy, innocent, undefiled, set apart from sinners' (Heb 7:26)" (PO, 12b/558).

In no. 12c the priest is confronted with Christ whom the Father sanctified or consecrated and sent into the world and who dedicated himself wholly to men and, through his passion, entered into glory. "Likewise, consecrated by the anointing of the Holy Spirit and sent by Christ, priests mortify in themselves the deeds of the flesh and devote themselves entirely to the service of men. Thus they can grow in the sanctity with which they are endowed in Christ, to the point of perfect manhood" (PO, 12c/558-59).

The central teaching is contained in no. 12d-e: "And so it is that they are grounded in the life of the Spirit while they exercise the ministry of the Spirit and justice, as long as they are docile to Christ's Spirit, who vivifies and leads them. For by their everyday sacred actions themselves, as by the entire ministry which they exercise in union with the bishop and their fellow priests, they are being directed toward perfection of life" (12c/559). The Council at this point hastens to correct a possible ambiguity. Some people might be led to think that there is a kind of sanctification which is automatically effected by the simple exercise of the ministry without the need for any personal, conscious effort on the priest's part. The Council therefore stresses the favorable effect which the priest's holiness has upon his ministry: "Priestly holiness itself contributes very great-

ly to a fruitful fulfillment of the priestly ministry. True,
the grace of God can complete the work of salvation even
through unworthy ministers. Yet ordinarily God desires to
manifest His wonders through those who have been made
particularly docile to the impulse and guidance of the Holy
Spirit. Because of their intimate union with Christ and
their holiness of life, these men can say with the Apostle:
'It is now no longer I that live, but Christ lives in me' (Gal
2:20) " (PO, 12e/559). For the exercise of the ministry to
have a genuinely sanctifying effect, a purely material, automatic fulfillment of it is not enough. It must be carried
out "with holiness, eagerness, humility, and courage" (LG,
41b/68), "sincerely and tirelessly in the Spirit of Christ"
(PO, 13a/559), as a "conscious exercise" (PO, 18a/569),
and on condition that priests "are docile to Christ's Spirit,
who vivifies and leads them" (PO, 12/559).

The Synod of Bishops repeats this doctrine, but does not
give it the same importance as a principle and even puts it
in last place. It gives the impression, moreover, of wanting
to reduce the ministry to a simple occasion of sanctification
instead of a true means and a means specific to priests.
Thus it says: "The activities of the apostolate for their part
furnish an indispensable nourishment for fostering the
spiritual life of the priest," and it explains: "In the exercise of his ministry the priest is enlightened and strengthened
by the action of the Church and the example of the faithful.
The renunciations imposed by the pastoral life itself help
him to acquire an ever greater sharing in Christ's Cross and
hence a pure pastoral charity" (74). But that is how we
used to speak before the Council. What the Synod is saying
here is, of course, important and deserves our consideration
and acceptance, but the Synod overlooks the most essential
and meaningful element in the teaching of Vatican II, namely, the intrinsic value of pastoral activity as "the principal
means of their own [the shepherds'] sanctification" (LG,
41b/68).

In the next number of the Decree on the Ministry and Life of Priests the Council begins by restating the principle: "Priests will attain sanctity in a manner proper to them if they exercise their offices sincerely and tirelessly in the Spirit of Christ" (PO, 13a/559). Throughout the rest of the section the Council attempts a practical application of the principle. As it does in systematic fashion in every document when the topic is the apostolate, the Council here divides the ministerial activity of the priest into three parts: teaching, sanctifying, and shepherding.

It begins by considering priests as "ministers of God's word"; as such they ought every day to read and listen to the word which they are to teach to others. "If they are at the same time preoccupied with welcoming this message into their own hearts, they will become ever more perfect disciples of the Lord. For as the Apostle Paul wrote to Timothy: 'Meditate on these things, give yourself entirely to them, that your progress may be manifest to all, Take heed to yourself and to your teaching, be earnest in them. For in so doing you will save both yourself and those who hear you' (1 Tim 4:15-16). As priests search for a better way to share with others the fruits of their own contemplation, they will win a deeper understanding of 'the unfathomable riches of Christ' (Eph 3:8) as well as the manifold wisdom of God. Remembering that it is the Lord who opens hearts and that sublime utterance comes not from themselves but from God's power, in the very act of preaching His word they will be united more closely with Christ the Teacher and be led by His Spirit" (PO, 13b-c/560).

The Council next looks at priests as "ministers of sacred realities," referring to those actions in which priests represent Christ in a special way. "Hence priests are invited to imitate the realities they deal with" (PO, 13d/560). Vatican II then takes advantage of the occasion to urge the daily celebration of holy Mass, "even if the faithful are unable to be present" (PO, 13e/560-61). It also refers to Pope

Paul VI's encyclical *Mysterium Fidei* with its theological justification for daily Mass. "For each and every Mass is not something private, even if a priest celebrates it privately; instead, it is an act of Christ and of the Church. In offering this sacrifice, the Church learns to offer herself as a sacrifice for all and she applies the unique and infinite redemptive power of the sacrifice of the Cross to the salvation of the whole world. For every Mass that is celebrated is being offered not just for the salvation of certain people, but also for the salvation of the whole world. . . . And so, we recommend from a paternal and solicitous heart that priests, who constitute our greatest joy and our crown in the Lord, . . . celebrate Mass daily in a worthy and devout fashion."[1]

The Synod of Bishops, too, urges daily celebration, "even if the Eucharist should be celebrated without participation by the faithful." For the mystery of the Eucharist "remains the centre of the life of the entire Church and the heart of priestly existence" (72). After the Council and wholly adopting its outlook, the Sacred Congregation of Rites, as it was then known, published an instruction on Eucharistic worship which can be very helpful to us as we endeavor to cultivate a correct and orthodox understanding of and mentality concerning the Eucharistic mystery.[2]

The text of the Decree on Priests continues: "So it is that while priests are uniting themselves with the act of Christ the Priest, they are offering their whole selves every day to God. While being nourished by the Body of Christ, their hearts are sharing in the love of Him who gives Himself as food for His faithful ones" (PO, 13f/561). In this context the Council also speaks of the recitation of the divine office or, as it is called today, the Liturgy of the Hours: "By reciting the divine office, they lend their voice to the Church as in the name of all humanity she perseveres in prayer along with Christ, who 'lives always to make intercession for us' (Heb 7:25)" (PO, 13g/561). Elsewhere, in the Decree on the Sacred Liturgy, the Council teaches that when the priests recites the Liturgy of the Hours, "then is truly the voice of the bride addressing her bridegroom; it is the very prayer which Christ Himself, together with His body, addresses to the Father" (SC, 84/163). There is a good deal that might be said on the theology of this noble kind of prayer, but we cannot go into it here. The Congregation for Divine Worship, in February, 1971, published a richly detailed general instruction on the subject; all priests should read and reflect on it.[3]

In the final paragraphs of no. 13, the Council considers priests as "guiding and nourishing God's people" (PO, 13h/561). As such, they are prompted by the love of the Good Shepherd to give their lives for their flock. Being themselves men of faith, they are teachers who bring others to the faith. They are also men of hope who can console those in distress. And "as rulers of the community, they ideally cultivate the asceticism proper to a pastor of souls, renouncing their own conveniences, seeking what is profitable for the many and not for themselves, so that the many may be saved" (PO, 13j/561-62). In this they follow the Apostle's example: "I try to please all in any way I can by seeking, not my own advantage, but that of the many, that they may be saved" (1 Cor 10:33).

3. *The priest should integrate his spiritual life by uniting himself to Christ in the acknowledgment of God's will and in self-dedication to men.* "A personal and immediate relationship with Christ in the Church should still sustain for the faithful of today their whole spiritual lives" (Synod, no. 26). For the priest, however, this relationship to Christ takes on a quite special cast. As we have already seen, the sacrament of orders effects in the priest an objective "configuration to Christ the Priest." This new objective reality at the very roots of his being as minister demands of the priest an unremitting effort toward subjective assimilation to the mind of Christ who gave his life out of love. In Jesus the most complete dedication to men coincides with a total

surrender to the will of the Father. The more the Son abandons himself to the Father, the more the Father can make himself known to the Son and, through him, to men. Here is the center of Christ's spiritual life; here too must be the center of a priest's spirituality.

In the document of the Synod of 1971 on *Justice in the World* there is a rather compact passage (nos. 31-35) on the unity of surrender to God and dedication to men. The Synod begins by stressing the fact that "Christ united in an indivisible way the relationship of man to God and the relationship of man to other men" (31), for he lived his life as a total gift of himself to God for the salvation and liberation of men. He identified himself with his "least brothers": "I assure you, as often as you did it for one of my least brothers, you did it for me" (Mt 25:40). Faith in God and love of neighbor are the basic theme of the New Testament. As Christ, so the Christian surrenders himself to God for the liberation of man. "According to the Christian message, therefore, man's relationship to his neighbor is bound up with his relationship to God; his response to the love of God, saving us through Christ, is shown to be effective in his love and service of men" (34). Since every man is really the image of God, the Christian meets God himself in every man. The Synod concludes this section with a strong statement: "The mission of preaching the Gospel dictates at the present time that we should dedicate ourselves to the liberation of man even in his present existence in this world" (35).

In Christ himself there was no dichotomy or opposition between a total surrender to the Father ("verticalism") and a complete dedication to men ("horizontalism"). His life derived its unity from his unceasing attitude of obedience to his Father. It must be the same in the priest's life: its unity (despite apparent dichotomies between personal spiritual life and apostolate, between surrender to God and commitment to men, between verticalism and horizontalism) will have its source in an attitude of unremitting obedience to the will of God. On this point Vatican II provides us with a text that has been carefully thought out (PO, 14); we should read the six paragraphs of this number with care.

In the first two paragraphs the Council sketches the problem: how find "a way which will enable them [priests] to unify their interior lives with their program of external activities" (PO, 14b/562)? The Fathers assert that such a unity of life is not to be obtained either by a purely external arrangement of one's ministerial activities or by the mere practice of exercises of piety, although these can play their part in fostering such unity. Then the Council offers as a possible solution the example of Christ whose food was to do the will of the One who sent him to accomplish his work (cf. Jn 4:34).

In the next two paragraphs the Council teaches that in in order constantly to carry out the Father's will through the Church (the "mystery" concept of the Church is here implied; cf. LG, chapter 1), Christ makes use of the ministry of priests. Consequently, "Christ forever remains the source and origin of their unity of life" (PO, 14c/562). And the Council is able to draw the conclusion: "Therefore priests attain to the unity of their lives by uniting themselves with Christ in acknowledging the Father's will and in the gift of themselves on behalf of the flock committed to them. Thus, by assuming the role of the Good Shepherd, they will find in the very exercise of pastoral love the bond of priestly perfection which will unify their lives and activities. This pastoral love flows mainly from the Eucharistic Sacrifice, which is therefore the center and root of the whole priestly life. The priestly soul strives thereby to apply to itself the action which takes place on the altar of sacrifice. But this goal cannot be achieved unless priests themselves penetrate ever more deeply through prayer into the mystery of Christ" (PO, 14c-d/562-63). (In footnote 172 the Council quotes St. Augustine, *Sermons on St. John* 123:5; PL, 35:1967:

"May it be a duty of love to feed the Lord's flock." It was these words that suggested the conciliar phrase, "pastoral love," which was to occur frequently in later documents of the Council.) It is worth our while here to recall PO, 18b/ 570: "With the light of a faith nourished by spiritual reading, priests can carefully detect the signs of God's will and the impulses of His grace in the various happenings of life, and thus can become more docile day by day to the mission they have undertaken in the Holy Spirit."

In the final two paragraphs the Council links the principle of fidelity to Christ to that of fidelity to the Church, since "loyalty toward Christ can never be divorced from loyalty toward His Church" (PO, 14e/563). "That they may be able to verify the unity of their lives in concrete situations, too, they should subject all their undertakings to the test of God's will,[4] which requires that projects should conform to the laws of the Church's evangelical mission. For loyalty toward Christ can never be divorced from loyalty toward His Church. Hence pastoral love requires that a priest always work in the bond of communion with the bishop and with his brother priests, lest his efforts be in vain.[5] If he acts in this way, a priest will find the unity of his own life in the very unity of the Church's mission. Thus he will be joined with the Lord, and through Him with the Father in the Holy Spirit. Thus he will be able to be full of consolation and to overflow with joy" (PO, 14e-f/563).

In the immediately ensuing paragraph the Council says, therefore, that "among the virtues most necessary for the priestly ministry must be named that disposition of soul by which priests are always ready to seek not their own will, but the will of Him who sent them. For the divine work which the Holy Spirit has raised them up to fulfill transcends all human energies and human wisdom: 'the foolish things of the world God has chosen to put to shame the wise' (1 Cor 1:27). Therefore, conscious of his own weakness, the true minister of Christ labors in humility, testing what is God's will. In a kind of captivity to the Spirit he is led in all things by the will of Him who wishes all men to be saved" (PO, 15a-b/563-64).

It is in this context that we can best understand the difficult virtue of obedience in the Church, for it is a necessary prolongation of obedience to God himself. The Council makes this point in PO, 15c/564: "Since the priestly ministry is the ministry of the Church herself, it can be discharged only by hierarchical communion with the whole body." Obedience is thus a free and voluntary insertion of oneself into the hierarchic communion.

But the "configuration to Christ the Priest" has other effects in the life of the priest. As Christ has power to represent the Father in the measure that he is humble and detached from himself (cf. Jn 5:19: "The Son cannot do anything by himself — he can do only what he sees the Father doing. For whatever the Father does, the Son does likewise"), so the priestly ministers of the New Testament have the power to represent Christ in the measure that they identify themselves with the mystery of the humble and detached Christ. If taken seriously, this principle will have enormous consequences for the spiritual life of the priest. It is a door that opens on to poverty (that is, to self-emptying in order to give place to Christ and the Father's will), to obedience (that is, the free act of self-determination which allows Christ to act in and through us), to humility (the general atmosphere which makes possible a ministry conceived as the instrumental action of Christ), to authority (that of the suffering Servant of Jahweh). After the curious incident of James and John who sought places of honor and thus irritated the other ten, Jesus called the Apostles together and said to them: "You know how among the Gentiles those who seem to exercise authority lord it over them; their great ones make their importance felt. It cannot be like that with you. Anyone among you who aspires to greatness must serve the rest; whoever wants to rank first among you must serve the needs of all. The Son of Man has not come to be served but to serve — to give his life in ransom for the many" (Mk 10:42-45). Here Christ teaches his followers the basic law of discipleship.

In a tightly packed and felicitously worded text (LG, 8c-d/23-24), Vatican II establishes a parallel between the action of Christ and the analogous action of the Church. As Christ did his work of redemption amid poverty and persecution, so the Church must amid poverty and persecution communicate to men the fruits of redemption. As Christ became poor and a servant, so the Church must walk in the paths of humility and self-sacrifice, for "she is not set up to seek earthly glory" (LG, 8c/23). As Christ was sent to bring the good news to the poor, so the Church must go out to all who are afflicted with human weakness. In another context the Council exclaims: "Prompted by the Holy Spirit, the Church must walk the same road which Christ walked: a road of poverty and obedience, of service and self-sacrifice to the death, from which death He came forth a victor by His resurrection. For thus did all the Apostles walk in hope. On behalf of Christ's body, which is the Church, they supplied what was wanting of the sufferings of Christ by their own many trials and sufferings (cf. Col 1:24)" (AG, 5e/590).

4. "That priests may be able to foster union with Christ in all the circumstances of life, they enjoy, *in addition to the conscious exercise of their ministry, those means, common and particular, new and old, which the Spirit of God never ceases to stir up* in the people of God and which the Church commends and indeed at times commands for the sanctification of her members" (PO, 18a/569—italics added). The spiritual life of the priest, as traditionally led, used to find its chief nourishment in the ample field of spiritual exercises. The priest had at his disposition an abundant and varied tradition of devotions and pious practices which were

recommended by the example of the saints, the revelations of visionaries, the eloquence of preachers, the urging of moralists, the scrupulous advice of spiritual directors, the obligation of rules, the heritage of schools of spirituality, and personal taste and inclination. But all this, as we have seen, has now entered a critical stage. For some the crisis has meant an authentic and profitable emancipation. For others it has been a source of scandal and they have thrown everything over. The problem is not with prayer, but with the forms and formulas of prayer. The problem is not with self-sacrifice but with the methods of self-denial. The problem is not with the sacrament of penance but with the manner in which it is now administered. In short, here too the crisis is a crisis not of substance but of forms. Men are looking for ways, methods, and forms which are adequate for the events, requirements, aspirations, and fears of our world. The Synod explicitly accepts this analysis when it says: "This same charity of priests will also cause them to adapt their spiritual lives to the modes and forms of sanctification which are more suitable and fitting for the men of their own times and culture. Desiring to be all things to all men, to save all (cf. 1 Cor 9:22), the priest should be attentive to the inspiration of the Holy Spirit in these days" (75).

Nontheless, in the search for new ways and methods, we must avoid indiscriminately throwing out everything that is old or established in order to make room for the new and the spontaneous. It is beyond doubt that there are obsolete devotions, forms, and formulas. It is equally beyond doubt that we have inherited much that is beautiful, expressive, well formulated, profound, and abidingly valuable. It is beyond doubt that spontaneity can be rich and creative; it is equally beyond doubt that the spontaneous can be stale, mediocre, primitive, and totally uncreative. We may never forget that formalism exists in the subject and his subjectivity, in man and his personal attitude, rather than in objects,

forms, or formulas. Formalism generates routine and the
corrupting power of habit, but it springs from a lack of intelligence or the lack of effort to understand formulas and
to attune oneself to them. Objective forms, such as we have
in the liturgy, must be given the subjective, personal dimension in our lives which they objectively possess. We must
"subjectivize" objective prayer. In order to fend off the
danger of an excessively objective, formalist, and ritualist
liturgical piety, the Council stresses the need of subjective
concern and of conscious, internal participation. "In order
that the sacred liturgy may produce its full effect, it is
necessary that the faithful come to it with proper disposi-
tions, that their thoughts match their words, and that they
cooperate with divine grace lest they receive it in vain" (SC,
11/143). Let us not forget, too, that there are times in
life (fatigue, apathy, dryness, depression) when spontaneity
dies out; at such times a man needs the support of forms
and formulas if he is not to abandon God.

After saying that the Spirit stirs up new means of sanctification in the Church, the Council speaks in particular of
"the twofold table of sacred Scripture and the Eucharist"
(PO, 18a/569-70). This would be the time to dwell on the
riches of "the table of God's word" (SC, 51/155) as a primary means of sanctification. We shall not do so,[6] but shall
simply recall the lively hope expressed by Vatican II: "We
may hope for a new surge of spiritual vitality from intensi-
fied veneration for God's word" (DV, 26a/128).

In speaking of the spiritual life of the priest, the Council
goes on to recommend *devotion to our Lady,* mother of the
eternal high priest and queen of the apostles. "With the
devotion and veneration of sons, priests should lovingly honor
this mother" (PO, 18c/570). The Synod of Bishops likewise
stresses this devotion: "With his mind raised to heaven and
sharing in the communion of saints, the priest should very
often turn to Mary the Mother of God, who received the
Word of God with perfect faith, and daily ask her for the

grace of conforming himself to her Son" (73).

No ecumenical council has ever spoken so eloquently and with such a depth and wealth of theological insight concerning the holy Virgin Mary as has Vatican II in the eighth chapter of its Dogmatic Constitution on the Church. Popular devotion to our Lady was doubtless subject to excesses and exaggerations (the Council acknowledged this fact in LG, 67/94-95), and there was therefore a need of revising and renewing it. However it is now time to stir up anew a solid Christian devotion to Mary. The study of chapter eight of the Constitution on the Church will be helpful to us here. Without stopping for such a study at this point, we ought at least call attention to LG, 61-62; for, in them we find the theological basis for our devotion.

The Council teaches that "in an utterly singular way she [the Mother of God] cooperated by her obedience, faith, hope, and burning charity in the Savior's work of restoring supernatural life to souls. For this reason she is a mother to us in the order of grace" (LG, 61/91). The Council then goes on to say: "This maternity of Mary in the order of grace began with the consent which she gave in faith at the Annunciation and which she sustained without wavering beneath the Cross. This maternity will last without interruption until the eternal fulfillment of all the elect. For, taken up to heaven, she did not lay aside this saving role, but by her manifold acts of intercession continues to win for us gifts of eternal salvation. By her maternal charity, Mary cares for the brethren of her Son who still journey on earth surrounded by dangers and difficulties, until they are led to their happy fatherland" (LG, 62a-b/91). This is the basis of our confidence and our devotion. We should meditate on it.

The Council closes its recommendations on the priest's spiritual life with these words: "That they [priests] may discharge their ministry with fidelity, they should prize daily conversation with Christ the Lord in visits of personal devotion to the most Holy Eucharist. They should gladly undertake spiritual retreats and highly esteem spiritual direction. In manifold ways, especially through approved methods of mental prayer and various voluntary forms of prayer, priests should search for and earnestly beg of God that Spirit of genuine adoration by which they themselves, along with the people entrusted to them, can unite themselves intimately with Christ the Mediator of the New Testament. Thus, as sons of adoption, they will be able to cry out: 'Abba, Father' (Rom 8:15) " (PO, 18d/570) .

Notes

[1] Paul VI, *Mysterium Fidei: On the Doctrine and Worship of the Holy Eucharist,* September 3, 1965, in TPS, 10 (1964-65), 317.

[2] Sacred Congregation of Rites, *Eucharisticum Mysterium: On the Worship of the Eucharistic Mystery,* May 25, 1967, in TPS, 12 (1967), 211-36.

[3] Sacred Congregation for Divine Worship, *General Instruction on the Liturgy of the Hours,* February 2, 1971 (Washington, D.C.: National Conference of Catholic Bishops, 1971).

[4] Cf. Rom 12:2: "Do not conform yourselves to this age but be transformed by the renewal of your mind, so that you may judge what is God's will, what is good, pleasing, and perfect."

[5] Cf. Gal 2:2: "I went [to Jerusalem to meet the Apostles] prompted by a divine revelation, and I laid out for their scrutiny the gospel as I present it to the Gentiles — all this in private conference with the leaders, to make sure the course I was pursuing, or had pursued, was not useless."

[6] I would be limited to repeating what I have already said in *O Cristao Secularizado,* pp. 264-268.

IV

Christian Celibacy and
the Priest

Among the numerous crises through which the Church is passing today, people include a "crisis of celibacy." Bishop Emilio Calagiovanni of the Sacred Congregation for Doctrine and Faith (one of the tasks of which is to process requests for reduction to the lay state) has made a detailed examination of 8,287 cases of laicized priests (the book was printed in 1971, but not published). He found that for 75% of the priests dispensed since 1967 the main reason for their decision was "celibacy as such": the burden of loneliness, the lack of adequate formation in the seminary, and the felt need of parenthood, affection, and love were responsible for the abandonment of the priesthood. For another 15% celibacy was "part of the reason." Another study of Brazilian priests, sponsored by CERIS, showed that 80% of those interviewed thought celibacy ought to be optional; the 20% who favored obligatory celibacy were chiefly elderly men and foreigners. The study also showed that priests in general

95

have difficulty in living a celibate life; 80% of those interviewed said they knew that "many"—even "very many" or
"all"—of their fellow-priests find difficulty in observing
celibacy. Celibacy is felt to be a sacrifice, a burden the priest
must carry, but not as something which is a help, even in
the exercise of the ministry. When questioned about the
reasons for living a celibate life, only 47% gave the "official"
reasons urged by the Church. Others gave various less con-
vincing reasons such as fidelity to an oath once taken, the
fact that it is a condition for priesthood, or reasons of a
practical order ("it's cheaper"; "being single is easier than
being married"). Many said they had no reasons at all.

The study thus shows that *less than half of the priests had
solid reasons for living as celibates*; they simply were putting
up with this kind of life. Their views on celibacy are therefore negative; indeed they are often bitter and lack understanding and Christian spirit.

— "The law is a mistake and ought to be changed. It's too
heavy a burden and can't be borne. A charism is a free gift.
It's wrong to make celibacy a condition for priesthood.
Psychologically speaking, the law is absurd and manicheistic.
Celibacy has great value but only when freely chosen."

— "In a Christian culture celibacy makes sense because the
social conditions required for living it are present. Today
a celibate life is very difficult, and the law ought to be
changed. I'm not referring, of course, to the chairsm of
celibacy; that has its value."

— "The law of obligatory celibacy depended on a negative
view of marriage. Today it's criminal to make celibacy
obligatory."

— "Obligation in this matter is repugnant. If the priesthood
were not connected with celibacy, no one would have any
reason to make celibacy obligatory. If a man finds freedom
to love more by being a celibate, let him be celibate; otherwise, let him marry."

— "I have changed my mind. I used to think obligatory

celibacy was a necessity; now I think it ought to be optional. Celibacy is the ideal, but the law ought nonetheless to be changed."

— "I am for total freedom. It was with this in mind that I chose the priesthood. I even saw how I could sustain it. If I think I have a vocation to celibacy, I'll continue in the priesthood; if I don't, I'll take some other road. The bishop knows what's going on and doesn't disagree."

From a comprehensive poll and study of the Spanish clergy (cut-off date: October, 1971), it emerged that 21% of the clergy considered chastity an unattainable virtue; 16% indicated that they were living pretty much in accordance with this view. During the Synod of Bishops, 1971, the Canadian bishops stressed the fact that concrete data show many priests to be living celibate lives for reasons far inferior to those officially urged by the Church. The real crisis is to be seen not so much in the departures from the celibate life as in the difficulties many priests feel in living their celibacy in a positive way and as an enrichment of their priestly lives.

In the *Testimonies of Priests (Documentos dos Presbyteros)* which were collected in Brazil in 1969 by the Departamento Nacional do Ministério Hierárquico (of the National Conference of Brazilian Bishops) we find numerous allusions to the difficulties in the way of a joyful celibate life among our priests. These difficulties are:

1. Defective formation with a view to the celibate life. Contributing to this are the premature separation from family, the lack of any education of the affective life in the seminaries, an individualist formation, and an education grounded in a false vision of chastity and women and a flight from sexuality. Celibacy is thus chosen at too early an age and against an inadequate background. The bishops at the Synod granted that "celibacy, as a gift of God, cannot be preserved unless the candidate is adequately prepared for it" (84). A strong statement, and one that perhaps

excuses many defections.

2. The obligatory and externally imposed character of celibacy. In the Decree on the Ministry and Life of Priests Vatican II notes that "celibacy was at first recommended to priests. Then, in the Latin Church, it was imposed by law" (PO, 16e/566). Because of the link thus established by Church law, many priests regard the priesthood as inseparable from celibacy. Because the distinction between celibacy and ministry is not made sufficiently clear, it was difficult for them to make a personal, free choice of celibacy itself. Instead, the man who wanted the ministry saw himself simply obliged to take celibacy as well. Thus celibacy was not accepted as a value in itself but only as a prior condition of being a priest.

3. Difficulties of the practical order, arising from the solitude which celibacy creates for priests who live in a world in which man, depersonalized into crowds, finds intimacy only in his home. The isolation of the priest may be geographical, cultural, affective, and social. His loneliness is increased and becomes psychologically unbearable when he loses his grasp on ideals or when he is frustrated in apostolic work or is not supported by superiors and colleagues. There is something moving about the testimonies of priests when they speak of loneliness. One priest, already on in years, admits: "Loneliness is the greatest, the only really serious problem of the priest. I am not concerned for myself, for I am old now, but I think it inhuman and criminal. . . ." Another says: "I do not feel the loneliness that comes for lack of fellow-workers, but I do feel an affective loneliness. Something is missing."

4. The conquest of a kind of Manicheism that still lurks in Catholic moral and ascetical literature; a more positive evaluation of sexuality and an esteem for and fascination with earthly realities.

5. Theological upgrading of marriage and conjugal life as a possible means of sanctification and love for God.

"Authentic married love is caught up into divine love and is governed and enriched by Christ's redeeming power and the saving activity of the Church. Thus this love can lead the spouses to God with powerful effect and can aid and strengthen them in the sublime office of being a father or a mother. For this reason Christian spouses have a special sacrament by which they are fortified and receive a kind of consecration in the duties and dignity of their state. By virtue of this sacrament, as spouses fulfill their conjugal and family obligations, they are penetrated with the spirit of Christ. Thus they increasingly suffuse their whole lives with faith, hope, and charity. Thus they increasingly advance their own perfection, as well as their mutual sanctification, and hence contribute jointly to the glory of God" (GS, 48e-f/251).

6. Understanding of the requirements of full solidarity, for which celibacy is not a favorable condition. "Alienated from the ongoing transformation of our world and from the realities of life in Brazil, priests are not forced to confront the problems of their milieu and consequently are unaware of these problems. They follow the lead of Rome in analyzing and proffering solutions to regional problems and do not share the real anxieties of the faithful. When they do make an effort to break out of their isolation, they fall into artificial and unbalanced attitudes and at times even become demagogues."[1]

7. Pressure from the eroticism which pervades the contemporary culture with its exaltation of sex. The wave of sexualism which is spread far and wide by the mass-communications media, especially film and television, pervades our civilization and even the religious sphere, for it does not stop at the doors of the church. Some people, even in the seminaries and convents, think they must practice brinkmanship, for they attempt real balancing acts when they seek and cultivate friendships with persons of the opposite sex.

8. False notions on the part of some priests who think

marriage to be the solution for problems of emotional imbalance or chastity.

9. Lack of involvement in the ministry, which is the chief
reason for the Christian celibacy of the priest.

10. Natural deficiencies (biological and psychological) of
the priest's person.

11. Unconvincing and rather un-Christian arguments in
favor of celibacy.

12. A disbelief among the people about the value of celibacy as such and especially about the real fidelity of priests
to the law of celibacy (priests lead a "double life" according
to the study, to which we have already referred, of the laity's
view of the priest's situation) ; the attitude shaped by the
communications media; the levity with which the matter is
treated, even in clerical circles.

In view of all this, and especially since celibacy really
requires a free personal choice, we see a growing demand
for "optional celibacy" or celibacy left to the free choice of
each priest. This tendency has clearly claimed the adherence
of the majority of priests, but it is still a minority view
among bishops. On this account, the Synod of Bishops, 1971,
decided to take the position that "the law of celibacy existing
in the Latin Church is to be kept in its entirety" (90). Here
we are once again confronted with a law and thus, at least
on the surface, with an "imposition by law," to use the
fortunate phrase of Vatican II's Decree on the Ministry and
Life of Priests (PO, 16e/566). We must, then, especially in
view of the attack on law today, attempt honestly to understand the meaning and importance of this particular law.[2]
It is our part, after all, to live this law of the Church. We
ought to live it with joy.

The Synod maintains that the Church has the right and
duty to determine the concrete shape of priestly ministry
and therefore the right as well to choose more suitable
candidates who will have certain natural and supernatural
qualifications.[3] In requiring celibacy, "she [the Church]

does not do so out of a belief that this way of life is the only path to attaining sanctification. She does so while carefully considering the concrete form of exercising the ministry in the community for the building up of the Church" (85).

The thrust of the law of celibacy is therefore that only they will be ordained priests who have made an authentic, responsible, personal free choice of Christian celibacy. In the law ("imposition") of ecclesiastical celibacy, the Church is, strictly speaking, asking not that priests become celibates but that celibates become priests. It is important that we see clearly that the Church accepts the distinction between celibacy and ministry. In its Decree on Priests, Vatican II expressly states that celibacy is not required by the nature of the priesthood (PO, 16a/565). The juridical link between celibacy and ministry arises not from doctrinal necessity but from pastoral considerations. As the Church today concretely sees the Christian priesthood, being a priest involves a double vocation: the divine call to virginity and the divine call to ministry. Consequently, a double response is required of the priest: he must choose first (with logical priority) celibacy, then priesthood. The Synod of Bishops explains this point: Anyone who seeks a total self-giving, which is the distinctive mark of the ministry, freely accepts the celibate life as well (unfortunately the necessary logical priority of celibacy is not brought out by the way the Synod speaks). The bishops go on to say that this way of life should be regarded "not as having been imposed from outside, but rather as a manifestation of his [the candidate's] free self-giving, which is accepted and ratified by the Church through the bishop. In this way the law becomes a protection and safeguard of the freedom wherewith the priest gives himself to Christ, and it becomes an 'easy yoke' " (86).

The intention of the law, then, is not to "impose" celibacy or to remove the full freedom of personal choice. Such freedom is, on the contrary, always supposed and affirmed. After speaking of celibacy as "imposed by law," Vatican II goes on to say: "This holy Synod likewise exhorts all priests who, trusting in God's grace, have freely undertaken sacred celibacy in imitation of Christ to hold fast to it magnanimously and wholeheartedly. May they persevere faithfully in this state, and recognize this surpassing gift which the Father has given them, and which the Lord praised so openly" (PO, 16f/566). In its Decree on Priestly Formation the Council says of seminarians: "May they deeply sense how gratefully this state deserves to be undertaken — not only as a requisite of Church law but as a previous gift which should be humbly sought of God" (OT, 10a/447). For the rest, we can discern in these texts that the Council itself is aware of the odious aspect of the law as involving an imposition and sees that it would be much better, nobler, and more Christian to insist only on the charismatic aspect of the divine gift.

The basic and essential point to be made is that if the priest is to be able to make (or remake) this free choice, he must learn to see in celibacy a divine gift and an evangelical value which is its own justification.

The Synod of Bishops urges us to look more to the positive reasons for celibacy and not to let ourselves be overly impressed by the difficulties which build up and weigh upon us (cf. 88). The admonition is valid and necessary if we are to live out joyfully our choice of celibacy. In considering the positive reasons, however, we ought to fix our attention chiefly on evangelical motives and not on those which are either non-Christian (from the Old Testament or paganism) or ecclesiastical. The ideal of Christian celibacy in fact originates in Christ; it arises prior to any of the motivations excogitated at a later date (especially in the patristic period) and is wholly independent of the latter. Before Origen, Jerome, or Augustine set down their reflections on chastity, numerous groups of people in the Church were already living lives of perfect continence, and were certainly not living thus for the reasons that were elaborated later on.

This point seems to me important today because of the valid criticisms that are directed, and even ought to be directed, against certain kinds of motivation. In speaking of celibacy it is important to distinguish Christian celibacy (celibacy accepted for reasons indicated by Christ) from non-Christian celibacy, even if the latter be ecclesiastical (not everything "ecclesiastical" is automatically "Christian"). Some of the motivations invoked in the course of history as grounds for the law of celibacy have derived in fact from philosophical world-views, political situations, and ecclesiastical interests (including economic interests) which were not very evangelical or were even objectively false. We are not convinced today by the Old Testament prescriptions which obliged priests to abstain from conjugal relations at periods when they were exercising their cultic ministry. Yet in the patristic period (and even later) the argument based on these prescriptions was widely accepted. Neither are we persuaded by the cultically or ritually inspired continence which we find in pagan surroundings (even today, for example, in Umbandist strongholds); the value of such continence is magical rather than moral.

In the early Christian centuries the idea was also commonly accepted that sexual relations, even those legitimate and necessary for procreation, imply an uncleanness or impurity. The rather full explanations of Origen on this point had a great deal of influence on later writers and provided the basis for the doctrinal positions of St. Damasus, St. Ambrose, and especially St. Jerome. Many of the Fathers were also influenced by Greek philosophy, chiefly that of the Stoics who were pessimists and hostile to the whole sphere of the passions and pleasure, but also that of the Pythagoreans and Neo-Platonists who recommended holding the body in check through ascetical discipline in order to enable the soul to achieve contemplation of the divinity. Such notions occur frequently in Clement of Alexandria, Origen, Tertullian, Cyril of Alexandria, and Jerome. They found their synthesizer in St. Augustine who in turn clearly inspired some statements of Pope Leo the Great and Pope Gregory the Great.

Taking our cue from the Synod of Bishops we can indicate the following motives for the Christian celibacy of the priest:

1. *Celibacy as charism or divine gift for love of the kingdom of God.* The Synod unfortunately does not speak of celibacy as a charism; it refers to it as a "divine gift," but only in no. 88 and then only in passing. Vatican II, however, speaks of "that precious gift of divine grace which the Father gives to some men" (LG, 42e/71), of the "surpassing gift which the Father has given them [priests]" (PO, 16f/566), of a "special grace" (PO, 12b/558), and of "a precious gift which should be humbly sought of God" (OT, 10a/447). When they speak in these terms, the texts refer us to Mt 19:10-12. The Scriptural text is the logion on spiritual eunuchs and reads as follows: "His disciples said to him, 'If that is the case between man and wife, it is better not to marry.' He said, 'Not everyone can accept this teaching. Some men are incapable of sexual activity from birth; some have been deliberately made so; and some there are who have freely renounced sex for the sake of God's reign. Let him accept this teaching who can.' "

Some observations on the text:

(a) In its paradoxical expression (close to the Semitic outlook) and its prophetic radicalism the text has an archaic quality which justifies us in thinking that we have in it an authentic logion from the Master himself, his *ipsissima verba.*[4]

(b) It is significant that the words are introduced with the observation that not everyone will understand them, but only those to whom such understanding is given. The understanding is a gift, and what is to be said is one of the mysteries, given from on high, of the kingdom of heaven: "To you has been given a knowledge of the mysteries of the reign of God" (Mt 13:11). We are confronted here with the mystery

of election and calling and with the mystery of the harden-
ing of hearts (cf. Mt 13:14-15). We can prepare ourselves
for such a gift, but cannot give it to ourselves. In this particular instance the gift consists in "understanding" and not
in any change in the person's biological functioning.

(c) Jesus distinguishes three kinds of celibate life; only
the third is "Christian."

(d) Jesus seems to be addressing himself to those who
blame him (and perhaps John the Baptist as well) for not
having married and for thus departing from the accepted
ways of their people.

(e) Jesus was not hostile to marriage, as Mt 19:3-9 shows.

(f) The preposition *dia* ("*for the sake of* God's reign")
can signify either causality or purpose; the latter is the
meaning required here. But what is the precise meaning
of the "for the sake of" here? The purpose is either to have
access to the kingdom or to be able to work better for the
kingdom or to verify the condition — virginity — which
one has understood to correspond best to the nature of the
kingdom ("The children of this age marry and are given in
marriage, but those judged worthy of a place in the age to
come and of resurrection from the dead do not" — Lk 20:
34-35). We have, then, a person who remains chaste for the
sake of God's kingdom. The kingdom requires a total commitment from man, and this includes the renunciation of
marriage. The need to seek first the kingdom of God and
its holiness (Mt 6:33) holds, of course, for all the disciples.
Some, however, have a mission which demands a holy courage and dedication to the point of renouncing the human
destiny of complete sexual fulfillment. In this way all the
vital powers of the human person are freed to put themselves
at the service of God's lordship. Such people are the ones
who receive the charismatic gift of "understanding" this.
More than this, they receive the gift of commiting themselves to this further vocation beyond simple discipleship.
No one who does not first understand is cut out for such a

generous renunciation. The life of the Church through the
centuries is proof that this kind of generous courage is to
be found ever anew.

(g) In this text the Lord proposes apostolic celibacy as
an example of which his own life and, perhaps, that of John
the Baptist are a model, but he does not express a direct
invitation to embrace such a state. The invitation is, however, to be found, possibly in Lk 14:21 and certainly in Lk
18:20-30: "Peter said, 'We have left all we own to become
your followers.' His answer was, 'I solemnly assure you, there
is no one who has left house or wife or brothers, parents or
children, for the sake of the kingdom of God who will not
receive a plentiful return in this age and life everlasting in
the age to come'" (Lk 18:28-30).

In the parallel passages to this (Mt 19:27-29; Mk 10:28-
30), the invitation to leave one's wife does not occur; it
seems rather to be an especially interesting variant in Luke.
(Instead of "for the sake of the kingdom of God," Mark has
"for me and the gospel.") The Lord is enumerating the requirements of total renunciation for becoming the complete
disciple and following Jesus everywhere and in every circumstance. Luke concludes that a total renunciation must include the renunciation of marital union. "Leaving — or
renouncing — a wife" must here mean renouncing the idea
of having a wife. The text does not seem to envisage only
the man already married who abandons his wife in order to
devote himself to the service of the kingdom; indeed such
a practice would be wholly alien to the Biblical tradition
and even to apostolic practice (cf. 1 Cor 9:5: "Do we not
have the right to marry a believing woman like the rest of
the apostles and the brothers of the Lord and Cephas?").[5]

The Apostle St. Paul, known to be a celibate for the sake
of the Gospel and God's kingdom, declares: "Given my
preference, I should like you to be as I am. Still, each one
has his own gift from God, one this and another that" (1
Cor 7:7). Christian celibacy, then, is a gift, a charism, a

present from the Father. We do not have it from our mother's womb and therefore cannot draw it out of ourselves. We do not receive it from any other human being, not even from the Church. The Lord instituted no sacrament in order to give this gift to us, nor can we acquire it by our natural efforts at asceticism. It will not come from fine meditations on the words and example of the Lord. It is purely and simply a gift from God which makes us able to hear the call of Christ. It is the expression of a response to a divine vocation which brings us into the service of Christ and the Gospel. It is the proof of a mysterious obedience to God and must be renewed in unremitting fidelity. "Not everyone can accept this teaching, only those to whom it is given to do so. . . . Let him accept this teaching who can" (Mt 19:11-12).

2. *Through celibacy the priest follows Christ.* The Synod speaks of "the vocation to an apostolic following of Christ" (76). Before the Apostles were called to exercise the ministry as "men sent," they were called by Christ to leave all and follow him alone (Mk 3:13). And "they immediately abandoned their nets" (Mk 1:18), simply in order to follow Christ's path in a very literal sense (they walked behind him) and to share his unusual way of life in the exclusive service of man's redemption. The theological consideration of the Christian priestly ministry turns our attention to the close union that exists between Christ and his priests, inasmuch as the latter are "living instruments of Christ the eternal priest" (PO, 12b/558). The priest therefore has in Christ his direct model and supreme ideal.

Christ "remained throughout His whole life in the state of celibacy, which signified His total dedication to the service of God and men."[6] Through his own celibacy the Christian in turn becomes a witness to Christ as the absolute value and supreme truth which can lay hold upon a human life in its totality (cf. Synod, no. 80). Celibacy presupposes a profound knowledge of Christ and an intense, passionate love of Jesus and his Church. In this exclusive dedication the Christian bears public witness that Christ is the supreme and indispensable personal value for all men, but a value that cannot be wrested by force or violence but can only be received as gift and grace. In celibacy the believer attests that the calling of man as man does not coincide with a temporal vocation and much less with sexual fulfillment and that the values of the present life are sound only to the extent that they are open and positively referred and ordered to him who is their source: God who reveals himself in Christ.

3. *By celibacy the priest shows himself more completely at the service of others* (cf. Synod, no. 76). This was already St. Paul's argument: "The unmarried man is busy with the Lord's affairs, concerned with pleasing the Lord; but the married man is busy with this world's demands and occupied with pleasing his wife. This means he is divided. . . . I am going into this with you for your own good. I have no desire to place restrictions on you, but I do want to promote what is good, what will help you to devote yourselves entirely to the Lord" (1 Cor 7:32-35). Vatican II also stresses this motive when it details how "celibacy accords with the priesthood on many scores" (PO, 16c/565) and observes that the "chastity which is practiced 'on behalf of the heavenly kingdom' . . . liberates the heart in a unique way and causes it to burn with greater love for God and all mankind" (PC, 12a/474). The Synod picks up this motive again in no. 82. It is because he is thus set free that the Apostle regards himself as "set apart to proclaim the gospel of God" (Rom 1:1).

4. *In adopting celibacy and simultaneously taking up pastoral service, the priest gives an unconditional response to the divine call* (cf. Synod, no. 76). When the Church links celibacy to ministry, it does not do violence to the charism but only brings its inner nature into play (it exists "for the sake of the Gospel and the kingdom") as well as its necessary reference to the community (since charisms are always given

for the sake of the community, not of the individual). A radical dissociation between charism and ministry indicates a failure to grasp the specific nature of Christian celibacy and of the very mission of the Church. "This total continence embraced on behalf of the kingdom of heaven has always been held in particular honor by the Church as being a sign of charity and stimulus towards it, as well as a unique fountain of spiritual fertility in the world" (LG, 42e/71-72). Pope Paul's encyclical on celibacy explains that it is the sign of a love without reservation and the stimulus to a charity that is open to all.[7] Speaking of what he calls "the peasants' revolt of the spirit," Nietzsche, himself the son and grandson of Protestant ministers, wrote in 1886: "One overlooks the fact readily enough at present that as regards all cardinal questions concerning power Luther was badly endowed; he was fatally short-sighted, superficial, and imprudent . . . so that his work, his intention . . . became involuntarily and unconsciously the commencement of a work of destruction. . . . He gave back to the priest sexual intercourse: but three-fourths of the reverence of which the people (and above all the women of the people) are capable, rests on the belief that an exceptional man in this respect will also be an exceptional man in other respects. It is precisely here that the popular belief in something superhuman in man, in a miracle, in the saving God in man, has its most subtle and insidious advocate. After Luther had given a wife to the priest, he had to take from him auricular confession; that was psychologically right: but thereby he practically did away with the Christian priest himself, whose profoundest utility has ever consisted in his being a sacred ear, a silent well, and a grave for secrets."[8]

5. *By celibacy the priest embarks upon the way of the Cross,* but *with Paschal joy in his heart* and desires to be consumed in an offering comparable to the Eucharist (cf. Synod, no. 76). No one denies that perfect continence is difficult for human nature and can at times be a genuine

cross. We cannot but admit that Jesus was hard and demanding in this respect: "If anyone comes to me without turning his back on [literally, "hating," i.e. loving less: cf. Mt 10:37] his father and mother, his wife and his children, his brothers and sisters, indeed his very self, he cannot be my follower. Anyone who does not take up his cross and follow me cannot be my disciple" (Lk 14:25-26).

6. *By celibacy the priest becomes an eschatological sign* (cf. Synod, no. 80). The celibate is a sign which cannot remain hidden and which effectively proclaims Christ to the men of our day (cf. no. 77). For modern man sets a high value on the witness given by a life which reveals the radical character of the Gospel. But, as the Synod points out, this is true only of the celibacy that is "lived in the spirit of the Gospel, in prayer and vigilance, with poverty, joy, contempt of honors, and brotherly love" (77). The encyclical on celibacy likewise stresses the sign-vaule which celibacy has for today's world: it is in this world which is in a crisis of growth and transformation and so proud of human values and man's conquests, that there is the greatest need of witness, in the form of dedicated lives, to the highest and holiest spiritual values.[9] Further on, in no. 79, the Synod notes that in a culture like our own, in which spiritual values have become so obscured, the celibate life of the priest is a sign of the presence of the Absolute God. But celibacy does not therefore imply a downgrading of temporal values. It is rather that the Christian is, above all else, a sign of the transcendent. Such a sign does not ignore, much less condemn, the values of the present world but refers them to a personal God who is the origin and goal of everything. It is in the light of this God that the world reveals its meaning and achieves its purpose. The Synods insists especially, in this same passage, that "where the value of sexuality is so exaggerated that genuine love is forgotten, celibacy for the sake of the Kingdom of Christ calls men back to the sublimity of faithful love and reveals the ultimate meaning of life."

7. *Through celibacy the priest can aid human and Christian progress.* The Synod develops this thought as follows: "Celibacy, as a personal option for some more important good, even a merely natural one, can promote the full maturity and integration of the human personality. This is all the more true in regard to celibacy undertaken for the kingdom of heaven, as is evident in the lives of so many saints and of the faithful who, living the celibate life, dedicated themselves totally to promoting human and Christian progress for the sake of God and men" (78). The reason for this is that Christian celibacy has a unique spiritual fruitfulness or generative power "by which the apostle knows that in Christ he is the father and mother of his communities" (80).

8. *A joyful celibacy requires a corresponding asceticism.* The Synod is not unaware that "in the world of today particular difficulties threaten celibacy from all sides" (87). But the Synod is convinced these difficulties can be overcome "if suitable conditions are fostered" (*ibid.*). Celibacy can, in fact, be lived only in the atmosphere of a protective asceticism; a Christian celibacy that is unprotected and undefended cannot survive, for the divine gift does not transform man's sexual nature. Pope Paul VI likewise notes: "The priest must not think that ordination makes everything easy for him or screens him once and for all from every temptation or danger. Chastity is not acquired all at once but results from a laborious conquest and daily affirmation."[10] "This treasure we possess in earthen vessels" (2 Cor 4:7). The vessel is fragile indeed and needs careful protection. For the rest, today's difficulties in this matter are essentially those of every age: "Priests have indeed already repeatedly experienced them in the course of the centuries," says the Synod (87). And since today's difficulties are substantially the same as those of other times, we can and ought to learn from the successful celibates of other times how to live our celibate lives today. "Let them not neglect to

follow the norms, especially the ascetical ones, which have been tested by the experience of the Church and which are by no means less necessary in today's world" (PO, 16g/567). The Synod, for its part, makes the following recommendations:

(a) "Growth of the interior life through prayer, renunciation and fervent love for God and one's neighbor and by other aids to the spiritual life" (87). Here some advice given to religious by Vatican II will be useful to priests as well: "Trusting in God's help rather than presuming on their own resources, let them practice mortification and custody of the senses. They should take advantage of those natural helps which favor mental and bodily health. As a result they will not be influenced by those erroneous claims which present complete continence as impossible or as harmful to human development. In addition a certain spiritual instinct should lead them to spurn everything likely to imperil chastity" (PC, 12b/474).

(b) "Human balance through well-ordered integration into the fabric of social relationships" (87).

(c) "Fraternal association and companionship with other priests and with the bishop, through pastoral structures better suited to this purpose and with the assistance also of the community of the faithful" (87). Here once again we may apply a valuable bit of advice from Vatican II to religious: "Above all, everyone should remember — superiors especially — that chastity has stronger safeguards in a community when true fraternal love thrives among its members" (PC, 12b/474-75).

To these suggestions the following recommendation should be added: to live according to the ideal of Christian celibacy in the priestly ministry. After all, the chief motive for Christian celibacy is now, as always: "for the sake of God's reign" (Mt 19:12), "for me and for the gospel" (Mk 10:29), "for the sake of the kingdom of God" (Lk 18:29), or in order to be "busy with the Lord's affairs" (1 Cor 7:32). If the priest does not live his celibacy for these reasons and if, consequently, he does not dedicate himself to Christ, the Gospel, and God's reign or the affairs of the Lord, then he will inevitably feel the burden of frustration and uselessness and the meaninglessness of celibacy. If, on the contrary, he devotes himself wholly to the Lord's affairs, the Christian celibate will be able to promote effectively "the full maturity and integration of the human personality" (Synod, no. 78). Then, and only then, he will be able to live his Christian celibacy to the full.

The contemporary discussion on celibacy has unfortunately remained excessively negative and has created around us a heavy, tense atmosphere. This not only sets obstacles to the free choice of celibacy by those who feel themselves called by the Lord; it also seems to make celibacy impossible for those who have already chosen it. Celibates, too, have the human right to be respected and allowed to live out their choice in a joyful way! Constant criticism of this choice, often coming precisely from those who ought to show understanding and love for it, can deeply shake a decision that was once made freely and joyously. The surroundings in which we now live and the spiritual air we breathe influence us in ways unknown to us but therefore affecting us all the more deeply. We are all subject to suggestion, whether we like it or not. And there is almost no defence against the lingering, persistent suggestion that comes from the whole atmosphere in which we live, especially when we do not want to take refuge in a harmful kind of reactionism. Then slowly, insensibly, without any conscious, voluntary connivance on our part, we find the symptoms of a treacherous poison showing up within us. We must therefore change the atmosphere in which we live if we are to make use in a satisfactory way of the divine gift of celibacy for the sake of the heavenly kingdom and if we are to devote ourselves unreservedly to the ministry entrusted to us. It is for this that God has chosen, called, and qualified us.

Notes

[1] "Inquéritos entre leigos sobre a situacao do padre," REB, 29 (1969), 641.

[2] On this subject Fr. Eduardo Andrade Ponte has offered some excellent and very opportune reflections in "Celibato sacerdotal e lei do celibato," REB, 27 (1967), 545-69. At the end of this article the author promises another, "God willing," which will analyze the theological and pastoral reasons for Christian celibacy; but this further article has never appeared.

[3] This obviously presupposes that the Church has enough candidates to allow it to pick and choose. For, the Church also has the duty of providing enough priests for the communities of the faithful. We have already observed that the common priesthood of the faithful can only be exercised, at least in respect to the Eucharistic celebration (the center and source of Christian life) "through the ministry of priests" (PO, 2e/535) and that without the celebration of the Eucharist (and therefore without the presence of the ministerial priesthood) Christian communities do not exist (cf. PO, 6g/545). To bestow the common priesthood on men (through baptism) and then to refuse them the possibility of exercising it would be either to frustrate one of the great effects of baptism or to deny in practice the need of the Christian ministerial priesthood. If we take seriously the urgent teaching of the Church on the necessity of the ministerial priesthood, then a community of baptized people which is condemned to live without priests is in a truly unjust situation. The Apostles were aware that they must provide each Christian community with priests: "In each church they installed presbyters" (Acts 14:23). Paul writes to Titus: "My purpose in leaving you in Crete was that you might accomplish what had been left undone, especially the appointment of presbyters in every town" (Tit 1:5). In Brazil we do not have such fully authorized Tituses.

[4] Cf. Joseph Coppens (ed.), *Sacerdoce et célibat: Etudes historiques et théologiques* (Louvain: Peeters, 1971), p. 308 (with reference to J. Blinzler).

[5] On this verse, cf. Heinz-Jürgen Vogels, "O Sentido de 1 Cor 5:9," in *Atualidades Bíblicas* (Petrópolis: Vozes, 1971), pp. 558-575. On this whole question of the Lord's call to virginity, cf. the summary of current research in "L'appel du Seigneur a la virginité" (Conseil de Redaction), in Coppens, *op. cit.*, pp. 307-314.

[6] Paul VI, *Sacerdotalis Caelibatus: On Priestly Celibacy*, June 24, 1967, no. 21, in TPS, 12 (1967), 297.

[7] *Op. cit.*, no. 24, in TPS, 12 (1967), 298.

[8] Nietzsche, *The Joyful Wisdom*, Book 5, section 358, tr. by Thomas Common, in *The Complete Works of Friedrich Nietzsche*, ed. by Oscar Levy (1909-1911; reprinted, New York: Russell & Russell, 1964), pp. 312-313.

[9] *Op. cit.*, no. 46, in TPS, 12 (1967), 305.

[10] *Op. cit.*, no. 73, in TPS, 12 (1967), 312.

V

The Possibility of
Ordaining Married Men

The Synod of Bishops, 1971, officially opened up for the Latin Church the question of priestly ordination for married men (cf. no. 91). The problem is a pastoral and disciplinary problem rather than a theological one. For, from a purely theological viewpoint, and in terms of the data of Christian revelation, it is clear that married men can receive the sacrament of orders in all its degrees. We are aware, of course, that celibacy puts the minister of the new covenant in an unusually favorable position for exercising his functions. It was for this reason that "celibacy was at first recommended to priests. Then, in the Latin Church, it was imposed by law on all who were to be promoted to sacred orders" (PO, 16e/566). Today, however, because of the fall-off in vocations to the celibate life and because of the "particular difficulties" (Synod, no. 87) which the celibate life encounters in the modern world, the question of ordaining married men has arisen and cannot be suppressed.

Thus, in a letter (1970) to Cardinal Villot Pope Paul VI wrote: "While we feel obliged thus to reassert the norm of sacred celibacy very clearly, we do not forget a question that has been urgently proposed to us by a number of bishops whose zeal and attachment to the venerable tradition of the priesthood in the Latin Church, and to the eminent values it expresses, we know very well, but who also have pastoral anxieties in the face of certain very particular needs of their apostolic ministry. They have asked us whether it might not be possible, in areas where there is an extreme shortage of priests, and in such areas only, to consider eventually ordaining to the sacred ministry men of advanced years who have given good witness to model family life and professional life in their own environment. We cannot hide the fact that such an eventuality gives rise to grave reservations on our part. Would it not be, among other things, a very dangerous illusion to believe that such a change in the traditional discipline could, in practice, be limited to local cases where there is a real and extreme need? Would it not be a temptation to others to look in this direction for an apparently easier solution to the current shortage of vocations? In any case, the consequence would be so serious and would raise such new questions for the life of the Church that, should the occasion rise, they would have to be examined carefully beforehand by our brothers in the episcopate, in union with us, keeping in mind before God the good of the universal Church as inseparable from that of the local churches."[1]

The working document prepared for the Synod of Bishops, 1971, therefore proposes that the episcopal conferences throughout the world should poll the bishops for their views. The question: In the present great lack of priests, must we not think of conferring priestly ordination on married men of advanced years, who have given proof of a holy family and professional life? Is this not the way to meet the needs of the faithful and their legitimate desire to profit by the blessings which the ministerial priesthood can bring the People of God? But stress was also laid on the reasons for doubting that such a change in the traditional discipline could be kept within the narrow limits of carefully determined cases of real and urgent necessity. Would the temptation not arise of seeking in such a change of discipline an apparently easier solution to the problem of a lack of vocations? For, in this whole matter, we must look to the good not only of this or that local Church but to the general good of the Church as a whole.

After the Synod had convened, the Fathers debated this question from October 8 to October 14 (along with other problems indicated in the practical section of the synodal document on priestly ministry). Because the question is so important at the present time, I shall reproduce here a part of the report I wrote on it during the Synod in Rome.[2] I shall begin with an alphabetical list of the episcopal conferences which officially expressed their views at the Synod (though not all expressed themselves very clearly), whatever their position:

Africa (in general). Cardinal Zoungrana gave some valuable information on the position of Africa as a whole, when he reported that the symposium of the thirty episcopal conferences of Africa and Madagascar, with only one exception, declared that the law of celibacy should be retained, as Vatican II had determined; the group accepted the principle of ordaining married men as long as the Church would proceed without haste and without permitting any abuse that could open the way to the abolition of the law of celibacy.

Africa, Central. Bishop N'Dayen of Bangui reported that more than a year before the Central African Episcopal Conference had asked the Holy Father for permission to study as soon as possible the conditions favorable to the priestly ordination of married men. The answer given them was that they should wait for the Synod. Now the question had arisen in the Synod: What should be done in mission lands when the number of missionaries has fallen off, when the local clergy is non-existent, when Christians are left without a priest, and when there are married laymen who would like to exercise the priestly ministry? Why are we to reject the latter? If the Synod does not approve the ordination of married men, then the bishops with larger numbers of priests must immediately send to the missions the needed priests. But this is by no means an ideal solution. Everyone tells us we must discern and read the signs of the times. Here is such a sign! We must read it without delay, for tomorrow may be too late.

Africa, South. After reaffirming celibacy, the bishops asked that favorable consideration be given to the possibility in particular cases of ordaining married men, especially when urgent pastoral needs require it, but also because we perceive a sign (concretized in the desire expressed by many bishops and priests throughout the world) of the Holy Spirit who works in our world even with regard to the priestly ministry.

Angola. Any definitive solution would be premature. Other solutions should be tried first: married deacons, laymen with more extensive powers, etc. Married priests would form a second-class or third-class clergy. Exceptions would lead to generalizations and to the abolition of the law of celibacy.

Antilles. Bishop Carter of Kingston reported that, even before the Episcopal Conference of the Antilles held its general meeting, the priests had, at the questioning of the bishops, unanimously resolved that priestly ordination could be conferred on married men. The bishops agreed with them, on condition that the possibility be allowed only in those places where the Episcopal Conference made such a request. The bishops did not base their view simply on the lack of priests. They were also motivated by the sign-value which the ordination of married men would have in indicating that celibacy is not the only thing chosen for the sake of the kingdom. The bishops trusted that the Holy Spirit would see to it that the charism of celibacy would continue to make itself manifest in the Church and in the lives of the Church's ministers.

Arab Countries (Latin rite). Archbishop Beltritti, Latin Patriarch of Jerusalem reported: the bishops think that if any locale in the Latin Church feels the need of ordaining married men, recourse should be had to the Holy See which will not refuse to recognize local needs.

Argentina. The bishops are of the opinion that such ordinations would not be timely or useful in Argentina. They would, however, be willing to admit the ordination of married men by way of exception and in special circumstances to be judged by the pope. — An official document of the Episcopal Conference of Latin American Bishops, distributed at the Synod, reported that 77% of the priests of Argentina favor the ordination of married men.

Australia. The bishops are disposed to listen to good reasons and eventually to admit the ordination of married men.

Austria. The bishops are in favor. Their reasons are not reducible simply to the lack of priests. The situation will become more critical with time. If we do not come to grips with the problem now, we shall in the near future be forced to do so by the pressure of inevitable events. Let us entrust celibacy to the Holy Spirit.

Belgium. Yes. Thus the majority of the bishops. A large majority of the Belgian clergy and laity are also in favor. Cardinal Suenens said that he favored the proposal for the following reasons: (1) The bishops have not only the power but also the duty to ordain a sufficient number of priests for the People of God. This duty, imposed by divine law, takes priority over all ecclesiastical legislation which may limit the recruiting of candidates by requiring qualifications not demanded in Sacred Scripture. (2) The Christan people has the right to the number of priests it needs. The Cardinal suggested that all the Episcopal Conferences set up commissions to study the problem in as honest a way as possible.

Bolivia. In some areas, on an experimental basis, and in accord with norms to be determined by the Holy See, the ordination of married men may be permitted.

Brazil. "The possibility of ordination should be opened for married men, as pastoral need shall require and the episcopal conferences, with the approval of the Holy See, shall judge." This was the resolution taken in August, 1971, by the commission which the National Conference of Brazilian Bishops had established; the vote was 26 to 8. The resolution was challenged, however, by Bishop Manuel Pedro da Cunha Cintra of Petrópolis in a letter to the pope, September 25, 1971 (published in *O Estado de Sao Paulo*, November 20, 1971). The bishop claims that the representative commission of the National Conference had relied on an equivocal vote taken in 1969. He also states that the ordination of married men "would mean the end of celibacy, the closing of the seminaries, and the moral decadence of the clergy." The bishop also makes it known that he has written a letter "to a certain number of bishops," asking them to make their views known in the matter, and that he has received replies from 77 bishops who unanimously prefer that "the present discipline, prohibiting the ordination of married men, be kept." He assures the pope that the replies to his letter would have been more numerous had time not been so short and our postal and telegraphic communications so plagued by delays; in any event, the replies represent "the thinking of the majority in the national episcopate." Among those replying affirmatively to the letter of the bishop of Petrópolis were two of the four representatives of the National Conference at the Synod: Cardinal Vicente Scherer and Cardinal Eugénio de Araújo Sales.

Canada. The Canadian bishops are almost unanimously in favor of ordaining married men, wherever necessary. Some of the bishops would be in favor of it even without this restriction. Of the clergy 90% are of the same opinion, believing that such priests would have a better understanding of daily life, the world's problems, etc., and that some forms of ministry would of their nature be more effectively carried out by married priests.

Ceylon. Absolutely opposed. In this country the discipline of celibacy has two thousand years of tradition behind it, dating from the time when Buddhism became widespread, two hundred years before Christ.

Chad. Accepts such ordinations and hope the subject will receive penetrating treatment at the Synod.

Chile. The Conference does not reject the solution which consists of ordaining married men.

China. The bishops do not exclude the possibility.

Congo (Kinshasa). The bishops admit the proposal in principle.

Cuba. Yes, wherever pastoral need requires it.

England. The Conference supports the other conferences in their acceptance of the proposal. The official speaker, Bishop Bowen of Brighton, expresses the view that the ordination of married men not only underlines the dignity of Christian marriage and our unity with the Eastern Catholics but can also be a form of sympathetic contact with the Anglicans and other separated Christians.

Ecuador. By no means. The official speaker, Archbishop Echeverria of Guayaquil, states that experiments in Ecuador lead to the conclusion that the same goals can be achieved by educated laymen which are sought through married deacons and priests. — The document published by CELAM, however, shows that 62% of the priests of Ecuador favor the ordination of married men and 52% favor optional celibacy.

France. For France itself, no. But if other episcopal conferences judge the move necessary, let authorization be granted, under the following conditions: that it be rendered necessary by inescapable needs in the mission; that it be requested and granted to the episcopal conferences of a homogenous geocultural area; that the Holy See be the final judge of the conditions under which the authorization is to be applied.

Germany. Although there are no doctrinal arguments which weigh against the ordination of married men, the bishops think the means sought is an uncertain one for resolving the pastoral problem created by a lack of priests. Until more cogent reasons are found for the move, the bishops are opposed to it.

Ghana. A questionnaire distributed to the priests shows that 60% of the priests find themselves in a crisis situation; that almost all are for optional celibacy; that married men to be ordained priests would have to meet certain conditions.

Holland. The authorization should be given to the conferences which ask for it. Criteria for selection should be established according to the norm of Sacred Scripture, especially the Pauline Letters to Timothy and Titus.

Indonesia. Yes.

Ireland. Such ordinations do not seem timely now. The matter should be given further study.

Italy. No. The lack of priests can be met with married deacons and a better sharing of ministries with the laity, including women.

Latin America (in general). The President of CELAM, Bishop Avelar Brandao Vilela, reports that although the ordination of married men cannot be considered an ideal solution, many bishops believe the experiment should be made under specific conditions and with the approval of the episcopal conferences and the Holy See. — A bulletin from the Department of Hierarchic Ministry of CELAM sums up the results of a survey of opinion among the clergy of Latin America: (1) a clear decision in favor of ordaining married laymen; (2) revision of the current discipline of celibacy, the majority requesting that it be made optional for present and future ministers; (3) acceptance by a notable majority of the readmission of laicized and married priests to the

exercise of the ministry. Another official document issued
by CELAM and approved at the Fourth Inter-American Meeting of Bishops (May, 1971) with a view to the coming Synod,
likewise looks very sympathetically on the possibility of ordaining married men: "The door should thus be opened
to an experiment which not only would enrich the Church
but also seems to meet the present needs of many Latin
American communities."

Madagascar. Only in case of extreme need and only
through the personal intervention of the pope.

Malaysia-Singapore. In view of the urgent need for a
native clergy, the Conference asks permission to ordain married men. A categorical official rejection of this request
and of proposals intended to meet the concrete needs of the
local churches may have catastrophic consequences. The
official speaker, Bishop Galvin of Miri, also said that the institutional Church shows little flexibility in regard to ordaining married men, even when circumstances seem to require such a change. Yet the proposal involves no lessening
of faith and no downgrading of celibacy but simply a genuine
concern for the kingdom of God. Christ came to serve and
not to be served; his compassionate love for the multitudes
seems sharply contrasted with the static, intellectualist, juridical outlook of the instutional Church. We must listen and
not be deaf to the cry of the multitudes who ask for priests
to administer the sacraments to which, as the baptized, they
have a right. The needed priests should be fathers of families
if they are to make the Church fully a part of local structures.
There is no time for preparing priests in the traditional way.
The need is pressing, especially since it is quite possible that
in the not too distant future foreign missionaries will be
expelled. What will we do then?

Malawi. The episcopal conference should be authorized
to ordain married men. Such a move deserves our attention
beyond all else.

Malta. Only for some countries, for reasons of pressing

pastoral need, and as an exception.

Mexico. The majority of the bishops does not oppose the granting of priesthood to married men, in certain circumstances and when the pope judges it opportune.

Mozambique. The priests' councils are for such ordination, but the official speaker, Bishop Alvim Pereira, is against it.

Nicaragua. Lacking vocations, we must make use of married men.

Nigeria. No, under no circumstances. The negative effects would outweigh the advantages. The good of a particular Church should not cause us to lose sight of the good of the universal Church. Married deacons are the solution to the problem.

New Zealand. No.

Peru. Yes, so that we can provide enough priests for a rapidly growing population.

Poland. No. The experience of the Eastern Church in Poland proves that married parish priests become in practice unremovable. If we start with exceptions we shall soon have a law.

Portugal. The majority of the bishops is opposed. The official speaker, Bishop Aleida Trindade of Aveiro, thinks we should not let ourselves be overly impressed with the results of socio-religious pollings and by public opinion: if Christ had been guided by such norms, he would never have proclaimed the Good News.

Puerto Rico. Only by way of exception.

Rhodesia. Yes.

Rwanda-Burundi. No. Moreover, the foreign clergy working here must respect the views of the native clergy, "the great majority of whom are opposed to this solution of the problem."

Scandinavia. After discussing the problem with the priests, the Episcopal Conference is unanimous in thinking that the ordination of mature married men would be a benefit in this part of the world. For here the problem is a wide-ranging one. Some Scandinavian priests live in great isolation and, especially if they are young, find the solitude very difficult. For this reason the Conference asks whether it would not be better to leave the candidate for priesthood free to choose marriage or renounce it, especially in view of the fact that the Church holds Christian marriage in such high esteem.

Spain. The majority of the bishops is opposed.

Tanzania. No. In this country celibacy is not a problem.

Togo. No. The official speaker, Bishop Oguki-Atakpah of Atakpamé, judges that the mere fact of now being permitted to debate the subject will prove fatal for the future, even if the Synod does not approve such ordinations. As for example of the Apostles—no one, even today, has shown us the tombs of the Apostles' wives at Rome!

United States. The bishops do not favor a quick solution to this problem at the present Synod, but they do not exclude further study of the timeliness of ordaining married men.

Upper Volta. The bishops ask the Synod to give favorable consideration to the request to ordain married men, under specific conditions and with authorization from the Holy See.

Venezuela. Absolutely not. The ordination of married men will not solve our problem and will give rise to two classes of priests. Moreover, the Eastern Church's experience of married priests does not seem a very happy one.

Vietnam. No. Even non-Christians have their celibate ministers.

Yugoslavia. The matter requires further study. For the time being, the answer should be No. — But the conference of 700 priests at Zagreb (January, 1971) was strongly in favor of ordaining married men.

Zambia. A qualified yes.

Superiors General. In their name Tarcisio Amaral, C.SS.R., said that the Synod should accept the idea of ordaining married men as a new fact in the Church's life and not be afraid to face up to it.

International Theological Commission. In the document it presented to the Synodal Fathers, the Commission said: "The position that the life of a disciple of Christ, lived in poverty, virginity, and joyful service of one's neighbor is the condition which the hierarchy ought to consider the best for one who would take up the apostolic ministry, does not mean that the hierarchy should require these qualification at all times and from all candidates in the same degree. If those who live virginal lives bear witness to certain aspects and values of the Gospel they preach, those who are married can, if called to the ministry, bear witness to other values of this same Gospel."[3]

The *Congregation of the Laity* (organ of the Holy See). This Congregation sent the Synodal Fathers a document suggesting the ordination of married men and pointing to instances in which laymen or deacons had raised up a believing community which then had no priest to celebrate the Eucharist for them.

In summary: in regard to the ordination of married men the episcopal conferences which voiced their opinion at the Synod (for not all spoke with sufficient clarity) can be divided into four groups:

1. Those simply opposed and not admitting even an exception were thirteen in number: Ceylon, Ecuador, Italy, Nigeria, New Zealand, Poland, Portugal, Rwanda-Borundi, Spain, Tanzania, Togo, Venezuela, Vietnam.

2. Those who took the position that we must wait and see were: Angola, Australia, Germany, Ireland, United States, and Yugoslavia.

3. Those who accept the proposed solution but only by way of exception were eight: Arab countries (Latin rite), Argentina, China, France, Madagascar, Malta, Puerto Rico, and Rhodesia.

4. Those more or less openly favorable were twenty-four:

Antilles, Austria, Belgium, Bolivia, Brazil, Canada, Central
Africa, Chad, Chile, Congo, Cuba, England, Ghana, Holland,
Indonesia, Malaysia-Singapore, Malawi, Mexico, Nicaragua,
Peru, Scandinavia, South Africa, Upper Volta, and Zambia.
In addition, the religious Superiors General and, as we shall
now see, almost all the Eastern Churches.

It is profitable, in this context, to hear the views and
position of the *Eastern Catholic Churches,* both because of
the long practical experience they have had with married
priests and, above all, because one of the reasons frequently
given at the Synod against the ordination of married men
was precisely the experience of the Eastern Churches, which
experience, it was claimed, was rather negative. Such claims
ignored, of course, the testimony given by Vatican II in
regard to the married priests of the Eastern Churches who
were described as "married priests of outstanding merit"
(PO, 16a/565).

What was the testimony of the Eastern Catholic Churches
themselves, through their representatives at the Synod in
1971?

Maronite Church. Cardinal Meouchi, the Patriarch, spoke
twice on the subject. On October 1 he complained of the
way celibacy was treated in the preparatory document, for
the impression was there given that the Church took priority
over the charisms and the Holy Spirit had to obey the
Church. He then defended the Eastern way of life; despite
a married clergy, there has always been and still is great
esteem for celibacy. In his address of October 8, he expressed
the fear that the exaltation of priestly celibacy would dis-
credit the sacrament of matrimony and downgrade the Eastern tradition. He stressed the fact that nowhere in Scripture
or Tradition do we find such a close connection made between priesthood and celibacy that the Church may be allowed to exclude from the service of the altar those who
wish to enter marriage. It would be more in accord with
man's freedom and therefore with the dignity of the human

person that the candidate for priesthood should be allowed
to choose his state for himself. Cardinal Meouchi also maintained that the current reflections of many theologians on
celibacy are motivated by society's decadent morals and by
the defection of priests. The problem should, in fact, be
approached not under the pressure of temporary situations
but in an objective way; to do otherwise is to show a lack
of faith. The Cardinal also was of the opinion that married
priests in the Eastern Church who have lost their wives
should be allowed to enter a second marriage.

Ukrainian Church. Cardinal Slipyj, head of this Church,
also spoke twice on the subject. On October 4 he defended
the Eastern custom of admitting a married clergy as normal,
after the example of the way Christ himself acted. It is not
readily to be granted that the celibate priest is more like
Christ, inasmuch as marriage too is a sign of the union between Christ and his Church. The Cardinal also rejected
the proposal that in the West priests of the Eastern rites
should have to follow the norms of the Latin Church; in
that event, he said, Latins working among Easterners should
have to adapt themselves to Eastern ways! On October 14,
at the end of the debate on the ordination of married men,
Cardinal Slipyj gave his main reply to the difficulties alleged
against the Eastern discipline. He said that by and large the
Eastern Churches defended their traditional practice of ordaining even married men. To expect a uniform discipline
of celibacy throughout the whole Church is an illusion and
premature hope. After all, in the Latin Church ten thousand
priests and five thousand religious are seeking dispensation
from the ties of celibacy. A celibacy that is not observed has
always been a scandal and still is. It is also a fact that candidates for the priesthood are losing heart because of celibacy;
the seminaries and convents are emptying, and the lack of
priests is growing. Just how far is celibacy responsible for
this situation? Some people argue that the Anglicans and
Protestants likewise lack vocations even though they do not

observe celibacy; but among them the cause is clear: the lack of faith and the negligence of the faithful. Cardinal Slipyj also observed that in the Eastern Churches vocations are on the increase, both to the married priesthood and to the celibate life. He stressed the fact that many married priests are truly oustanding ministers. During the persecution they acted with great courage. In Poland too they showed heroic zeal and were a great help to their brothers in the Latin rite.

Greco-Melkite Church. Twenty-two bishops of this Church gathered in August, 1971, in preparation for the Synod. After clearly reaffirming the canonical practice which authorized them to ordain married men to the priesthood, they declared: "The Greco-Melkite Catholic Church considers this view of the priesthood a completely legitimate one and has always regarded it as profitable and praiseworthy to entrust the priestly ministry to married men as need dictates. It calls our attention to the basic and heroic function which these priests have carried out during the difficult times through which our Church has passed. These married priests had the merit not only of keeping the faith alive in the people but also of preventing a gulf from widening between the laity on the one hand and, on the other, the celibate clergy and bishops who have always been chosen from the celibate clergy. The married priests, by remaining in the midst of the people and sharing their life, have greatly contributed to unifying the community of believers around their shepherds. The example of a Christian family life, in which the role of the wife who shares her husband's pastoral and missionary exertions must by no means be underestimated, has frequently produced from within itself vocations to the priesthood and religious life and brought forth priests and bishops renowned for their scholarship and sanctity." On October 2, the Patriarch, Maximus V Hakim, defended the same system for the Latin Church. In another address he criticized the lack of sincere and honest courage that would face up to the advantages of a married clergy.

This determination to carry on the traditional practice of having two kinds of clergy, married and celibate, was also expressed by other patriarchs of the Eastern churches. Cardinal Slipyj reported that only very recently did some Eastern Catholic churches (e.g., the Bulgarian and Coptic churches and the Malabar church in India) show a tendency to ordain only celibates; but this phenomenon was having no influence on the other Eastern Churches. Such unanimity among churches with a long experience of married clergy cannot but be a weighty and valid *a posteriori* argument. We can see also how worthless and aprioristic the argument is that optional celibacy would mean the end of celibacy in the Church. The example of the Eastern churches, which have an extensive celibate clergy despite the fact that celibacy is optional, is eloquent testimony to the contrary. The authentic celibate, the charismatic celibate, will always be exclusively the work of the Holy Spirit, not of the Church; his existence will not depend on ecclesiastical laws. The Church does not and cannot bestow the charism. For this reason, the urging of some of the Synodal Fathers that the Church should trust the Holy Spirit to keep celibacy alive has profound theological justification.

During the Synod numerous bishops spoke in their own name, almost all of them in opposition to the ordination of married men. Thus Cardinals Bengsch of Germany, Carberry of the United States, Conway of Ireland, Dell'Acqua of Rome, Garrone of Rome, Höffner of Germany, Sales of Brazil, Seper of Rome, and Siri of Italy. Almost all stressed one argument: the ordination of married men would certainly open the way to optional celibacy in the Latin Church; to all of them, this would be a catastrophe.

Cardinal Seper, Prefect of the Sacred Congregation for the Doctrine of the Faith, saw in the ordination of married men "a real psychological, economic, sociological revolution." With fright in his voice he asked: Who can take on such a

grave responsibility? He added that current pressures cannot be elevated into "a sign of the times," as some were
arguing. He even proposed that the right to vote on the
matter be withdrawn from the religious present (the Superiors General had shown that they would cast a favorable
vote) and from the representatives of the Eastern Churches.

Cardinal Bengsch called attention to the fact that Vatican
II, assisted by the Holy Spirit, had confirmed the law of
celibacy; he found it difficult to believe that the Holy Spirit
should now want to express himself through those opposed
to this law. Cardinal Conway made a dramatic appeal.
Cardinal Dell'Acqua spoke of the possibility of ordaining
widowers. Cardinal Sales reminded the assembly that they
must stress the qualitative rather than the quantitative aspect
of the priesthood; he did not see that every Christian community had the right to its own priest. Cardinal Siri claimed
that the Latin Church should not take this step because it
still did not have enough experience in the matter (how
could it, if it did not allow a married clergy?).

Of the curial cardinals only Cardinal Samoré showed any
understanding of pastoral needs. Quoting the text of Pope
Paul's letter to Cardinal Villot, he stressed the fact that there
was no question of granting the requested permission to
episcopal conferences, but rather that each bishop, "if he
found himself in dire need of priests," could present his individual case to the pope. In this way, the exception would
confirm the rule.

Among these addresses by individuals in their own name
was one by Bishop Aloisio Lorscheider, president of the
National Conference of Brazilian Bishops, who raised some
theological questions. Why can a married man be ordained
a priest, yet, once his wife has died, be unable to enter a
new marriage? What are the theological and pastoral reasons
for this law? What is the nature of this tradition? For the
same reason it is difficult to understand why those who
admit married men to the priesthood should exclude from

the ministry those who marry after ordination. He also found it strange that no one spoke of the possibility of consecrating married men as bishops. He was not suggesting that this be done, but simply raising the theoretical question as a way of helping us reflect on the opportuneness of ordaining married men.

Willem Goossens, superior general of the Congregation of the Immaculate Heart of Mary, was another who spoke in his own name, as superior of an essentially missionary congregation. As such he is very much concerned with the formation of a native clergy and favored admitting to the priesthood men, married or not, who already have experience in the apostolate; this not simply to meet pastoral needs but also because it is more in conformity with the ways of the early Church. He insisted that the incarnation of the Church in various cultures will come to pass only if we entrust the greatest share in the ministries to members of the local churches.

Thus the Synod was rather divided on this key issue of the present time. Archbishop Diraviam of Madhurai, India, stressed how necessary it was that before making any decision, favorable or unfavorable, the Synod should openly and freely discuss the doctrinal and practical reasons for the proposed change. Otherwise the Synod's decision would not be acceptable or in fact accepted in the Synod itself or in the Church at large for want of credibility. Those in opposition to the decision taken would always be able to allege that it was the result of prefabricated solutions, and that is something which today's priests are not disposed to accept. Bishop Carter of Canada pointed to the existence, in some episcopal synods, of a "mad obsession with celibacy." So preoccupied are they with saving this discipline, he claimed, that they even alter the very nature of the ministerial priesthood and deny its necessity.

As a matter of fact one of the cardinals even argued that it is enough to have one priest celebrate the Eucharist in each diocese; then the whole diocese shares in this "breaking of the bread." An archbishop maintained that good laymen can achieve the results for which the help of married deacons and priests is deemed necessary. Put into other words, this amounts to saying that we can dispense with the ministerial priesthood or at least reduce it to a single celebrant in each diocese. Cardinal Bengsch saw a solution in the following pastoral experiment that has been carried on in his area: about ninety tested and faithful laypeople presided over gatherings for prayer and distributed Communion; this had been going on for seven years, with fine results; one of these laypeople asked to be ordained a priest, and only a few showed any desire to be deacons; everything was fine without priests and deacons, and only Communion was needed.

Such a solution introduces a radical dichotomy into the concept of the Eucharist, and this dichtonomy is, theologically speaking, doubtful and even indefensible. The solution loses sight of the principal element of the Eucharist, namely the sacrificial, and of the indispensable for the real, physical presence of the altar in the midst of concrete, living, Christian community, so that here and now (and not at a distant altar somewhere in the diocese) the sacrifice of the Cross may once again become present and the faithful may unite themselves to it in offering themselves to the Father through Christ. "No Christian community . . . can be built up unless it has its basis and center in the celebration of the most Holy Eucharist" (PO, 6h/545). However well the laity, religious, and even deacons may organize the community, however flourishing its condition from the human and social point of view, if the Eucharistic sacrifice be missing from it, then the source, root, axis, center, and apex of the supernatural life is missing as well. The possible presence of the Eucharistic sacrament for adoration and Communion is not enough; the presence of the Sacrifice is a necessity. Without this presence the faithful cannot transform their spiritual sacrifices (cf. Rom 12:1) into a living sacrifice that is holy and acceptable to God, through Christ, with Christ, and in Christ present on our altars. "For all their works, prayers, and apostolic endeavors, their ordinary married and family life, their daily labor, their mental and physical relaxation, if carried out in the Spirit, and even the hardships of life, if patiently borne—all of these become spiritual sacrifices acceptable to God through Jesus Christ (cf. 1 Pet. 2:5). During the celebration of the Eucharist, these sacrifices are most lovingly offered to the Father along with the Lord's body" (LG, 34b/60). That is the law of the new covenant. That is what all Christian communities need and have a divine right to: "Such participation . . . is their right and duty by reason of their baptism" (SC, 14a/144). — Such was the reasoning of Bishop Valfredo Tepe, when in the name of the Brazilian bishops he presented the majority opinion of the latter in favor of ordaining married men.

To give ourselves a good overall view of the question I shall draw up a list of the reasons in favor of ordaining married men:

1. The example of Jesus Christ who chose even married men for his own apostolic college.

2. Apostolic tradition which continues to be observed down to the present in the Eastern Churches.

3. The experience of the Eastern Catholic Churches, an experience they regard as positive and as reason for holding fast to their received tradition.

4. The theological possibility of separating priestly ministry from celibacy and of thus allowing for an authentic divine call of married men to the priestly ministry.

5. The element of complementarity: if those who live in virginity bear witness to certain aspects and values of the Gospel they preach, married men who are called to the ministry can bear witness to other values of the same Gospel.

6. The evident lack and even lessening in the numbers of celibate priests in many areas of the world at a time of population explosion.

7. The crisis in the seminaries and the lack of vocations to a priestly ministry to which obligatory celibacy is attached.

8. The duty of the bishop to ordain priests in sufficient numbers to meet the legitimate needs and requirements of the baptized; a duty which is of divine law and takes priority over any ecclesiastical law limiting the influx of candidates by requiring qualifications not provided for in Sacred Scripture.

9. The divine law and the consequent need in Christian communities for the sacrament of reconciliation and for the Eucharistic sacrifice.

10. The need of incarnating the Church in varying cultures and of forming a native clergy out of local people, married or not.

11. The married priest is better able to enter into the current problems facing the world and the Christian family.

12. Some forms of priestly ministry can be better carried out by married priests.

13. The daily growing trend even among the clergy and some bishops to have celibacy made optional (this is something new which is a "sign of the times").

14. The sign-value of a priestly ministry of married men in today's world, especially for the purpose of stressing the dignity of Christian marriage.

15. The real difficulty of living a joyous celibate life in the context of a shifting view of man (greater knowledge of the importance of sexuality and of the complementarity of the sexes, etc.).

16. The painful solitude of many priests who work entirely in lonely isolation.

17. The example of a Christian family life, in which the wife's active part in her husband's pastoral and missionary efforts is not to be undervalued, often gives rise to religious and priestly vocations, even of priests and bishops who become renowned for their learning and sanctity (thus the testimony of the Greco-Melkite Eastern Church).

The arguments against the ordination of married men:

1. The law of celibacy which has been in force for centuries in the Latin Church and has recently been reaffirmed by Vatican II, with all its well-known advantages and motivations.

2. The fear that any innovation will not remain a simple exception but become the first and irreversible step toward optional celibacy in the Latin Church.

3. The experience of the Eastern Churches on the negative side (lack of sufficient preparatory study; difficulties in transferring ministers to other places; financial problems of the family; etc.).

4. There would be a twofold clergy, with married priests forming a second or third class.

5. The move would not be an answer to the chief problem which it is intended to meet, namely, the lack of vocations; for the same fall-off exists among Easterners, Anglicans, and Protestants who do not follow a law of celibacy.

6. The need to study more fully the possibility opened up by Vatican II of ordaining married men to the permanent diaconate; a better distribution of ministries among religious and laypeople of both sexes; a better distribution of ordained ministers.

7. The serious psychological consequences of such a move in relation to those already priests and seminarians.

Thus, in the presence of Paul VI, the Synodal Fathers openly and freely laid their cards on the table.

On November 5, 1971, the Fathers of the Synod were presented with two alternative propositions on which a final vote was to be taken. "Formula A: Excepting always the right of the Supreme Pontiff, the priestly ordination of married men is not permitted, even in particular cases. Formula B: It belongs solely to the Supreme Pontiff, in particular cases, by reason of pastoral needs and the good of the universal Church to allow the priestly ordination of married men, who are of mature age and proven life" (91).

With 198 votes being cast, Formula A received 107 votes and Formula B 87 (there were two abstentions and two invalid votes). Since neither proposition received a necessary two-thirds majority (133 votes), the question remains open in the Latin Church.

Notes

[1] Paul VI, *Le dichiarazioni: Letter to Cardinal Jean Villot on Priestly Celibacy,* February 2, 1970, in TPS, 15 (1970), 43.
[2] The report appeared in REB, 31 (1971), 891-936.
[3] *Le ministère sacerdotal,* pp. 105-106. Cf. Appendix I, below.

VI

The Priest and
Temporal Activities

The bishops at the Synod noted that: "Many priests, experiencing within themselves the questionings that have arisen with the secularization of the world, feel the need to sanctify worldly activities by exercising them directly and so bringing the leaven of the Gospel into the midst of events. Similarly, the desire is developing of cooperating with the joint efforts of men to build up a more just and fraternal society. In a world in which almost all problems have political aspects, participation in politics and even in revolutionary activity is by some considered indispensable" (8). Further on, the document twice returns to this problem with a view to offering norms for attitude and behavior: first in the doctrinal section of the document (44-46) and then in the practical section (62-69). The thought of the Synod on this matter may be systematized into the following propositions:

1. *Affairs of the temporal order are essentially subordinate to the reign of God* (44). The documents of Vatican II lay a great deal of stress on this principle which is once again, and more clearly, emerging into the Christian consciousness. In fact it is one of the great novelties with which the recent Council presented us. We have today a more unified vision of human and Christian life. We are on the way to over-coming the dangerous dualism that lurks in such pairs of terms as: temporal-spiritual, profane-sacred, civilization-evangelization, creation-redemption, world-Church, nature-grace. All these realities, after all, were brought into exist-ence by the same Word who became man and dwelt among us as our Redeemer. There is no opposition between the Creator-Word and the Redeemer-Word. The incarnate Word who is Redeemer seeks not to destroy but to complete what the Creator-Word began.

Thus, what we call "profane" or "temporal" or "secular" is also the work of the Creator-Word and as such has an intrinsic value which must be gratefully acknowledged and joyously accepted by those who have entered the Mystical Body of the Redeemer-Word, for he seeks to take to him-self and sanctify the very universe itself. Vatican II empha-sizes the identity of the Word of God who made all things with the Word who became man and dwelt on earth: "He entered the world's history as perfect man, taking that his-tory up into Himself and summarizing it" (GS, 38b/236). The Creator-Lord is also our Savior; the Lord of human history is also the Lord of the history of salvation (GS, 41f/240). The order of redemption (the "supernatural" order) subsumes the order of creation (the "natural" order); for "the entire world, which is primarily related to man and achieves its purpose through him, will be perfectly re-estab-lished in Christ" (LG, 48a/78-79). The kingdom of God will involve "the consummation of the earth and of human-ity" (GS, 39a/237), and the service rendered to men in their earthly affairs is preparing the material of the heavenly kingdom (cf. GS, 38a/236). We have here one of the essential doctrinal principles set forth by Vatican II; it needs to be emphasized at the present time as we seek to understand man's activity in the temporal order. The Synod recalls it when it says, rather brusquely: "Every reality of this world must be subjected to the lordship of Christ" (44).

2. *The autonomy of the temporal order sets limits to the Church's competence in this area.* After affirming the first of our propositions the bishops of the Synod immediately add a second: "This however does not mean that the Church claims technical competence in the secular order, with disregard for the latter's autonomy" (44). This further point was also clearly taught in various documents of Vatican II. In its Dogmatic Constitution on the Church, for example, the Council said: "It must be recognized that the temporal sphere is governed by its own principles, since it is properly concerned with the interests of this world" (LG, 36f/63). We note that according to this text "the interests of this world" are entrusted to the Earthly City, not to the Church. The Council speaks with equal firmness and even greater explicitness in its Decree on the Apostolate of the Laity. After stating that "God's plan for the world is that men should work together to restore the temporal sphere of things and to develop it unceasingly" (AA, 7a/497), the Council continues: "Many elements make up the temporal order: namely, the good things of life and the prosperity of the family, culture, economic affairs, the arts and professions, political institutions, international relations, and other matters of this kind, as well as their development and progress. All of these not only aid in the attainment of man's ultimate goal but also possess their own intrinsic value. This value has been implanted in them by God, whether they are considered in themselves or as parts of the whole temporal order. 'God saw all that he had made, and it was very good' (Gen. 1:31). This natural goodness takes on a special dignity as a result of their relation to the human person, for whose

service they were created. Last of all, it has pleased God to unite all things, both natural and supernatural, in Christ Jesus 'that in all things he may have the first place' (Col. 1:18). This destination, however, not only does not deprive the temporal order of its independence, its proper goals, laws, resources, and significance for human welfare but rather perfects the temporal order in its own intrinsic strength and excellence and raises it to the level of man's total vocation on earth" (AA, 7b/497).

In the Pastoral Constitution on the Church in the Modern World, Vatican II again stresses this teaching which is so basically important for the relationship between the Church and today's world. "If by the autonomy of earthly affairs we mean that created things and societies themselves enjoy their own laws and values which must be gradually decipher-ed, put to use, and regulated by men, then it is entirely right to demand that autonomy. Such is not merely required by modern man, but harmonizes also with the will of the Creator. For, by the very circumstances of their having been created, all things are endowed with their own stability, truth, goodness, proper laws, and order. Man must respect these as he isolates them by the appropriate methods of the individual sciences or arts" (GS, 36b/233-34). The state-ment is incisive, firm, and clear. The Council even took the opportunity to "deplore certain habits of mind, some-times found too even among Christians, which do not suffi-ciently attend to the rightful independence of science" (GS, 36d/234; note 99 indicates that the Council had the Galilei affair in mind here).

The competence of the Church is thus limited by the prin-ciple of the autonomy of the temporal order. "Moreover, in virtue of her mission and nature, she is bound to no particu-lar form of human culture, nor to any political, economic, or social system" (GS, 42e/242). "The role and competence of the Church being what it is, she must in no way be con-fused with the political community, nor bound to any political system" (GS, 76b/287). In all these pronouncements the Council evidently supposes a clear distinction (not a separation!) or duality (not a dualism!) between world and Church, between temporal-secular human society and Christian-religious human society, between progress in human development and growth of the kingdom of God, between temporal order and spiritual order—"realms" which, "although distinct, are so connected in the one plan of God, that He Himself intends in Christ to appropriate the whole universe into a new creation, initially here on earth, fully on the last day" (AA, 5/495).

This clear statement of the autonomy of the temporal order and the Church's lack of technical competence in this area does not, however, strip the Church of its right and duty faithfully and freely to preach the Gospel. She must indeed bring the Gospel to men and utter moral judgments on concrete situations, "even on matters touching the political order, whenever basic personal rights or the salvation of souls make such judgments necessary. In so doing, she may use only those helps which accord with the gospel" (GS, 76g/289).

3. *"All truly Christian undertakings are related to the salvation of mankind, which, while it is of an eschatological nature, also embraces temporal matters"* (Synod, no. 44). In his encyclical on the Church as Mother and Teacher, Pope John XXIII had already stated: "Since they [Christians] are united in mind and spirit with the divine Redeemer, even when they are engaged in the affairs of the world, their work becomes a continuation of His work, penetrated with redemptive power."[1] The same teaching is repeated in the Pastoral Constitution on the Church in the Modern World, of Vatican II: "We hold that by offering his labor to God a man becomes associated with the redemptive work itself of Jesus Christ" (GS, 67b/275).

Jesus himself, in fact, redeemed the world with hands clasped in prayer but also with hands calloused by hard work; with the bloody Cross of Calvary but also with the daily cross of exhausting labor in the workshop at Nazareth; with the blood that spurted from his veins but also with the sweat that dripped from his brow. The virtue or asceticism involved in labor thus makes human weariness a means of sustaining life but also a means of redemption and sanctification; a means to a more perfect material and intellectual state but also a means of spiritual, supernatural perfection; a source of life and development for body and spirit alike.

If work in the temporal order is to have a sanctifying value, it must, as the texts indicate, be "Christian," "carried out in union with Jesus," or "offered to God": "The fact is that whether you eat or drink — whatever you do — you should do all for the glory of God" (1 Cor 10:31) ; "Whatever you do, whether in speech or in action, do it in the name of the Lord Jesus. Give thanks to God the Father through him" (Col 3:17) . Against those who reject the use of certain foods the Apostle teaches that "God created [these foods] to be received with thanksgiving by believers who know the truth. Everything God created is good, nothing is to be rejected when it is received with thanksgiving, for it is made holy by God's word and by prayer" (1 Tim 4:3-5) .

In our present situation this Christian understanding of work in the temporal order is very important. That is why Vatican II put into the first part of its Pastoral Constitution on the Church in the Modern World the third chapter: "Man's Activity throughout the World," which really deals with "the profound meaning of human activity" (GS, 40a/ 238) . I have given an analysis of this text elsewhere[2] and shall here only attempt in a set of propositions to sum up the thought of the Council and its development. (1) Human activity in the temporal order is part of God's plan and is a glorification of the Creator. (2) Human activity in the temporal order is ambivalent, for it has been touched by sin. (3) Human activity in the temporal order has been embraced by the redemptive work of Christ and becomes part of the Paschal Mystery. (4) Human activity in the temporal order finds its proximate norms in man himself. (5) Human activity in the temporal order has its own value and its own legitimate autonomy. (6) Human activity in the temporal order is a serious duty for Christians as bearers of the eschatological hope. (7) Human activity in the temporal order is the proper and specific object of the lay apostolate.

4. *"The proper mission entrusted by Christ to the priest, as to the Church, is not of the political, economic, or social order, but of the religious order"* (Synod, no. 45). Here the synodal document refers us to the Pastoral Constitution on the Church in the Modern World (42b/241) and situates the priest's specific role within that of the Church itself. The text of Vatican II, in turn, is inspired by the words of Pius XII: "Her Divine Founder, Jesus Christ, gave her no mandate and established no objective of a cultural nature. The goal which Christ assigns to her is strictly religious. . . . The Church should lead men to God, in order that they may give themselves wholeheartedly to Him. . . . The Church can never lose sight of this exclusively religious, supernatural end. All her activities, down to the very last canon of her code, can take this direction only — to contribute, directly or indirectly, to this end."[3] We notice, however, that the Council's statement is not so incisive as that of Pope Pius XII; it is nonetheless sufficiently clear.

If we are to look for the specific work of the priest in the mission proper to the Church, we must evidently study the latter first. I refer the reader to what I have written elsewhere on this point.[4] The synodal document, *Justice in the World,* distinguished between the mission of the Church in general, the special mission of the hierarchy, and the mission of Christians (36-38).

The Church's mission is to preach the Gospel message, including man's vocation to turn from sin to love of the Father and universal brotherhood and consequently to the quest for justice in the world. This is why the Church has the right and duty to call for justice at the social, national, and international levels, and to decry injustice where it occurs.

The mission of the hierarchy (and the priest is part of the hierarchy; cf. LG, chap. 3) is not to offer concrete solutions to social, economic, and political problems, but it does involve the defence and promotion of the dignity and basic rights of the human person.

The mission of Christians, insofar as they are members of civil society, includes the right and duty of seeking the common good, along with other citizens. In undertaking civil activity as Christians, they act, generally speaking, on their own account, and the hierarchy is not responsible for their decision. In a measure, however, they do fasten some responsibility for it upon the Church whose members they are.

In several documents Vatican II speaks of the possible profane or secular activities of the priest:

LG, 31b/57: "A secular quality is proper and special to laymen. It is true that those in holy orders *can at times engage in secular activities, and even have a secular profession.* But by reason of their particular vocation they are chiefly and professedly ordained to the sacred ministry" (italics added).

GS, 43d/243: "Secular duties and activities belong properly *although not exclusively* to laymen" (italics added).

PO, 8b/549-50: "All priests are sent forth as co-workers in the same undertaking, whether they are engaged in a parochial or supraparochial ministry, whether they devote their efforts to scientific research or teaching, whether by manual labor they share in the lot of the workers themselves — if there seems to be need for this and competent authority approves — or whether they fulfill any other apostolic tasks or labors related to the apostolate. All indeed are united in the single goal of building up Christ's Body, a work requiring manifold roles and new adjustments, especially nowadays."

The Apostolic Letter *Octogesima Adveniens,* in 1971, made the following, somewhat triumphalistic, statement (no. 48): "In the social sphere, the Church has always wished to assume a double function: first, to enlighten minds in order to assist them to discover the truth and to find the right path to follow amid the different teachings that call for their attention; and secondly, to take part in action and to spread, with a real care for service and effectiveness, the energies of the gospel. Is it not in order to be faithful to this desire that the Church has sent on an apostolic mission among the workers priests who, by sharing fully the condition of the worker, are at that level the witnesses to the Church's solicitude and seeking?"[5]

The Synod of Bishops, after describing the priestly ministry as a fully valid form of human activity, and even one superior to other activities, states that *"sharing in the secular activities of men is by no means to be considered the principal end* nor can such participation suffice to give expression to priests' specific responsibility" (62). Each priest must therefore take it as his general guiding principle that he is to give full time to the priestly ministry. The latter can never become a secondary or accessory occupation. Further on, the Synod says again that "the priority of the specific mission which pervades the entire priestly existence must therefore always be kept in mind" (69). What men expect from the priest, after all, is that he will speak to them of God and bring them to God.

Nonetheless, the Synod points out (in no. 45, the main paragraph on which we have been commenting), even while remaining strictly within the bounds of his specific ministry, the priest can do much for the establishment of a just temporal order, especially in those regions of the world in which the problems of injustice and oppression are greater. We may find help here in the passage from the Pastoral Constitution on the Church in the Modern World to which the Synod document refers in no. 46: "The good news of Christ constantly renews the life and culture of fallen man. It combats and removes the errors and evils resulting from sinful allurements which are a perpetual threat. It never ceases to purify and elevate the morality of peoples. By riches coming from above, it makes fruitful, as it were from within, the spiritual qualities and gifts of every people and of every age. It strengthens, perfects, and restores them in Christ. Thus by the very fulfillment of her own mission the Church stimulates and advances human and civic culture. By her action, even in its liturgical form, she leads men toward interior liberty" (GS, 58d/264-65). In this context Vatican II makes its own a statement of Pius XI: "It is necessary never to lose sight of the fact that the objective of the Church is to evangelize, not to civilize. If it civilizes, it is for the sake of evangelization" (note 192 on GS, 58/264).

5. *Any action of the priest in the temporal order must always take place within the ecclesial communion.* Such is a first requirement implicit in what the Synod says in no. 45. Further on, in speaking more concretely of such activity, the bishops indicate that by action within "ecclesial communion" they mean that this "within" it to be "judged by the local bishop with his presbyterium, and if necessary in consultation with the episcopal conference" (63; cf. 68). The Synod had earlier taught that "the priestly ministry . . . is essentially communitarian within the presbyterium and with the bishop who, preserving communion with the successor of Peter, is a part of the body of bishops" (41). The theological reason for this is given in the conciliar Decree on the Ministry and Life of Priests: *"Since the priestly ministry is the ministry of the Church herself,* it can be discharged only by hierarchical communion with the whole body" (PO, 15c/564; italics added). For this reason, "that they may be able to verify the unity of their lives in concrete situations too, they should subject all their undertakings to the test

of God's will, which requires that projects should conform to the laws of the Church's evangelical mission. For loyalty toward Christ can never be divorced from loyalty toward His Church. Hence pastoral love requires that priest always work in the bond of communion with the bishop and with his brother priests, lest his efforts be in vain" (PO, 14e-f/ 563).

It is absolutely certain, then, that "no priest can in isolation or singlehandedly accomplish his mission in a satisfactory way. He can do so only by joining forces with other priests under the direction of Church authorities" (PO, 7f/549). Like the bishop, the priest is by nature a "collegial being" (he belongs to the Order or College of Priests) and functions well only within the "hierarchical communion." The bishop or priest who lacks the "collegiate sense" (LG, 23f/46) is straying from his vocation; the priest who isolates himself is walking the wrong road and running in vain. The synodal Fathers add that the communitarian nature of the priesthood "holds also for priests who are not in the immediate service of any community or who work in remote and isolated territories" (41). The Church is of its very essence a "communion," for God's will is "to make men holy and save them not merely as individuals without any mutual bonds" (LG, 9a/25) but in communion with one another.

6. *Violence in word or deed is a non-evangelical attitude* (cf. Synod, no. 45). In his address at the opening of the Second General Assembly of the Latin American Bishops (1968) Pope Paul VI said: "We must encourage every honest effort to improve the lot of the poor and of those who live in conditions of human and social inferiority. We cannot be linked with systems and structures that cloak and foster serious, oppressive inequalities among citizens and social classes within the same country. Effective measures must be implemented to remedy the insufferable and unequal plight that is often visited on the less prosperous. Yet,

having said this, we must repeat what we have said before: the strength of our charity is not to be found in hatred and violence. Of the various ways leading to a just reordering of society, we cannot choose that of atheistic Marxism or organized revolt, much less that of anarchy and bloodshed. We must distinguish our obligation and purpose from those who exalt violence into a noble ideal, a glorious heroism, an obliging theology. Let us not commit new wrongs to repair past errors and present ills. To do this would be contrary to the Gospel, contrary to the spirit of the Church, contrary to the real interests of the people, and contrary to the hopeful outlook of the present era, which is marching under the banner of justice toward brotherhood and peace."[6]

The previous day, at Bogotá, Pope Paul had stated: "Violence is not in accord with the Gospel, that is, not Christian."[7] The Christian is a man of peace and not ashamed of the fact. He is not a pacifist pure and simple, for he is capable of fighting, but he prefers peace to war. He knows that "sudden or violent changes of structures would be deceitful, would be ineffective of themselves, and certainly would not be in conformity with the dignity of the people. Their dignity demands that the needed changes be realized from within — in other words, through an appropriate coming to awareness, an adequate preparation, and that real participation by all which ignorance and sometimes inhuman living conditions keep from being assured at present."[8]

The Medellin document on peace observes: "As the Christian believes in the productiveness of justice in order to achieve peace, he also believes that justice is a prerequisite for peace. He recognizes that in many instances Latin America finds itself faced with a situation of injustice that can be called institutionalized violence, when, because of a structural deficiency of industry and agriculture, of national and international economy, of culture and political life, 'whole towns lack necessities, live in such dependence as hinders all initiative and responsibility as well as every

possibility for cultural promotion and participation in social and political life,' thus violating fundamental rights.
This situation demands all-embracing, courageous, urgent
and profoundly renovating transformations. We should not
be surprised, therefore, that the 'temptation to violence' is
surfacing in Latin America. One should not abuse the
patience of a people that for years has borne a situation that
would not be acceptable to anyone with any degree of awareness of human rights."[9]

The same document, however, says elsewhere: "If it is
true that revolutionary insurrection can be legitimate in
the case of evident and prolonged 'tyranny that seriously
works against the fundamental rights of man, and which
damages the common good of the country,' whether it pro-
ceeds from one person or from clearly unjust structures, it
is also certain that violence or 'armed revolution' generally
'generates new injustices, introduces new imbalances and
causes new disasters; one cannot combat a real evil at the
price of a greater evil.' "[10] In *Justice in the World,* the
Synod of Bishops in its turn stresses that "there are sources
of progress other than conflict, namely love and right. This
priority of love in history draws other Christians to prefer
the way of non-violent action and work in the area of public
opinion." (39).

7. *In each concrete case we must determine whether and
to what extent specific temporal duties or activities of the
priest effectively serve the mission of the Church, the Christian community, and those not yet evangelized* (cf. Synod,
no. 62). Personal desire or inclination ("charism") is not
an adequate criterion, for we must not lose sight of the
meaning of a vocation to priestly ministry or of its specific
functions. If we neglect this principle, we are in danger
of missing the meaning of that personal consecration by
which we were called to the priestly ministry. In this context the bishops note: "When activities of this sort, which
ordinarily pertain to the laity, are as it were demanded by

the priest's very mission to evangelize, they must be harmonized with his other ministerial activities, in those circumstances where they can be considered as necessary forms
of true ministry" (64). For there can indeed be real in-
compatibilities: an advocate cannot at the same time be
the judge. Since he is to be a sign of catholicity and a
minister of unity, the priest must attentively consider how
far this or that activity or duty is really compatible with
his very being and specific function, even though the temporal initiatives may be in themselves good, positive, and
even necessary.

8. *Priests should try to form the consciences of the laity
in their efforts to create a Christian temporal order* (cf. no.
65). Such efforts are, after all, the specific field of the lay
apostolate: "The laity, by their very vocation, seek the
kingdom of God by engaging in temporal affairs and by
ordering them according to the plan of God. . . . It is therefore his [the layman's] special task to illumine and organize
these affairs in such a way that they may always start out,
develop, and persist according to Christ's mind, to the praise
of the Creator and Redeemer" (LG, 31c-d/57-58). "The
laity must take on the renewal of the temporal order as
their own specific obligation. Led by the light of the gospel
and the mind of the Church, and motivated by Christian
love, let them act directly and definitively in the temporal
sphere" (AA, 7e/498).

In this situation it is the priest's task (and part of his
specific function) to form the consciences of laypeople so
that they can with real competence do their apostolic duty
in the temporal order. In the Medellin document on justice, the bishops said: "We wish to affirm that it is indispensable to form a social conscience and a realistic per-
ception of the problems of the community and of social
structures. We must awaken the social conscience and communal customs in all strata of society and professional
groups regarding such things as dialogue and community

living within the same group and relations with wider social groups (workers, peasants, professionals, clergy, religious, administrators, etc.). This task of *'concientización'* and social education ought to be integrated into joint Pastoral Action at various levels."[11] In their document on *Justice in the World* the bishops of the synod declare: "Christians' specific contribution to justice is the day-to-day life of the individual believer acting like the leaven of the Gospel in his family, his school, his work, and his social and civic life. Included with this are the perspectives and meaning which the faithful can give to human effort. Accordingly, educational method must be such as to teach men to live their lives in its entire reality and in accord with the evangelical principles of personal and social morality which are expressed in the vital Christian witness of one's life" (49). The whole of this important section on "Educating to Justice" (49-58) should be carefully read and studied. Here the priest will find an immense field for his labors and a field that is truly his as minister of the Gospel.

9. *"In circumstances in which there legitimately exist different political, social, and economic options, priests like all citizens have a right to select their personal options"* (Synod, no. 66). He must, however, always be extremely careful to avoid presenting other Christians with his views as though they were the only legitimate ones or letting them become a cause of discord among the faithful. "Often enough the Christian view of things will itself suggest some specific solution in certain circumstances. Yet it happens rather frequently, and legitimately so, that with equal sincerity some of the faithful will disagree with others on a given matter. Even against the intentions of their proponents, however, solutions proposed on one side or another may easily be confused by many people with the gospel message. Hence it is necessary for people to remember that no one is allowed in the aforementioned situations to appropriate the Church's authority for his opinion. They

should always try to enlighten one another through honest discussion, preserving mutual charity and caring above all for the common good" (GS, 43f/244). The bishops of the Synod remind the priest: "Let priests be mindful of the laity's maturity, which is to be valued highly when it is a question of their specific role" (67). Some involvements presuppose a technical competence which a priest does not have, at least by dint of his formation for the priesthood. Here again we must remember the Church's lack of technical competence in this area.

10. *The priest must keep his distance from any political office or responsibility* (cf. Synod, no. 66). For, "political options are by nature contingent and never in an entirely adequate and perennial way interpret the Gospel" (*ibid.*). Politics is an area in which opposition is the general rule, even among Christians. Moreover, difficult though it is to admit this, it is a fact that political success and evangelical sincerity are not easily united in one person. For his part, as minister of Christ at the service of the ecclesial community, the priest must always act as sign and instrument of unity and as preacher of the Gospel. If he is to be able to persevere as a valid sign of unity and if he is always to be in a position freely to preach the Gospel in its fulness, the priest must in some concrete situations surrender the exercise of his own political rights (Synod, no. 67). Moreover, as a general rule, "leadership or active militancy on behalf of any political party is to be excluded by every priest" (68). For "it is their [priests'] task . . . to reconcile differences of mentality in such a way that no one will feel himself a stranger in the community of the faithful" (PO, 9e/553). For this reason, Vatican II warned that "in building the Christian community, priests are never to put themselves at the service of any ideology or human faction. Rather, as heralds of the gospel and shepherds of the Church, they must devote themselves to the spiritual growth of the Body of Christ" (PO, 6j/546).

Notes

[1] John XXIII, *Mater et Magistra: A Re-evaluation of the Social Question in the Light of Christian Teaching,* May 15, 1961, in TPS, 7 (1961), 342.
[2] Cf. *O Cristao Secularizado,* chapter 7.
[3] Pius XII, *C'est biens volontiers: Address to the International Union of Archaeological Institutes,* March 9, 1956, in TPS, 3 (1956-1957), 158-159.
[4] Cf. *The Ecclesiology of Vatican II,* chapter 4.
[5] Paul VI, *Octogesima Adveniens: Apostolic Letter to Cardinal Roy,* May 14, 1971, in *Catholic Mind,* 69 (November, 1971), 56.
[6] Address of August 24, 1968, in TPS, 13 (1968-1969), 256.
[7] Address at Bogotá, August 23, 1968, in TPS, 13 (1968-1969), 240.
[8] *Ibid.*
[9] *The Church in the Present-Day Transformation of Latin America in the Light of the Council* (Second General Conference of the Latin American Bishops, Bogotá, August 24, 1968, and Medellin, August 26—September 6, 1968), edited by Louis Colonnese (Bogotá: General Secretariat of CELAM, 1970), vol. 2, p. 78 (no. 16). The first quotation within this text is from Paul VI, *Populorum Progressio,* no. 30.
[10] *Op. cit.,* p. 78 (no. 19). The two quotations are from *Populorum Progressio,* no. 31.
[11] *Op. cit.,* p. 65 (no. 17).

VII

Relationship of
Priest and Bishop

Here we have what seems to be the most difficult and delicate aspect of the modern priest's life. It is also, however, an important and even essential aspect, because of that indispensable "hierarchical communion" without which the Church would lack one of its chief constitutive elements. To speak of the bishop is to speak of authority. Consequently when priests speak of a "crisis of authority," we might well substitute "crisis concerning the bishop." Recent inquiries conducted among priests in Brazil, Latin America, the United States, Spain, etc., all show the reality and seriousness of this crisis among a large part of the clergy. We mentioned earlier, in chapter 1, the painful distance that exists between bishops and priests. There are of course many priests, especially older ones, who have a fairly good relationship with the bishop. But a growing number admit to an increasing dissatisfaction on this head. During the past three years I have met many groups of priests throughout Latin America, in courses and spiritual retreats. One of the major problems voiced at these meetings — whether in general sessions or in private conversations — is invariably the problem of the priests' relations with their bishops.

The causes of this "crisis concerning the bishop" have been pointed out by priests themselves:[1]

—The conception which people and priests have of the bishop's position: in general they see him as set apart and and enveloped in myth;

—The decidedly juridical ecclesiology which bishops hold, with its highly juridical conception of the episcopal office; an excessive concentration of powers which are guaranteed by a canonically or juridically oriented dogmatism, and a mystique of doctrinal infallibilism;

—The juridical organization which still exists and predominates but which is regarded, in theory, as now overcome and obsolete;

—The lack of theological vision and pastoral courage needed for putting the principles of Vatican II into practice in the present critical time of the Church: there is a discontinuity in the attitude of bishops toward the Council;

—Theological and pastoral uncertainty on the part of the bishops;

—Bureaucratic exercise of authority;

—Personal whims of the bishops, translated into orders and decisions;

—Conflict between the conceptions of the hierarchy as power and as service;

—Disproportion between the increasingly rapid rate of changes in mentality and the slow changes in pastoral structures;

—The feudal mentality of those in authority, who often listen as a formality but make decisions on their own;

—The life-time duration of episcopal responsibility;

—The social situation in which we live, where bishops are identified with the social elite and often brought into contact more with the upper classes than with the people;

—Participation of the bishops in social ceremonies that have no pastoral meaning;

—A kind of nepotism or favoritism that enters into the exercise of the pastoral office: favorites are given preference and thus incompetent people easily get to the top.

The deepest cause of the crisis, however, is brought home to us by the many priests who are moving more and more to the periphery of the ecclesiastical organization and in practice no longer accept the Church as an institution.[2]

However, the Church, in addition to being a "mystery," is in fact also a *social institution*. The historical fact of Christianity with its world-view and value-system must always take shape, when lived by the faithful, within a particular society. Here its world-view and value-system are translated into concrete ways of thinking and acting. This process of concretization or translation into concrete forms is called *institutionalization*. From it flow specific structures which depend not only on the content of the Christian message but also on the culture and social system in which the Christian lives his life. We cannot conceive of a Church or Chrisitan community that has no structures! The question therefore is not whether the Church needs structures. The question is whether certain structures are those which best enable Christianity to be incarnated and lived in a concrete society. In other words, what we question is not institutionalization as such but the forms of institutionalization. Such forms are not and need not be definitive and eternal. They have in fact changed often, and radically, in the course of history, whenever the Church has encountered new cultures and entered along with mankind into new historical eras. Antiquity, the Middle Ages, and the Modern Period each have required new and often deep-going adaptations and changes.

"Today," as Vatican II points out, "the human race is passing through a new stage of its history. Profound and rapid changes are spreading by degrees around the whole world" (GS, 4b/202). Again: "The living conditions of modern man have been so profoundly changed in their social and cultural dimensions, that we can speak of a new age in human history" (GS, 54a/260). In his Letter *Octogesima Adveniens* on "the new needs of a changing world," Paul VI does not hesitate to speak of a "new civilization" and says: "In the present changes, which are so profound and rapid, each day man discovers himself anew, and he questions himself about the meaning of his own being and of his collective survival. Reluctant to gather the lessons of a past he considers over and done with, and too different from the present, man nevertheless needs to have light shed upon his future — a future that he perceives to be as uncertain as it is changing — by permanent eternal truths. These are truths that are certainly greater than man; but, if he so wills, he can himself find their traces."[3]

We are, then, entering upon a new historical era. Like other such periods, this one too will make its demands upon the Church. We are entering a world of new aspirations, new values, and new forms of social fellowship. As it faces this new world the Church finds itself shaped by institutional forms (ways of thinking, structures of authority, juridical system, type of organization, etc.) which still correspond at bottom to a now outdated model ("Christendom"). The priests who say they no longer accept the Church as an institution are in fact simply unable to conform to *this particular* institutional form; I do not think they are looking for the impossible, namely, a totally non-institutionalized Church. When those in authority persist in maintaining *this* institutional form, the crisis of authority inevitably appears.

But the problems which arise in this crisis are initially institutional; only in a second moment do they become personal as well. This being so, the personal problems are not to be resolved without first resolving the underlying institutional problem. The present serious crisis through which the Church is passing is wholly of this kind; it arises therefore not from bad will on the part of Christians but from the inadequacy of inherited institutional forms to new conditions, situations, and needs. The inadequacy is in ways of thinking (or in the way in which the revealed data of Christianity have been understood and expressed in categories which are no longer ours or applied to problems which are no longer ours). The inadequacy is in organizational forms (or in the organizational structures which still characterize the institutional Church: the relationship between the episcopal college and its head, between bishop and priests, between clergy and laity; structures for the exercise of authority; diocesan and parochial organizations; forms of the aposotlate; etc.). The inadequacy is in ways of acting (or in the manner in which the Church directly relates to men, for whose sake alone she exists; the manner in which the Church is able to integrate itself into human society and become able to carry out her mission).

The concrete case of the tension between bishops and priests is a typically institutional one, not a personal one. Unless deep-going, radical (getting at the "root") changes are made, such as are perfectly possible while maintaining complete fidelity to the Lord's will and institution, the problems which today trouble so many of our best priests and bishops will go unresolved. Precisely because this kind of crisis is in its root institutional and not personal, both bishops and priests, who may be excellent human beings, will continue to suffer under this unfortunate tension.

One thought frequently recurs when priests suggest ways of overcoming the crisis. The priests of the North I Region of Brazil, for example, think that we will break through the impasse "only if there is a decentralization away from Rome, so that bishop, priests, and people, can really assume their own responsibilities and become a church which is a vital community rather than a juridically organized society."[4] The priests of the Inter-Regional Northeast expressed the same view: "If the bishop and his priests are to carry out their mission, each region and diocese must have greater pastoral autonomy, and stimulus must be given to the creation of new expressions of interecclesial relationships."[5]

The bishops in their 1971 Synod felt the same need to look for something new in these relationships: "New forms of hierarchical communion between bishops and priests (cf. PO; 7) must be found, to facilitate contacts between local churches. A search must be made for ways whereby priests may collaborate with bishops in supra-diocesan bodies and enterprises" (102).

In the search for "new forms of hierarchical communion" the following basic principles must be respected:

1. *"All priests, together with bishops, share in one and the same priesthood and ministry of Christ"* (PO, 7a/546). The priest shares in the authority of Christ himself and not, strictly speaking, in that of the bishop. It is true, of course, that the bishop transmits this authority to the priest, but in so doing the bishop is but the instrument of Christ. "Through the ministry of the bishop, God consecrates priests" (PO, 5a/541). It is therefore theologically inaccurate to say that the priest is a "minister of the Church"; he can however be said to act "in the name of the Church," but always as "minister of Christ and acting in the name of Christ." It is also inaccurate to say that the priest acts "in the name of the bishop" or that he "represents the bishop," but accurate to say that he acts and should always act "in communion with the bishop." In addition, it is not true that the priest "depends for his power on the bishop," but correct to say that he depends on the bishop "in the exercise of his power." The power (*potestas* or *exousia*) he receives directly from Christ and not from the bishop. Since Vatican II we may no longer say that the bishop communicates to the priest a part of his own priesthood. In the days when it was thought that priests received all they

have and are from the bishop, there was good theological
reason to emphasize the fatherhood of the bishop: he was
the father, the priests his sons. The basis for this has now
vanished; the priest is related directly to Christ. For "all
priests, both diocesan and religious, participate in and exercise the one priesthood of Christ" (CD, 28a/416). The
Council therefore adds: "On account of this communion
in the same priesthood and ministry, the bishop should regard priests as his brothers and friends" (PO, 7c/547).

2. *Priests are co-workers of the episcopal order.* The
college of bishops succeeds the apostolic college in the office
of teaching and pastoral guidance; it "succeeds" in the
sense that the apostolic body continues to exist in the form
of the episcopal order and that the bishops are successors of
the Apostles, having full and supreme power over the whole
Church (cf. LG, 22c/43). But the ministerial priesthood
of presbyters is wholly situated in the same line as the
ministry of bishops.

It may be in place here to give some documentation for
this last statement, which is rather important. Before Vatican
Council II the priest was usually regarded simply as the
man of sacrifice, and the essence of his priesthood was defined in terms of his relationship to the Eucharist. Such
was the conception expressed by the *Summa theologiae* of
St. Thomas Aquinas; such was the doctrine presupposed by
the Council of Trent. The conciliar commission which drew
up the text for Vatican II's Decree on the Ministry and Life
of Priests referred to this view as "the scholastic definition
of priesthood" and definitively abandoned it as an approach
to the priesthood. The official exposition, made when the
final, definitive version of the text was presented to the
conciliar Fathers, made it a point to explain: "The central
idea of this working paper, providing a center of coherence
for the whole, is that presbyters, being consecrated in the
sacrament of orders by the anointing of the Holy Spirit and
being made like Christ the Priest, are the ministers of

Christ the Head in his Church and are assigned to serve the people of God. In their ministry therefore they act in the person of Christ himself, who ceaselessly carries on, through them, the mission he has received from his Father." When suggestions for changes in the text were being made a group of conciliar Fathers tried to reintroduce the idea that "the essence of presbyterial priesthood lies in its relation to the Eucharist" (13th proposed modification), but the commission simply rejected the proposal and, in reply to the 14th proposed modification, answered: "As is clear from observations expressed in the council hall or communicated in writing to the commission, the majority of the Fathers prefer that the priestly function of presbyters be shown as flowing, as it were, from the *episcopal* office and connected with it. The function of bishops, however, includes more than their role in the Eucharist, even if the Eucharistic celebration be the high point of their ministry. Their ministry is to be regarded as properly *apostolic,* as the Dogmatic Constitution *Lumen Gentium* (chapter 3) and the Decree on the Bishops' Pastoral Office in the Church make clear. All of us must keep these documents continually in mind, as the commission has. *The priesthood of presbyters is to be portrayed as in the same line as the priesthood of bishops, allowing for the necessary adaptations.*" In the general address on these proposed modifications, the official expositor said: "The commission cannot agree with those Fathers who think that this working paper should be controlled by the scholastic definition of priesthood which focuses on the power to consecrate the Eucharist. For it is the mind of this Council, manifested in numerous petitions from the Council Fathers, that the priesthood of presbyters be linked to the priesthood of bishops, the latter being the crown and fulness of priesthood." Thus, according to the mind and intention of the Council the nature of presbyteral priesthood is to be sought where the priesthood of bishops is sought: in their consecration and mission. This was the thinking behind chapter 2 of the Decree on the Ministry and Life of Priests.[6]

Thus the ministry proper to bishops has been entrusted to presbyters "in a limited degree" in order that they might be "co-workers of the episcopal order in the proper fulfillment of the apostolic ministry entrusted to the latter order by Christ" (PO, 2c/534). The expression "co-workers of the episcopal order" occurs sixteen times in the documents of Vatican II; it is taken from the Preface for the Ordination of Priests in the Roman Ritual and is found in some of the early Western liturgies.[7] The bishops receive the fullness of the sacrament of orders (LG, 21c/41) and therefore act in the person of Christ "in an eminent and visible way" (LG, 21e/42). Priests "do not possess the highest degree of the priesthood" and therefore "are dependent on the bishops in the exercise of their power" (LG, 28a/53).

3. *Priests can exercise their ministry only in hierarchic communion.* For, as the Synod states, "the priestly ministry . . . is essentially communitarian within the presbyterium and with the bishop" (41). The Council had already given the reason for this fact: "The very unity of their [the presbyters'] consecration and mission requires their hierarchical communion with the order of bishops" (PO, 7a/546). The formula, "hierarchical communion," is original with Vatican II and came into existence during the composition of LG, chapter 3, when there was question of describing the relations between bishops and the successor of Peter: the former can exercise their powers "only in hierarchical communion with the head and the members of the college" (LG, 21d/41).

The Church itself, after all, is a fellowship or communion (*koinonia, communio*). The communion consists first and foremost in an internal, invisible, sacramental, and supernatural unity which holds all the baptized in a vital union with Christ and, in Christ, with the other members. But the external or visible unity of the Church must also be sought and structured into the communion; the Council speaks in this context of a "unity of communion" (LG, 15a/33) or a "fellowship in unity" (UR, 2d/344). The unity of the Church is not the kind of unity that flows from domination and subjection; such would not be evangelical. Nor is the "unity of communion" which characterizes the Church of Christ the result of human efforts; instead, it is the Holy Spirit who "gives her a unity of fellowship and service" (LG, 4b/17). The Holy Spirit is "the principle of their coming together and remaining together . . . in fellowship" (LG, 13a/31).

As Christ himself tells us, there are, strictly speaking, no "superiors" or "subjects" in the Church. After sternly criticizing the outlook, titles, and pretensions of the Scribes and Pharisees, Christ bids his disciples follow these norms: "You, however, must not allow yourselves to be called Rabbi, since you have only one Master, and *you are all brothers.* You must call no one on earth your father, since you have only one Father, and he is in heaven. Nor must you allow yourselves to be called teachers, for you have only one Teacher, the Christ" (Mt 23:8-10, JB; italics added). You are all brothers! Including bishops and priests; bishops are not the "superiors" of priests, and priests are not the "inferiors" or "subjects" of bishops. The Gospel rejects this unfortunate terminology which came into use in a period when bishops were beginning to be regarded as "princes" or as something even worse and less Christian. "If by the will of Christ some are made teachers, dispensers of mysteries, and shepherds on behalf of others, yet all share a *true equality with regard to* the *dignity* and to the activity common to all the faithful for the building up of the Body of Christ" (LG, 32c/58). It would be most unevangelical to introduce a kind of superior caste into the Church.

There must indeed be a diversity of authorized *services* or ministries in the Church if the people of God is to be able to grow and if all are to advance freely in an ordered way to the kingdom of God. That is why the communion

must be a *hierarchic* one; a brotherhood hierarchically organized into distinct services, some of which are less important and depend on others, as in any other human organization. It is clear, moreover, that in rendering these services the priest cannot act as a loner: "Since the priestly
ministry is the ministry of the Church herself, it can be
discharged only by hierarchical communion with the whole
body" (PO, 15c/564).

The essential thing, then, is always communion. But
communion is not submission or subjection. "With the
bishop" need not change into "under the bishop." "With"
and "under" are little words but they sum up wholly distinct worlds and outlooks. In another age "under" may
have adequately expressed a predominant mentality and
therefore been respectfully accepted. Today the insistence
on "under" no longer has meaning and only causes useless
difficulties and tensions; in this respect the current crisis
of obedience is evidence more of maturation than of rebellion. But the insistence on "with" is wholly evangelical
and is, moreover, readily accepted by the modern mind.
The document of the Synod is therefore very much to the
point when it says that the principle of hierarchical communion "is considered fundamental to a practical restoration or renewal, with full confidence, of the mutual relationship between the bishop and the presbyterium over
which the bishop presides" (94).

4. *Priests are the chief helpers and natural advisers of
the bishop.* This is the necessary consequence of the second
principle indicated above, namely, that priests are "co-workers of the episcopal order." The Council therefore teaches
in the Decree on the Ministry and Life of Priests: "By
reason of the gift of the Holy Spirit which is given to priests
in sacred ordination, bishops should regard them as necessary helpers and counselors in the ministry and in the task
of teaching, sanctifying, and nourishing the People of God"
(PO, 7a/546-47). This is also the reason why the Council,

in defining a "diocese" in the Decree on the Bishops' Pastoral Office in the Church, says that it is "entrusted to a bishop to be shepherded by him with the cooperation of the presbytery" (CD, 11a/403). Not to the bishop all by himself! The Church is not a monarchy but a fellowship. The sixth doctrinal proposition formulated by the International Theological Commission for the Synod says: "The ministry of the new covenant has a collegial dimension, which is realized in analogical fashion, according as there is question of the bishops around the pope in the universal Church or of the priests around their bishop in a local church."[8]

5. *The fact of his being associated with the Church is not to deprive the priest of rights shared by all.* In its document on *Justice in the World* the bishops point out that before the Church can speak to men of justice, she must herself first be found just in the eyes of men, and that she must make a sincere examination of her own conscience (40). They then proclaim that "within the Church rights must be preserved" and that "no one [including priests and religious, who are explicitly mentioned] should be deprived of his ordinary rights because he is associated with the Church in one way or other" (41). It is further said that "the Church recognizes everyone's right to suitable freedom of expression and thought. This includes the right of everyone to be heard in a spirit of dialogue which preserves a legitimate diversity within the Church" (44). The Synod adds that when an accusation is made, "the form of judicial procedure should give the accused the right to know his accusers and also the right to a proper defence" (45). Finally, "the members of the Church should have some share in the drawing up of decisions" (46).

Since the Synod so generously grants that ordinary rights should be recognized even within the Church (including those of priests and religious), we might well mention some further "universal and inviolable" rights (GS, 26b/228) of the human person, as proclaimed either by the Council (for example, in the Pastoral Constitution on the Church in the Modern World) or by Pope John XXIII in his encyclical *Peace on Earth*. Such are, for example, the right to act according to the right norm of individual conscience, even when it does not agree with the objective norms of morality and truth; the right to seek the truth; the right to express and comunicate one's own ideas; the right to receive information; the right to strike; etc.

At the Tenth General Meeting of the National Conference of Brazilian Bishops (Sao Paulo, 1969), the bishops approved the following statements on the relationship of bishop to priests:

1. We should not stress the juridical aspect of the relationship but rather seek to live in a spirit of brotherhood, which will show itself in dialogue, pastoral zeal, unity, communion, and responsibility.

2. Elimination of barriers and formalities.

3. Brotherly gatherings for revision of life and for betterment of relations with priests.

4. Understanding of the difficulties and weaknesses of the priests, and concern for their circumstances and work.

5. In appointing and transferring priests the bishop will consult with the individuals in question.

6. The bishops are to take part in the main pastoral gatherings of priests, religious, and laity.

7. The bishops will try to keep up continuous informal contacts with the priests and to be always ready to hear them.

8. The bishops should truly take pastoral charge of the diocese and spur on the representative organs of the diocese (priests' council, pastoral council).

9. A suitable time should be set aside for reflecting on the themes that are the basis of unity.

10. Continuity in the discussions with priests.

11. Revitalization of clerical conferences with a view to dialogue.

12. Help given to priests going through crises.

13. Make use of group dynamics techniques in the bishop-priest relationship.

These are fine points and propositions. But the priests will have to help their bishops if the latter's projects are to be carried out in a spirit of joy. For, more than priests, the bishops are the great victims of a now outmoded form of institutionalization, which they have inherited. Only with great difficulty can they free themselves from it and discover new forms. "The union of priests with their bishops is all the more necessary today since in our present age for various reasons apostolic activities are required not only to take on many forms, but to extend beyond the boundaries of one parish or diocese. Hence no priest can in isolation or singlehandedly accomplish his mission in a satisfactory way. He can do so only by joining forces with other priests under the direction of Church authorities" (PO, 7f/549).

Notes

[1] The following list is drawn from *Documentos dos Presbíteros.*

[2] This cause is well described and amply documented in a summary of a study of the Spanish clergy, in *Asambleia Conjunta Obispos—Sacerdotes* (*Biblioteca de autores cristianos,* 328; Madrid: Editorial Católica, 1971), pp. 543-587. I shall here give only a summary of the introductory theoretical reflections, which seem to me especially well-done and illuminating. The complete text of the summary, in Portuguese, is in REB, 32 (172), 161-195.

[3] Paul VI, *Octogesima Adveniens: Apostolic Letter to Cardinal Roy,* May 14, 1971, in *Catholic Mind,* 69 (November, 1971), 40.

[4] *Documentos dos Presbíteros,* p. 10.

[5] *Op. cit.,* p. 39.

[6] On all this, cf. *The Ecclesiology of Vatican II,* chapter 9: "The Theology of Priesthood."

[7] Cf. the data given in Abbott, p. 534, note 17.

[8] *Le ministère sacerdotal,* p. 126. Cf. Appendix I, below.

VIII

Priestly Fellowship

The individualist outlook developed by formation received, lack of preparation for team work, lack of education for friendship, concern solely for the task of the moment, the absence of any ecclesial vision in planning and coordination, and, above all, the great diversity in mentalities are the chief reasons why priests today find it difficult to develop a fraternal, friendly fellowship among themselves. Tensions exist which are beginning to spur the formation of closed groups, systematic conflict, and blocs in opposition to one another, each of them setting up barriers to outside influences. The result is that encounter and dialogue inspired by charity are hindered. The priests of the South I Region of Brazil have described in a rather sensible way the impression given by various kinds of priests as they face reality.[1] There are, to begin with, the *anachronists:* men really cut off from reality, who continue in their "traditional" ways; they are frightened, often anxious, because they do not understand what is happening and because their pastoral efforts do not produce the results they used to.

There are the *perplexed,* who are beginning to be aware of changes going on and to grasp something of their meaning, but cannot manage to achieve a minimum of genuinely personal reaction to the facts. There are the *insecure* who also see the change that is taking place and the new demands it makes on them, but feel completely helpless and unprepared to respond to these demands; the insecurity can become so extreme that these men throw everything over. Finally, ever since Vatican II, there is the *new priest,* whose role is to stir men's faith as they live in a secularized, pluralist society; he does not deny he feels some insecurity but he is also able, with a confidence that flows from faith in Christ and in the divine character of the Church, to seek out the sources of initiative and creativity in his own life; he is optimistic as he sees himself helping to build a new Church in a new world.

According to another classification, there are the *nostalgic* men who will accept nothing but what has been and are opposed to any kind of renewal, purification, or modification. There are the *comfortable* people who have lost any genuine apostolic enthusiasm and make no effort to come abreast of the times. There are people with a *siege mentality* who have chosen the field they will defend and make no attempt to enlarge it. There are the *men in a hurry* who act without any solid doctrinal footing under them or who, without entertaining the possibility that good may come of it, want to abandon the renewal, whatever effects such abandonment may have; they are even ready to break entirely with the Church. There are the hasty, empty-minded *innovators* who, out of a taste for sensationalism and a concern for their own advantage, will accept anything new. Finally, there are the healthy *renovators* who question everything in order to retain what is still valid today.

The variety of outlooks creates deep divisions among the clergy and sets great difficulties in the way of the apostolate. The situation cannot, must not be allowed to continue.

Priests must recapture their sense of fellowship and rediscover the roots of their unity.

1. *"All priests are united among themselves in an intimate sacramental brotherhood"* (PO, 8a/549). The Dogmatic Constitution on the Church packs a good deal into a few lines on this subject: "In virtue of their common sacred ordination and mission, all priests are bound together in an intimate brotherhood, which should naturally and freely manifest itself in mutual aid, spiritual as well as material, pastoral as well as personal, in meetings and in a community of life, of labor, of charity" (LG, 28e/57-58). That says everything. It contains a whole program. First, the reason for the necessary fellowship is given: all share in the same special way in the priesthood of Christ and the mission of the Church. The result of this sharing is a union which is not only "intimate" (LG) but "sacramental" (PO): that is, the union is effected by an ontological bond established in ordination. The text next stresses the need for an external manifestation of this internal communion, and says that this manifestation should be "spontaneous and free." Finally, the text signals the various areas in which collaboration should take place (the material and the spiritual, the pastoral and the personal) and the ways in which it can be effected (meetings, community of life, work, and charity).

The Synod makes its own the same principle and expresses it as follows: "Since priests are bound together by an intimate sacramental brotherhood and by their mission, and since they work and plan together for the same task, some community of life or a certain association of life shall be encouraged among them and can take various forms, including non-institutional ones. This shall be allowed for by the law itself through opportune norms and by renewed or newly-discovered pastoral structures" (104).

2. Priests are *"established in the priestly order by ordination"* (PO, 8a/549). As there exists an order or college

of bishops, so there exists an order or college of priests. As the bishop is a being who is essentially collegial or "part of a college" and must develop in himself a sense of his "collegial nature and meaning" (LG, 22a/41), of "collegial union" (LG, 23a/44), a "collegiate sense' (LG, 23f/46; cf. AG, 6i/592), so too the priest is essentially "part of a college" and must develop his own collegial nature and the collegial union and awareness. A man who is introverted and individualistic has no vocation to the priesthood and should not be ordained. A non-collegial priest is a contradiction. This collegiality of priests had already found expression in what St. Ignatius of Antioch and St. Cyprian called the "presbytery"; we still use the term today: all the priests who work in a diocese "form one presbytery and one family" (CD, 28a/417). (The formation of a presbyteral council, or senate of priests, "representing the presbytery" was approved by Vatican II: PO, 7d/548).

3. *The free association of priests with each other can help them to this brotherly fellowship.* From the recent investigations conducted among the clergy, isolation (geographical, cultural, affective, social) has emerged as one of the major problems faced by priests today.[2] The bishops of Vatican II recognized this serious problem and tried to suggest ways of resolving it: "In order that priests may find mutual assistance in the development of their spiritual and intellectual lives, that they may be able to cooperate more effectively in their ministry and be saved from the dangers which may arise from loneliness, let there be fostered among them some kind or other of community life. Such a life can take several forms according to various personal or pastoral needs: for instance, a shared roof where this is feasible, or a common table, or at least frequent and regular gatherings" (PO, 8g/551); and "They will readily and joyfully gather together for recreation" (PO, 8f/551).

It is in this context that the Council urgently recommends the setting up of free associations which are not oriented or ruled by the bishop: "Worthy too of high regard and zealous promotion are those associations whose rules have been examined by competent Church authority, and which foster priestly holiness in the exercise of the ministry through an apt and properly approved rule of life and through brotherly assistance. Thus these associations aim to be of service to the whole priestly order" (PO, 8h/551). The Synod makes the ideas of this text its own (105).

The history of this conciliar text was somewhat stormy, but that very fact shows the importance the Council intended to give to these free associations. When the vote was being taken on this particular section, the suggestion was made that the associations be subject to the direction of the bishop or the episcopal conference. But the theological commission refused the suggestion and gave this explanation: "As far as the canonical regulation of these associations is concerned, it seems better that they not be made subject in law to the bishops or the episcopal conferences, for they have to do with the personal life of the priest and with the exercise of his legitimate freedom. Control by the bishops, therefore, does not seem right (1) in law: because when the bishop exercises his power in regard to his priests, a confusion between the internal and external forums would arise; (2) in practice: because many a priest would feel morally forced to become a member of an association directed by the bishop, thinking that he would be obeying his own ordinary, etc.; in fact, a serious division would arise in the diocese between those who belonged and those who did not belong to an association 'run' by the bishop." When suggestions for modifications were being offered, contrary suggestions were made by thirty bishops, to the effect that "the associations should be subject in law to the bishop" (Modification 129). The commission once again replied rather forcefully: "We cannot deny priests what we grant the laity in view of their dignity as men. The Council has declared this course of action a suitable one, inasmuch as it is according to natural law." In its reply to Modification 132 the Council insisted that such associations may be interdiocesan or even international. Some have even seen in this statement an invitation to the formation of real *trade-unions of priests*. The Council itself says in the Pastoral Constitution on the Church in the Modern World: "Among the basic rights of the human person must be counted the right of freely founding labor unions. These unions should be truly able to represent the workers and to contribute to the proper arrangement of economic life. Another such right is that of taking part freely in the activity of these unions without fear of reprisal. Through this sort of orderly participation, joined with an ongoing formation in economic and social matters, all will grow day by day in the awareness of their own function and responsibility" (GS, 68c/277). With the necessary adaptations, this statement can also be applied to priests, for they too have rights which are not infrequently ignored by authoritarian, unjust actions on the part of some ecclesiastical authorities; against such actions priests have no juridical recourse unless the Church provides a way.

We ought always bear in mind that in such associations there is the danger that groups or factions may be formed. This is why the Synod urges: "It is desirable that, as far as possible, ways be sought, even if they prove rather difficult, whereby associations which perhaps divide the clergy into factions may be brought back to communion and to the ecclesial structure" (106).

Notes

[1] *Documentos dos Presbiteros*, p. 93.
[2] Cf. Gregory, *art. cit.*, p. 933.

APPENDIXES

I. Doctrinal Propositions on the Ministerial Priesthood

II. Synod of Bishops, The Ministerial Priesthood

III. Synod of Bishops, Justice in the World

RESCRIPT OF THE AUDIENCE GIVEN BY THE HOLY FATHER TO THE CARDINAL SECRETARY OF STATE 30 NOVEMBER 1971:

The Holy Father has carefully examined the two documents containing the proposals expressed by the Second General Assembly of the Synod of Bishops on the themes, "The Ministerial Priesthood" and "Justice in the World", which had been put before the Assembly for study.

As he has already announced in his address at the General Audience of 24 November, the Holy Father desires that the aforementioned documents be made public.

His Holiness now accepts and confirms all the conclusions in the two documents that conform to the current norms: in particular, he confirms that in the Latin Church there shall continue to be observed in its entirety, with God's help, the present discipline of priestly celibacy.

The Holy Father reserves to himself to examine carefully in due course whether the proposals—and which of them—contained in the recommendations of the Synodal Assembly should be convalidated as directive guidelines or practical norms. — JOHN CARDINAL VILLOT, *Secretary of State.*

Appendix I

Doctrinal Propositions on the Ministerial Priesthood

Since the main theme of the Synod of 1971 was to be the ministerial priesthood, the International Theological Commission was asked to draw up some doctrinal propositions on the Christian ministerial priesthood. In its meeting of October, 1970, the Commission drew up, voted on, and approved six such propositions. As the Synod drew near, however, some further detailed position on the so-called "indelible character" was desired. Therefore, on September 25, 1971, four days before the opening of the Synod, the Commission drew up, voted on, and approved two more propositions on the "priestly character."

I. *Propositions on the Nature of Priestly Ministry*

1. Every hierarchic ministry in the Church is connected with the institution of the Apostles. The latter ministry was willed by Christ and is essential to the Church; through the mediation supplied by this ministry the Lord's saving act becomes sacramentally and historically present to all generations.

2. In the new covenant there is no other priesthood than

Christ's. His priesthood fulfills and transcends all the ancient priesthoods. In the Church all the faithful are called to share in it. The hierarchic ministry is necessary for building up the Body of Christ within which the call to the faithful is effectively given.

3. Only Christ has offered a perfect sacrifice by giving himself over to the will of the Father. The episcopal and presbyteral ministry is thus a priestly one in the sense that it makes Christ's ministry present in the effective proclamation of the Gospel message, in the gathering and guiding of the Christian community, in the forgiveness of sins, and in the Eucharistic celebration in which the one sacrifice of Christ is made present in a singular way.

4. The Christian who is called to the priestly ministry receives in his ordination not a purely external function but a new and unique share in the priesthood of Christ. In virtue of this sharing he represents Christ at the head of the community and, as it were, over against the community. The ministry is thus a specific way of living a life of Christian service in the Church. Its specific character appears most clearly in the minister's role of presiding at the Eucharist (a presidency that is required if Christian worship is to have its full reality). The preaching of the word and pastoral care are ordered to the Eucharist, for the latter consecrates the whole of the Christian's existence in the world.

5. Even while we recognize that there was a period in which ecclesial structures only gradually reached their full development, we may not set up an opposition between a purely charismatic constitution of the Pauline churches and a ministerial constitution in the other churches.

6. The ministry of the new covenant has a collegial dimension, which is realized in analogical fashion, according as there is question of the bishops around the pope in the universal Church or of the priests around the bishop in a local Church.

II. *Propositions on the Permanent Priestly Character*

1. There are no valid grounds for questioning the normative doctrinal teaching of Christian tradition, especially as expressed at the Council of Trent, regarding the existence and lifelong permanence of what we call the "sacramental character" of the ordained minister.

2. In order to understand this reality we may begin with the fact that a power of the Spirit is communicated through the imposition of hands (cf. 2 Tim 1:6).

The character gives the minister a share in the mission of Christ under the twofold aspect of authority and service. The authority does not belong to him as something of his own; it is, rather, a manifestation of the *exousia* (power and authority) of the Lord, and by reason of it the priest now has the role of ambassador in the eschatological work of reconciliation (cf. 2 Cor 1:20, 5:18-20). He is at the service of the conversion of man's freedom to God, for the building up of the Christian community.

The permanence of the character is related to the fact that Christ remains irrevocably associated with the Church for the salvation of the world and with the fact that the Church is irrevocably dedicated to Christ for the accomplishment of his work.

The minister, whose life bears the mark of the gift received in ordination, is a reminder to the Church that God's gift is without recall.

Within the Christian community, which lives by the Spirit, the minister, for all his deficiencies, is a pledge of Christ's saving presence.

The minister's special share in the priesthood of Christ does not cease to exist even if, for ecclesial or personal reasons, a priest is dispensed or removed from the exercise of the ministry.

Appendix II

The Ministerial Priesthood

INTRODUCTION

1) In recent times, especially since the close of the Second Vatican Council, the Church is experiencing a profound movement of renewal, which all Christians should follow with great joy and with fidelity to the Gospel. The power of the Holy Spirit is present to illumine, strengthen and perfect our mission.

2) Every true renewal brings the Church undoubted benefits of great value. We well know that through the recent Council priests have been fired with new zeal and that they have contributed much to fostering this renewal by their daily solicitude. We have before our minds our many heroic brothers who, in fidelity to their ministry, live lives dedicated to God with joy, either among the peoples where the Church is subjected to a harsh yoke or in mission lands. At the same time, however, the renewal also entails difficulties, which are especially felt by all in the priesthood, whether bishops or priests.

3)   We should all scrutinize the signs of the times in this age of renewal and interpret them in the light of the Gospel (cf. *GS* 4), in order that we may work together in distinguishing between spirits, to see if they come from God, lest ambiguity cloud the unity of the Church's mission or excessive uniformity hinder needed adaptation. Thus, by testing everything and holding fast to what is good, the present crisis can give occasion for an increase of faith.

4)   In accordance with its importance, the Holy Father put forward the ministerial priesthood for discussion by this year's Synod. Before the Synod many episcopal conferences examined this theme together with priests and quite frequently with lay people. Some priests were also called to the Synod as "auditores," to assist the bishops in dealing with important questions.

5)   We wish to fulfil our duty with the evangelical simplicity which befits pastors who are serving the Church. Considering our responsibility before the fraternal community of the Church, we desire to strengthen the faith, uplift the hope and stimulate the love both of our brothers in the ministerial priesthood and of all the faithful. May our words bring solace to the People of God and the priests dedicated to their service and renew their joy!

DESCRIPTION OF THE SITUATION

6)   The extent of the Church's mission was illustrated at length by the Second Vatican Council. Indeed, the Church's relationship with the world was the subject especially of the pastoral constitution *Gaudium et Spes*. Many good results followed from a closer consideration of this matter: it is more clearly seen that salvation is not an abstract category outside, as it were, of history and time, but that it comes from God and ought to permeate the whole of man and the

whole history of men and lead them freely to the Kingdom of God, so that at last "God may be all in all" (*1 Cor* 15:28).

7)   However, as is understandable, difficulties have also arisen: some priests feel themselves estranged from the movements which permeate society and unable to solve the problems which touch men deeply. Often too the problems and troubles of priests derive from their having, in their pastoral and missionary care, to use methods which are now perhaps obsolete to meet the modern mentality. Serious problems and several questions then arise, especially from real difficulties which they experience in exercising their function and not—although this is sometimes the case— from an exasperated spirit of protest or from selfish personal concerns. Is it possible to exhort the laity as if from the outside? Is the Church sufficiently present to certain groups without the active presence of the priest? If the situation characteristic of a priest consists in segregation from secular life, is not the situation of the layman better? What is to be thought of the celibacy of Latin-rite priests in present-day circumstances, and of the personal spiritual life of the priest immersed in the world?

8)   Many priests, experiencing within themselves the questionings that have arisen with the secularization of the world, feel the need to sanctify worldly activities by exercising them directly and bring the leaven of the Gospel into the midst of events. Similarly, the desire is developing of cooperating with the joint efforts of men to build up a more just and fraternal society. In a world in which almost all problems have political aspects, participation in politics and even in revolutionary activity is by some considered indispensable.

9)   The Council emphasized the pre-eminence of the proclamation of the Gospel, which should lead through faith to fullness of the celebration of the sacraments. But current thinking about the religious phenomenon fosters doubts in many minds concerning the sense of a sacramental and cultic ministry. Many priests not suffering from a personal identity

crisis ask themselves another question: What methods should be used so that sacramental practice may be an expression of faith really affecting the whole of personal and social life, in order that Christian worship should not be wrongly reduced to a mere external ritualism?

10)   Since priests are very concerned with the image of herself that the Church seems to present to the world, and at the same time are deeply conscious of the singular dignity of the human person, they desire to bring about a change within the Church herself in inter-personal relationships, in relations between person and institutions, and in the very structures of authority.

11)   And still, relationships between bishops and priests and between priests themselves are growing more difficult by the very fact that the exercise of the ministry is becoming more diversified. Present-day society is divided into many groups with different disciplines, which call for differing skills and forms of apostolate. This gives rise to problems concerning brotherhood, union and consistency in the priestly ministry.

12)   Happily the recent Council recalled the traditional and fruitful teaching on the common priesthood of the faithful (cf. *LG* 10). That, however, gives rise, as by a swing of the pendulum, to certain questions which seem to obscure the position of the priestly ministry in the Church and which deeply trouble the minds of some priests and faithful. Many activities which in the past were reserved to priests—for instance, catechetical work, administrative activity in the communities, and even liturgical activities—are today quite frequently carried out by lay people, while on the other hand many priests, for reasons already mentioned, are trying to involve themselves in the condition of life of lay persons. Hence a number of questions are being asked: Does the priestly ministry have any specific nature? Is this ministry necessary? Is the priesthood incapable of being lost? What does being a priest mean today? Would it not be enough

to have for the service of the Christian communities presidents designated for the preservation of the common good, without sacramental ordination, and exercising their office for a fixed period?

13) Still more serious questions are posed, some of them as a result of exegetical and historical research, which show a crisis of confidence in the Church: Is the present-day Church too far removed from its origins to be able to proclaim the ancient Gospel credibly to modern man? Is it still possible to reach the reality of Christ after so many critical investigations? Are the essential structures of the early Church well enough known to us that they can and must be considered an invariable scheme for every age, including our own?

14) The above-mentioned questions, some of them new, others already long familiar but appearing in new forms today, cannot be understood outside of the whole context of modern culture, which has strong doubts about its meaning and value. New means of technology have stirred up a hope based excessively on enthusiasm and at the same time they have aroused profound anxiety. One rightly asks whether man will be capable of being master of his work and directing it towards progress.

15) Some, especially the young, despair of the meaning of this world and look for salvation in purely meditative systems and in artificial marginal paradises, abandoning the common striving of mankind.

16) Others dedicate themselves with ardent utopian hope devoid of reference to God to the attainment of some state of total liberation, and transfer the meaning of their whole personal lives from the present to the future.

17) There is therefore a profound cleavage between action and contemplation, work and recreation, culture and religion, and between the immanent and the transcendental aspects of human life.

18) Thus the world itself is obscurely awaiting a solution

to this dilemma and is paving a way whereby the Church may go forward proclaiming the Gospel. Certainly, the only complete salvation offered to men is Christ himself, Son of God and Son of Man, who makes himself present in history through the Church. He joins inseparably together love for God and the love which God has until the end for men as they seek their way amid the shadows, and the value of human love whereby a man gives his life for his friends. In Christ, and only in him, do all of these become one whole, and in this synthesis the meaning of human life, both individual and social, shines forth. The mission of the Church, Christ's Body, far from being obsolete, is therefore rather of the highest relevance for the present and the future: the whole Church is the witness and effective sign of this union, especially through the priestly ministry. The minister's proper task in the Church's midst is to render present, by the word and sacrament, the love of God in Christ for us, and at the same time to promote the fellowship of men with God and with each other. All this of course demands that we should all, especially those who perform the sacred office, strive to renew ourselves daily in accordance with the Gospel.

19)   We know that there are some parts of the world in which that profound cultural change has hitherto been less felt, and that the questions raised above are not being asked everywhere, nor by all priests, nor in the same way. But since communications between men and peoples have today become more frequent and more speedy, we judge it good and opportune to examine these questions in the light of faith and to give humbly but in the strength of the Holy Spirit some principles for finding more concrete answers to them. Although this response must be applied differently according to the circumstances of each region, it will have the force of truth for all those faithful and priests who live in situations of greater tranquillity. Therefore, ardently desiring to strengthen the witness of faith, we fraternally

urge all the faithful to strive to contemplate the Lord Jesus living in his Church and to realize that he wishes to work in a special way through his ministers; they will thus be convinced that the Christian community cannot fulfil its complete mission without the ministerial priesthood. Let priests be aware that their anxieties are truly shared by the bishops, and that the bishops desire to share them still more.

* * *

20) Moved by this desire, the Synod Fathers, in the spirit of the Gospel, following closely the teaching of the Second Vatican Council, and considering also the documents and addresses of the Supreme Pontiff Paul VI, intend to set forth briefly some principles of the Church's teaching on the ministerial priesthood which are at present more urgent, together with some guidelines for pastoral practice.

PART ONE

PRINCIPLES OF DOCTRINE

1. *Christ, Alpha and Omega.*

21) Jesus Christ, the Son of God and the Word," whom the Father sanctified and sent into the world" (*Jn* 10:36), and who was marked with the seal of the fullness of the Holy Spirit (cf. *Lk* 4:1, 18-21; *Ac* 10:38), proclaimed to the world the Good News of reconciliation between God and men. His preaching as a prophet, confirmed by signs, reaches its summit in the paschal mystery, the supreme word of the divine love with which the Father addressed us. On the cross Jesus showed himself to the greatest possible extent to be the Good Shepherd who laid down his life for his sheep in order to gather them into that unity which

depends on himself (cf. *Jn* 10:15ff.; 11:52). Exercising a supreme and unique priesthood by the offering of himself, he surpassed, by fulfilling them, all the ritual priesthoods and holocausts of the Old Testament and indeed of the pagans. In his sacrifice he took on himself the miseries and sacrifices of men of every age and also the efforts of those who suffer for the cause of justice or who are daily oppressed by misfortune. He took on himself the endeavours of those who abandon the world and attempt to reach God by asceticism and contemplation as well as the labours of those who sincerely devote their lives to a better present and future society. He bore the sins of us all on the cross; rising from the dead and being made Lord (cf. *Phil* 2:9-11), he reconciled us to God; and he laid the foundation of the people of the New Covenant, which is the Church.

22)   He is the "one mediator between God and men, the man Christ Jesus" (*1 Tim* 2:5), "for in him were created all things" (*Col* 1:16; cf. *Jn* 1:3ff.) and everything is brought together under him, as head (cf. *Eph* 1:10). Since he is the image of the Father and manifestation of the unseen God (cf. *Col* 1:15), by emptying himself and by being raised up he brought us into the fellowship of the Holy Spirit in which he lives with the Father.

23)   When therefore we speak of the priesthood of Christ, we should have before our eyes a unique, incomparable reality, which includes the prophetic and royal office of the Incarnate Word of God.

24)   So Jesus Christ signifies and manifests in many ways the presence and effectiveness of the anticipatory love of God. The Lord himself, constantly influencing the Church by his Spirit, stirs up and fosters the response of all those who offer themselves to this freely given love.

2. *Coming to Christ in the Church.*

25)   The way to the person and mystery of Christ lies ever

open in the Holy Spirit through the Scriptures understood in the living tradition of the Church. All the Scriptures, especially those of the New Testament, must be interpreted as intimately inter-linked and inter-related by their single inspiration. The books of the New Testament are not of such differing value that some of them can be reduced to mere late inventions.

26) A personal and immediate relationship with Christ in the Church should still for the faithful of today sustain their whole spiritual lives.

3. *The Church from Christ through the Apostles.*

27) The Church which he had declared would be built on Peter, Christ founded on the Apostles (cf. *LG* 18). In them are already manifested two aspects of the Church: in the group of the Twelve Apostles there are already both fellowship in the Spirit and the origin of the hierarchical ministry (cf. *AG* 5). For that reason, the New Testament writings speak of the Church as founded on the Apostles (cf. *Rev* 21:14; *Mt* 16:18). This was concisely expressed by ancient tradition: "The Church from the Apostles, the Apostles from Christ, Christ from God".[1]

28) The Church, which was founded on the Apostles and sent into the world and is a pilgrim there, was established to be a sacrament of the salvation which came to us from God in Christ. In her, Christ is present and operative for the world as a saviour, so that the love offered by God to men and their response meet. The Holy Spirit stirs up in and through the Church impulses of generous free will by which man participates in the very work of creation and redemption.

---

[1] TERTULLIAN, *De Praescr. Haer.* XXI, 4; cf. also I Letter of CLEMENT *Ad Cor.* XLII, 1-4; IGNATIUS OF ANTIOCH *Ad Magn.* VI and passim; IRENAEUS *Adv. Haer.* 4, 21, 3; ORIGEN *De Princip.* IV, 2, 1; SERAPION, Bishop of Antioch, in EUSEBIUS *Hist. Eccl.* VI, 12.

4. *The origin and nature of the hierarchical ministry.*

29)   The Church, which through the gift of the Spirit is
made up organically, participates in different ways in the
functions of Christ as Priest, Prophet and King, in order
to carry out her mission of salvation in his name and by
his power, as a priestly people (cf. *LG* 10).

30)   It is clear from the New Testament writings that an
Apostle and a community of faithful united with one another by a mutual link under Christ as head and the influence of his Spirit belong to the original inalienable
structure of the Church. The Twelve Apostles exercised
their mission and functions, and "they not only had helpers
in their ministry (cf. *Ac* 6:2-6; 11:30; 13:1; 14:23; 24:17;
1 Th 5:12-13; *Phil* 1:1; *Col* 4:11 and *passim*), but also, in
order that the mission assigned to them might continue
after their death, they passed on to their immediate cooperators, as a kind of testament, the duty of perfecting and
consolidating the work begun by themselves (*Ac* 20:25-27;
2 Tim 4:6 taken together with *1 Tim* 5:22; *2 Tim* 2:2; *Tit*
1:5; Saint Clement of Rome to the Corinthians 44:3), charging them to attend to the whole flock in which the Holy
Spirit placed them to shepherd the Church of God (cf. *Ac*
20:28). They appointed such men, and made provision that,
when these men should die, other approved men would take
up their ministry (cf. Saint Clement of Rome to the Corinthians 44:2)" (*LG* 20).

31)   The letters of Saint Paul show that he was conscious
of acting by Christ's mission and mandate (cf. *2 Cor* 5:18ff.).
The powers entrusted to the Apostle for the Churches were
handed on to others insofar as they were communicable (cf.
2 Tim 1:6), and these others were obliged to hand them
on to yet others (cf. *Tit* 1:5).

32)   This essential structure of the Church—consisting of a
flock and of pastors appointed for this purpose (cf. *1 Pt*

5:1-4) —according to the Tradition of the Church herself was always and remains the norm. Precisely as a result of this structure, the Church can never remain closed in on herself and is always subject to Christ as her origin and head.

33)   Among the various charisms and services, the priestly ministry of the New Testament, which continues Christ's function as mediator, and which in essence and not merely in degree is distinct from the common priesthood of all the faithful (cf. *LG* 10), alone perpetuates the essential work of the Apostles: by effectively proclaiming the Gospel, by gathering together and leading the community, by remitting sins, and especially by celebrating the Eucharist, it makes Christ, the head of the community, present in the exercise of his work of redeeming mankind and glorifying God perfectly.

34)   Bishops and, on a subordinate level, priests, by virtue of the sacrament of Orders, which confers an anointing of the Holy Spirit and configures to Christ (cf. *PO* 2), become sharers in the functions of sanctifying, teaching and governing, and the exercise of these functions is determined more precisely by hierarchical communion (cf. *LG* 24, 27-28).

35)   The priestly ministry reaches its summit in the celebration of the Eucharist, which is the source and centre of the Church's unity. Only a priest is able to act in the person of Christ in presiding over and effecting the sacrificial banquet wherein the People of God are associated with Christ's offering (cf. *LG* 28).

36)   The priest is a sign of the divine anticipatory plan proclaimed and effective today in the Church. He makes Christ, the Saviour of all men, sacramentally present among his brothers and sisters, in both their personal and social lives. He is a guarantor both of the first proclamation of the Gospel for the gathering together of the Church and of the ceaseless renewal of the Church which has already been gathered together. If the Church lacks the presence and activity of the ministry which is received by the laying on

of hands with prayer, she cannot have full certainty of her fidelity and of her visible continuity.

5. *Permanence of the priesthood.*

37)   By the laying on of hands there is communicated a gift of the Holy Spirit which cannot be lost (cf. *2 Tim* 1:6). This reality configures the ordained minister to Christ the Priest, consecrates him (cf. *PO* 2) and makes him a sharer in Christ's mission under its two aspects of authority and service.

38)   That authority does not belong to the minister as his own: it is a manifestations of the "exousia" (i.e. the power) of the Lord, by which the priest is an ambassador of Christ in the eschatological work of reconciliation (cf. *2 Cor* 5: 18-20). He also assists the conversion of human freedom to God for the building up of the Christian community.

39)   The lifelong permanence of this reality, which is a sign, and which is a teaching of the faith and is referred to in the Church's tradition as the priestly character, expresses the fact that Christ associated the Church with himself in an irrevocable way for the salvation of the world, and that the Church dedicates herself to Christ in a definitive way for the carrying out of his work. The minister whose life bears the seal of the gift received through the sacrament of Orders reminds the Church that the gift of God is irrevocable. In the midst of the Christian community which, in spite of its defects, lives by the Spirit, he is a pledge of the salvific presence of Christ.

40)   This special participation in Christ's priesthood does not disappear even if a priest for ecclesial or personal reasons is dispensed or removed from the exercise of his ministry.

6. *For the service of fellowship.*

41)   Even if he exercises his ministry in a determined community, the priest nevertheless cannot be exclusively

devoted to a particular group of faithful. His ministry always tends towards the unity of the whole Church and to the gathering together in her of all men. Each individual community of faithful needs fellowship with the bishop and the universal Church. In this way the priestly ministry too is essentially communitarian within the prebyterium and with the bishop who, preserving communion with the Successor of Peter, is a part of the body of bishops. This holds also for priests who are not in the immediate service of any community or who work in remote and isolated territories. Religious priests also, within the context of the special purpose and structure of their institute, are indissolubly part of a mission which is ecclesially ordered.

42) Let the whole life and activity of the priest be imbued with a spirit of catholicity, that is, with a sense of the universal mission of the Church, so that he will willingly recognize all the gifts of the Spirit, give them freedom and direct them towards the common goal.

43) Let priests follow Christ's example and cultivate with the bishop and with each other that brotherhood which is founded on their ordination and the oneness of their mission so that their priestly witness may be more credible.

7. *The Priest and temporal matters.*

44) All truly Christian undertakings are related to the salvation of mankind, which, while it is of an eschatological nature, also embraces temporal matters. Every reality of this world must be subjected to the lordship of Christ. This however does not mean that the Church claims technical competence in the secular order, with disregard for the latter's autonomy.

45) The proper mission entrusted by Christ to the priest, as to the Church, is not of the political, economic or social order, but of the religious order (cf. *GS* 42) ; yet, in the pursuit of his ministry, the priest can contribute greatly to

the establishment of a more just secular order, especially in places where the human problems of injustice and oppression are more serious. He must always, however, preserve ecclesial communion and reject violence in words or deeds as not being in accordance with the Gospel.

46)   In fact, the word of the Gospel which he proclaims in the name of Christ and the Church, and the effective grace of sacramental life which he administers should free man from his personal and social egoism and foster among men conditions of justice, which would be a sign of the love of Christ present among us (cf. *GS* 58).

PART TWO

GUIDELINES FOR THE PRIESTLY LIFE AND MINISTRY

47)   Considering the priestly mission in the light of the mystery of Christ and the communion of the Church, the Fathers of this Synod, united with the Roman Pontiff and conscious of the anxieties which bishops and priests are experiencing in the fulfilment of their common role today, present the following guidelines to clarify certain questions and to give encouragement.

I. PRIESTS IN THE MISSION OF CHRIST AND THE CHURCH

1. *Mission: Evangelization and sacramental life.*

48)   *a*) "By their vocation and ordination, the priests of the New Testament are indeed set apart in a certain sense within the midst of God's people. But this is so, not that they may be made distant from this people or from any man, but that they may be totally dedicated to the work for which the Lord has raised them up" (*PO* 3). Priests thus

find their identity to the extent that they fully live the mission of the Church and exercise it in different ways in community with the entire People of God, as pastors and ministers of the Lord in the Spirit, in order to fulfil by their work the plan of salvation in history. "By means of their own ministry, which deals principally with the Eucharist as the source of perfecting the Church, priests are in communion with Christ the Head and are leading others to this communion. Hence they cannot help realizing how much is yet wanting to the fullness of that Body, and how much therefore must be done if it is to grow from day to day" (*AG* 39).

49)   *b*) Priests are sent to all men and their mission must begin with the preaching of God's Word. "Priests have as their duty the proclamation of the Gospel of Christ to all . . . For through the saving Word the spark of faith is struck in the hearts of unbelievers and fed in the hearts of the faithful" (*PO* 4). The goal of evangelization is "that all who are made sons of God by faith and baptism should come together to praise God in the midst of his Church, to take part in her sacrifice and to eat the Lord's supper" (*SC* 10). The ministry of the Word, if rightly understood, leads to the sacraments and to the Christian life, as it is practised in the visible community of the Church and in the world.

50)   The sacraments are celebrated in conjunction with the proclamation of the word of God and thus develop faith by strengthening it with grace. They cannot be considered of slight importance, since through them the word is brought to fuller effect, namely communion in the mystery of Christ.

51)   Let priests then perform their ministry in such a way that the faithful will "have recourse with great eagerness to the sacraments which were instituted to nourish the Christian life" (*SC* 59).

52)   An enduring evangelization and a well-ordered sacramental life of the community demand, by their nature, a *diaconia* of authority, that is, a serving of unity and a pre-

siding over charity. Thus the mutual relationship between evangelization and the celebration of the sacraments is clearly seen in the mission of the Church. A separation between the two would divide the heart of the Church to the point of imperilling the faith, and the priest, who is dedicated to the service of unity in the community, would be gravely distorting his ministry.

53)   Unity between evangelization and sacramental life is always proper to the ministerial priesthood and must carefully be kept in mind by every priest. And yet the application of this principle to the life and ministry of individual priests must be made with discretion, for the exercise of the priestly ministry often in practice needs to take different forms in order better to meet special or new situations in which the Gospel is to be proclaimed.

54)   *c*) Although the pedagogy of faith demands that man be gradually initiated into the Christian life, the Church must nevertheless always proclaim to the world the Gospel in its entirety. Each priest shares in the special responsibility of preaching the whole of the Word of God and of interpreting it according to the faith of the Church.

55)   The proclamation of the Word of God is the announcement in the power of the Spirit of the wonders performed by God and the calling of men to share the paschal mystery and to introduce it as a leaven into concrete human history. It is the action of God in which the power of the Holy Spirit brings the Church together interiorly and exteriorly. The minister of the word by evangelization prepares the ways of the Lord with great patience and faith, conforming himself to the various conditions of individuals' and peoples' lives, which are evolving more or less rapidly.

56)   Impelled by the need to keep in view both the personal and social aspects of the announcement of the Gospel, so that in it an answer may be given to all the more fundamental questions of men (cf. *CD* 13), the Church not only preaches conversion to God to individual men, but also, to

the best of her ability, as the conscience of humanity, she addresses society itself and performs a prophetic function in society's regard, always taking pains to effect her own renewal.

57)   As regards the experiences of life, whether of men in general or of priests, which must be kept in mind and always interpreted in the light of the Gospel, these experiences cannot be either the sole or the principal norm of preaching.

58)   *d*) Salvation, which is effected through the sacraments, does not come from us but from God; this demonstrates the primacy of action of Christ, the one priest and mediator, in his body, which is the Church.

59)   Since the sacraments are truly sacraments of faith (cf. *SC* 59), they require conscious and free participation by every Christian who has the use of reason. This makes clear the great importance of preparation and of a disposition of faith on the part of the person who receives the sacraments; it also makes clear the necessity for a witness of faith on the part of the minister in his entire life and especially in the way he values and celebrates the sacraments themselves.

60)   To bishops and, in the cases foreseen by law, to episcopal conferences is committed the role of authentically promoting, in accordance with the norms given by the Holy See, pastoral activity and liturgical renewal better adapted to each region, and also of determining the criteria for admission to the sacraments. These criteria, which must be applied by priests, are likewise to be explained to the faithful, so that a person who asks for a sacrament may become more aware of his own responsibility.

61)   Let priests, with consciousness of their office of reconciling all men in the love of Christ and with attention to the dangers of divisions, strive with great prudence and pastoral charity to form communities which are imbued with apostolic zeal and which will make the Church's missionary spirit present everywhere. Small communities, which

are not opposed to the parish or diocesan structure, ought to be inserted into the parochial or diocesan community in such a way that they may serve it as a leaven of missionary spirit. The need to find apt forms of effectively bringing the Gospel message to all men, who live in differing circumstances, furnishes a place for the multiple exercise of ministries lower than the priesthood.

2. *Secular and political activity.*

62) *a*) The priestly ministry, even if compared with other activities, not only is to be considered as a fully valid human activity but indeed as more excellent than other activities, though this great value can be fully understood only in the light of faith. Thus, as a general rule, the priestly ministry shall be a full-time occupation. Sharing in the secular activities of men is by no means to be considered the principal end nor can such participation suffice to give expression to priests' specific responsibility. Priests, without being of the world and without taking it as their model, must nevertheless live in the world (cf. *PO* 3, 17; *Jn* 17:14-16), as witnesses and stewards of another life (cf. *PO* 3).

63) In order to determine in concrete circumstances whether secular activity is in accord with the priestly ministry, inquiry should be made whether and in what way those duties and activities serve the mission of the Church, those who have not yet received the Gospel message and finally the Christian community. This is to be judged by the local bishop with his presbyterium, and if necessary in consultation with the episcopal conference.

64) When activities of this sort, which ordinarily pertain to the laity, are as it were demanded by the priest's very mission to evangelize, they must be harmonized with his other ministerial acitvities, in those circumstances where they can be considered as necessary forms of true ministry (cf. *PO* 8).

65)   *b*) Together with the entire Church, priests are obliged, to the utmost of their ability, to select a definite pattern of action, when it is a question of the defence of fundamental human rights, the promotion of the full development of persons and the pursuit of the cause of peace and justice; the means must indeed always be consonant with the Gospel. These principles are all valid not only in the individual sphere, but also in the social field; in this regard priests should help the laity to devote themselves to forming their consciences rightly.

66)   In circumstances in which there legitimately exist different political, social and economic options, priests like all citizens have a right to select their personal options. But since political options are by nature contingent and never in an entirely adequate and perennial way interpret the Gospel, the priest, who is the witness of things to come, must keep a certain distance from any political office or involvement.

67)   In order that he may remain a valid sign of unity and be able to preach the Gospel in its entirety, the priest can sometimes be obliged to abstain from the exercise of his own right in this matter. Moreover, care must be taken lest his option appear to Christians to be the only legitimate one or become a cause of division among the faithful. Let priests be mindful of the laity's maturity, which is to be valued highly when it is a question of their specific role.

68)   Leadership or active militancy on behalf of any political party is to be excluded by every priest unless, in concrete and exceptional circumstances, this is truly required by the good of the community, and receives the consent of the bishop after consultation with the priests' council and, if circumstances call for it, with the episcopal conference.

69)   The priority of the specific mission which pervades the entire priestly existence must therefore always be kept in mind so that, with great confidence, and having a renewed experience of the things of God, priests may be able to

announce these things efficaciously and with joy to the men who await them.

3. *The spiritual life of priests.*

70)   Every priest will find in his very vocation and ministry the deep motivation for living his entire life in oneness and strength of spirit. Called like the rest of those who have been baptized to become a true image of Christ (cf. *Rom* 8:29), the priest, like the Apostles, shares besides in a special way companionship with Christ and his mission as the Supreme Pastor: "And he appointed twelve; they were to be his companions and to be sent out to preach" (*Mk* 3:14). Therefore in the priestly life there can be no dichotomy between love for Christ and zeal for souls.

71)   Just as Christ, anointed by the Holy Spirit, was impelled by his deep love for his Father to give his life for men, so the priest, consecrated by the Holy Spirit, and in a special way made like to Christ the Priest, dedicates himself to the work of the Father performed through the Son. Thus the whole rule for the priest's life is expressed in the words of Jesus: "And for their sake I consecrate myself, that they also may be consecrated in truth" (*Jn* 17:19).

72)   Following the example of Christ who was continually in prayer, and led by the Holy Spirit in whom we cry, "Abba, Father," priests should give themselves to the contemplation of the Word of God and daily take the opportunity to examine the events of life in the light of the Gospel, so that having become faithful and attentive hearers of the Word they may become true ministers of the Word. Let them be assiduous in personal prayer, in the Liturgy of the Hours, in frequent reception of the sacrament of penance and especially in devotion to the mystery of the Eucharist. Even if the Eucharist should be celebrated without participation by the faithful, it nevertheless remains the centre of the life of the entire Church and the heart of priestly existence.

73)   With his mind raised to heaven and sharing in the
communion of saints, the priest should very often turn to
Mary the Mother of God, who received the Word of God
with perfect faith, and daily ask her for the grace of conforming himself to her Son.

74)   The activities of the apostolate for their part furnish
an indispensable nourishment for fostering the spiritual life
of the priest: "By assuming the role of the Good Shepherd,
they will find precisely in the pastoral exercise of love the
bond of priestly perfection which will unify their lives and
activities" (*PO* 14). In the exercise of his ministry the
priest is enlightened and strengthened by the action of the
Church and the example of the faithful. The renunciations
imposed by the pastoral life itself help him to acquire an
ever greater sharing in Christ's Cross and hence a purer
pastoral charity.

75)   This same charity of priests will also cause them to
adapt their spiritual lives to the modes and forms of sanctification which are more suitable and fitting for the men of
their own times and culture. Desiring to be all thing to all
men, to save all (cf. *1 Cor* 9:22), the priest should be attentive to the inspiration of the Holy Spirit in these days.
Thus he will announce the Word of God not only by human
means but he will be taken as a valid instrument by the
Word himself, whose message is "living and active and
sharper than any two-edged sword" (*Heb* 4:12).

4. *Celibacy.*

    a) The basis for celibacy.

76)   Celibacy for priests is in full harmony with the vocation to the apostolic following of Christ and also with the
unconditional response of the person who is called and
who undertakes pastoral service. Through celibacy, the
priest, following his Lord, shows in a fuller way his availability, and embarking upon the way of the Cross with

paschal joy he ardently desires to be consumed in an offering which can be compared to the Eucharist.

77)   If celibacy is lived in the spirit of the Gospel, in prayer and vigilance, with poverty, joy, contempt of honours, and brotherly love, it is a sign which cannot long be hidden, but which effectively proclaims Christ to modern men also. For words today are scarcely heeded, but the witness of a life which displays the radical character to the Gospel has the power of exercising a strong attraction.

   b) Convergence of motives.

78)   Celibacy, as a personal option for some more important good, even a merely natural one, can promote the full maturity and integration of the human personality. This is all the more true in regard to celibacy undertaken for the Kingdom of heaven, as is evident in the lives of so many saints and of the faithful who, living the celibate life, dedicated themselves totally to promoting human and Christian progress for the sake of God and men.

79)   Within modern culture, in which spiritual values are to a great extent obscured, the celibate priest indicates the presence of the Absolute God, who invites us to be renewed in his image. Where the value of sexuality is so exaggerated that genuine love is forgotten, celibacy for the sake of the Kingdom of Christ calls men back to the sublimity of faithful love and reveals the ultimate meaning of life.

80)   Furthermore, one rightly speaks of the value of celibacy as an eschatological sign. By transcending every contingent human value, the celibate priest associates himself in a special way with Christ as the final and absolute good and shows forth, in anticipation, the freedom of the children of God. While the value of the sign and holiness of Christian marriage is fully recognized, celibacy for the sake of the Kingdom nevertheless more clearly displays that spiritual fruitfulness or generative power of the New Law by

which the apostle knows that in Christ he is the father and mother of his communities.

81)   From this special way of following Christ, the priest draws greater strength and power for the building up of the Church; and this power can be preserved and increased only by an intimate and permanent union with Christ's Spirit. The faithful people of God wish to see in their pastors this union with Christ, and they are able to recognize it.

82)   Through celibacy, priests are more easily able to serve God with undivided heart and spend themselves for their sheep, and as a result they are able more fully to be promoters of evangelization and of the Church's unity. For this reason, priests, even if they are fewer in number, but are resplendent with this outstanding witness of life, will enjoy greater apostolic fruitfulness.

83)   Priestly celibacy furthermore, is not just the witness of one person alone, but by reason of the special fellowship linking members of the presbyterium it also takes on a social character as the witness of the whole priestly order enriching the people of God.

c) Celibacy to be kept in the Latin Church.

84)   The traditions of the Eastern Churches shall remain unchanged, as they are now in force in the various territories.

85)   The Church has the right and duty to determine the concrete form of the priestly ministry and therefore to select more suitable candidates, endowed with certain human and supernatural qualities. When the Latin Church demands celibacy as a necessary condition for the priesthood (cf. *PO* 16), she does not do so out of a belief that this way of life is the only path to attaining sanctification. She does so while carefully considering the concrete form of exercising the ministry in the community for the building up of the Church.

86)   Because of the intimate and multiple coherence be-

tween the pastoral function and a celibate life, the existing law is upheld: one who freely wills total availability, the distinctive characteristic of this function, also freely undertakes a celibate life. The candidate should feel this form of living not as having been imposed from outside, but rather as a manifestation of his free self-giving, which is accepted and ratified by the Church through the bishop. In this way the law becomes a protection and safeguard of the freedom wherewith the priest gives himself to Christ, and it becomes "an easy yoke."

   d) Conditions favouring celibacy.

87)   We know well that in the world of today particular difficulties threaten celibacy from all sides; priests have indeed already repeatedly experienced them in the course of the centuries. But they can overcome these difficulties if suitable conditions are fostered, namely: growth of the interior life through prayer, renunciation and fervent love for God and one's neighbour and by other aids to the spiritual life; human balance through well-ordered integration into the fabric of social relationships; fraternal association and companionship with other priests and with the bishop, through pastoral structures better suited to this purpose and with the assistance also of the community of the faithful.
88)   It must be admitted that celibacy, as a gift of God, cannot be preserved unless the candidate is adequately prepared for it. From the beginning, candidates should give attention to the positive reasons for choosing celibacy, without letting themselves be disturbed by objections, the accumulation and continual pressure of which are rather a sign that the original value of celibacy itself has been called in question. Let them also remember that the power with which God strengthens us is always available for those who strive to serve him faithfully and entirely.
89)   A priest who leaves the ministry should receive just and fraternal treatment; even though he can give assistance

in the service of the Church, he is not however to be admitted to the exercise of priestly activities.

e) The Law of Celibacy.

90) The law of priestly celibacy existing in the Latin Church is to be kept in its entirety.[2]

* * *

f) The ordination of married men.

91) Two formulas were proposed to the vote of the Fathers:[3]

Formula A: Excepting always the right of the Supreme Pontiff, the priestly ordination of married men is not permitted, even in particular cases.

Formula B: It belongs solely to the Supreme Pontiff, in particular cases, by reason of pastoral needs and the good of the universal Church to allow the priestly ordination of married men, who are of mature age and proven life.

* * *

II. PRIESTS IN THE COMMUNION OF THE CHURCH

1. *Relations between priests and bishop.*

92) Priests will adhere more faithfully to their mission the more they know and show themselves to be faithful to ecclesial communion. Thus the pastoral ministry, which is exercised by bishops, priests and deacons, is an eminent sign of this ecclesial communion, in that they have received a

---

[2] Result of the vote on this proposition: *Placet* 168. *Non placet* 10. *Placet iuxta modum* 21. Abstentions 3.

[3] According to the directives of the Presidents the vote was taken not by *Placet* or *Non placet*, but by the choice of the first or second formula. The first formula, *A*, obtained 107 votes; the second, *B*, obtained 87. There were 2 abstentions and also 2 null votes.

special mandate to serve this communion.

93)   But in order that this ministry may really become a sign of communion, the actual conditions in which it is exercised must be considered to be of the greatest importance.

94)   The guiding principle expressed by the Second Vatican Council in the decree *Presbyterorum Ordinis*, namely that the very unity of consecration and mission requires the hierarchical communion of priests with the order of bishops, is considered fundamental to a practical restoration or renewal, with full confidence, of the mutual relationship between the bishop and the presbyterium over which the bishop presides. This principle is more concretely to be put into practice especially by the diligence of the bishops.

95)   The service of authority on the one hand and the exercise of not merely passive obedience on the other should be carried out in a spirit of faith, mutual charity, filial and friendly confidence and constant and patient dialogue. Thus the collaboration and responsible cooperation of priests with the bishop will be sincere, human and at the same time supernatural (cf. *LG* 28; *CD* 15; *PO* 7).

96)   Personal freedom, responding to the individual vocation and to the charisms received from God, and also the ordered solidarity of all for the service of the community and the good of the mission to be fulfilled are two conditions which should shape the Church's proper mode of pastoral action (cf. *PO* 7). The guarantee of these conditions is the bishop's authority, to be exercised in a spirit of service.

97)   The Council of Priests, which is of its nature something diocesan, is an institutional manifestation of the brotherhood among priests which has its basis in the sacrament of Orders.

98)   The activity of this council cannot be fully shaped by law. Its effectiveness depends especially on a repeated effort to listen to the opinions of all in order to reach a consensus with the bishop, to whom it belongs to make the final decision.

99)   If this is done with the greatest sincerity and humility, and if all one-sidedness is overcome, it will be easier to provide properly for the common good.

100)   The Priests' Council is an institution in which priests recognize, at a time when variety in the exercise of their ministry increases every day, that they are mutually complementary in serving one and the same mission of the Church.

101)   It is the task of this Council, among other things, to seek out clear and distinctly defined aims, to suggest priorities, to indicate methods of acting, to assist whatever the Spirit frequently stirs up through individuals or groups, and to foster the spiritual life, whence the necessary unity may more easily be attained.

102)   New forms of hierarchical communion between bishops and priests (cf. *PO* 7) must be found, to facilitate contacts between local Churches. A search must be made for ways whereby priests may collaborate with bishops in supra-diocesan bodies and enterprises.

103)   The collaboration of religious priests with the bishop in the presbyterium is necessary, though their work is of valuable assistance to the universal Church.

2. *Relations of priests with each other.*

104)   Since priests are bound together by an intimate sacramental brotherhood and by their mission, and since they work and plan together for the same task, some community of life or a certain association of life shall be encouraged among them and can take various forms, including non-institutional ones. This shall be allowed for by the law itself through opportune norms and by renewed or newly-discovered pastoral structures.

105)   Priestly associations should also be fostered which in a spirit of ecclesial communion and being recognized by the competent ecclesiastical authority, "through an apt and properly approved rule of life and through brotherly assistance" (*PO* 8), seek to advance the aims which belong to

their function and "holiness in the exercise of the ministry"
(*ibid.*) .

106)   It is desirable that, as far as possible, ways be sought,
even if they prove rather difficult, whereby associations
which perhaps divide the clergy into factions may be brought
back to communion and to the ecclesial structure.

107)   There should be greater communication between religious priests and diocesan priests, so that true priestly fra-
ternity may exist between them and that they may provide
one another with mutual help, especially in spiritual matters.

3. *Relations between priests and laity.*

108)   Let priests remember "confidently to entrust to the
laity duties in the service of the Church, allowing them
freedom and room for action. In fact, on suitable occasions,
they should invite them to undertake works on their own
initiative" (*PO* 9) . The laity, "likewise sharing their cares,
should help their priests by prayer and work to the extent
possible, so that their priests can more readily overcome
difficulties and be able to fulfil their duties more fruit-
fully" (*ibid.*) .

109)   It is necessary to keep always in mind the special
character of the Church's communion in order that personal freedom, in accordance with the recognized duties and
charisms of each person, and the unity of life and activity of
the people of God may be fittingly combined.

110)   The pastoral council, in which specially chosen clergy,
religious and lay people take part (cf. *CD* 27) , furnishes by
its study and reflection elements necessary for enabling the
diocesan community to arrange its pastoral programme organically and to fulfil it effectively.

111)   In proportion as the co-responsibility of bishops and
priests daily increases (especially through priests' councils) ,
the more desirable it becomes that a pastoral council be
established in each diocese.

4. *Economic affairs.*

112)   The economic questions of the Church cannot be adequately solved unless they are carefully examined within the context of the communion and mission of the people of God. All the faithful have the duty of assisting the Church's needs.

113)   In treating these questions account must be taken not only of solidarity within the local Church, diocese or religious institute, but also of the condition of dioceses of the same region or nation, indeed of the whole world, especially of the Churches in the so-called mission territories, and of other poor regions.

114)   The remuneration of priests, to be determined certainly in a spirit of evangelical poverty, but as far as possible equitable and sufficient, is a duty of justice and ought to include social security. Excessive differences in this matter must be removed, especially among priests of the same diocese or jurisdiction, account also being taken of the average condition of the people of the region.

115)   It seems greatly to be desired that the Christian people be gradually instructed in such a way that priests' incomes may be separated from the acts of their ministry, especially sacramental ones.

CONCLUSION

116)   To priests exercising the ministry of the Spirit (cf. *2 Cor* 3:4-12) in the midst of the communion of the entire Church, new ways are open for giving a profoundly renewed witness in today's world.

117)   It is necessary therefore to look to the future with Christian confidence and to ask the Holy Spirit that by his guidance and inspiration doors may be opened to the Gospel,

in spite of the dangers which the Church cannot overcome by merely human means.

118)   Having always before our eyes the Apostles, especially Peter and Paul, as the examples for the renewal of the priesthood, we should give thanks to God the Father that he has given us all the opportunity of manifesting more faithfully the countenance of Christ.

119)   Already there are true signs of a rebirth of spiritual life, while men everywhere, amid the uncertainties of modern times, look forward to fullness of life. This renewal certainly cannot take place without a sharing in the Lord's Cross, because the servant is not greater than his master (cf. *Jn* 13:16). Forgetting the past let us strive for what is still to come (cf. *Phil* 3:13).

120)   With real daring we must show the world the fullness of the mystery hidden through all ages in God so that men through their sharing in it may be able to enter into the fullness of God (cf. *Eph* 3:19).

121)   "We proclaim to you the eternal life which was with the Father and was made manifest to us—that which we have seen and heard we proclaim also to you, so that you may have fellowship with us; and our fellowship is with the Father and with his Son Jesus Christ" (*1 Jn* 1:2-3).

Appendix III

Justice in the World

INTRODUCTION

1)   Gathered from the whole world, in communion with all who believe in Christ and with the entire human family, and opening our hearts to the Spirit who is making the whole of creation new, we have questioned ourselves about the mission of the People of God to further justice in the world.

2)   Scrutinizing the "signs of the times" and seeking to detect the meaning of emerging history, while at the same time sharing the aspirations and questionings of all those who want to build a more human world, we have listened to the Word of God that we might be converted to the fulfilling of the divine plan for the salvation of the world.

3)   Even though it is not for us to elaborate a very profound analysis of the situation of the world, we have nevertheless been able to perceive the serious injustices which

are building around the world of men a network of domination, oppression and abuses which stifle freedom and which keep the greater part of humanity from sharing in the building up and enjoyment of a more just and more fraternal world.

4)   At the same time we have noted the inmost stirring moving the world in its depths. There are facts constituting a contribution to the furthering of justice. In associations of men and among peoples themselves there is arising a new awareness which shakes them out of any fatalistic resignation and which spurs them on to liberate themselves and to be responsible for their own destiny. Movements among men are seen which express hope in a better world and a will to change whatever has become intolerable.

5)   Listening to the cry of those who suffer violence and are oppressed by unjust systems and structures, and hearing the appeal of a world that by its perversity contradicts the plan of its Creator, we have shared our awareness of the Church's vocation to be present in the heart of the world by proclaiming the Good News to the poor, freedom to the oppressed, and joy to the affilcted. The hopes and forces which are moving the world in its very foundations are not foreign to the dynamism of the Gospel, which through the power of the Holy Spirit frees men from personal sin and from its consequences in social life.

6)   The uncertainty of history and the painful convergences in the ascending path of the human community direct us to sacred history; there God has revealed himself to us, and made known to us, as it is brought progressively to realization, his plan of liberation and salvation which is once and for all fulfilled in the Paschal Mystery of Christ. Action on behalf of justice and participation in the transformation of the world fully appear to us as a constitutive dimension of the preaching of the Gospel, or, in other words, of the Church's mission for the redemption of the human race and its liberation from every oppressive situation.

I

JUSTICE AND WORLD SOCIETY

CRISIS OF UNIVERSAL SOLIDARITY

7) The world in which the Church lives and acts is held captive by a tremendous paradox. Never before have the forces working for bringing about a unified world society appeared so powerful and dynamic; they are rooted in the awareness of the full basic equality as well as of the human dignity of all. Since men are members of the same human family, they are indissolubly linked with one another in the one destiny of the whole world, in the responsibility for which they all share.

8) The new technological possibilities are based upon the unity of science, on the global and simultaneous character of communications and on the birth of an absolutely inter-dependent economic world. Moreover, men are beginning to grasp a new and more radical dimension of unity; for they perceive that their resources, as well as the precious treasures of air and water—without which there cannot be life— and the small delicate biosphere of the whole complex of all life on earth, are not infinite, but on the contrary must be saved and preserved as a unique patrimony belonging to all mankind.

9) The paradox lies in the fact that within this perspective of unity the forces of division and antagonism seem today to be increasing in strength. Ancient divisions between nations and empires, between races and classes, today possess new technological instruments of destruction. The arms race is a threat to man's highest good, which is life; it makes poor peoples and individuals yet more miserable, while making richer those already powerful; it creates a continuous danger of conflagration, and in the case of nuclear arms, it

threatens to destroy all life from the face of the earth. At the same time new divisions are being born to separate man from his neighbour. Unless combatted and overcome by social and political action, the influence of the new industrial and technological order favours the concentration of wealth, power and decision-making in the hands of a small public or private controlling group. Economic injustice and lack of social participation keep a man from attaining his basic human and civil rights.

10) In the last twenty-five years a hope has spread through the human race that economic growth would bring about such a quantity of goods that it would be possible to feed the hungry at least with the crumbs falling from the table, but this has proved a vain hope in underdeveloped areas and in pockets of poverty in wealthier areas, because of the rapid growth of population and of the labour force, because of rural stagnation and the lack of agrarian reform, and because of the massive migratory flow to the cities, where the industries, even though endowed with huge sums of money, nevertheless provide so few jobs that not infrequently one worker in four is left unemployed. These stifling oppressions constantly give rise to great numbers of "marginal" persons, ill-fed, inhumanly housed, illiterate and deprived of political power as well as of the suitable means of acquiring responsibility and moral dignity.

11) Furthermore, such is the demand for resources and energy by the richer nations, whether capitalist or socialist, and such are the effects of dumping by them in the atmosphere and the sea that irreparable damage would be done to the essential elements of life on earth, such as air and water, if their high rates of consumption and pollution, which are constantly on the increase, were extended to the whole of mankind.

12) The strong drive towards global unity, the unequal distribution which places decisions concerning three quarters of income, investment and trade in the hands of one third

of the human race, namely the more highly developed part, the insufficiency of a merely economic progress, and the new recognition of the material limits of the biosphere — all this makes us aware of the fact that in today's world new modes of understanding human dignity are arising.

THE RIGHT TO DEVELOPMENT

13)   In the face of international systems of domination, the bringing about of justice depends more and more on the determined will for development.

14)   In the developing nations and in the so-called socialist world, that determined will asserts itself especially in a struggle for forms of claiming one's rights and self-expression, a struggle caused by the evolution of the economic system itself.

15)   This aspiring to justice asserts itself in advancing beyond the threshold at which begins a consciousness of enhancement of personal worth (cf. *Populorum Progressio* 15; *A.A.S.* 59, 1967, p. 265) with regard both to the whole man and the whole of mankind. This is expressed in an awareness of the right to development. The right to development must be seen as a dynamic interpenetration of all those fundamental human rights upon which the aspirations of individuals and nations are based.

16)   This desire however will not satisfy the expectations of our time if it ignores the objective obstacles which social structures place in the way of conversion of hearts, or even of the realization of the ideal of charity. It demands on the contrary that the general condition of being marginal in society be overcome, so that an end will be put to the systematic barriers and vicious circles which oppose the collective advance towards enjoyment of adequate remuneration of the factors of production, and which strengthen the situation of discrimination with regard to access to opportunities and collective services from which a great part of

the people are now excluded. If the developing nations and regions do not attain liberation through development, there is a real danger that the conditions of life created especially by colonial domination may evolve into a new form of colonialism in which the developing nations will be the victims of the interplay of international economic forces. That right to development is above all a right to hope according to the concrete measure of contemporary humanity. To respond to such a hope, the concept of evolution must be purified of those myths and false convictions which have up to now gone with a thought-pattern subject to a kind of deterministic and automatic notion of progress.

17)   By taking their future into their own hands through a determined will for progress, the developing peoples— even if they do not achieve the final goal—will authentically manifest their own personalization. And in order that they may cope with the unequal relationships within the present world complex, a certain responsible nationalism gives them the impetus needed to acquire an identity of their own. From this basic self-determination can come attempts at putting together new political groupings allowing full development to these peoples; there can also come measures necessary for overcoming the inertia which could render fruitless such an effort—as in some cases population pressure; there can also come new sacrifices which the growth of planning demands of a generation which wants to build its own future.

18)   On the other hand, it is impossible to conceive true progress without recognizing the necessity—within the political system chosen—of a development composed both of economic growth and participation; and the necessity too of an increase in wealth implying as well social progress by the entire community as it overcomes regional imbalance and islands of prosperity. Participation constitutes a right which is to be applied both in the economic and in the social and political field.

19) While we again affirm the right of people to keep their own identity, we see ever more clearly that the fight against a modernization destructive of the proper characteristics of nations remains quite ineffective as long as it appeals only to sacred historical customs and venerable ways of life. If modernization is accepted with the intention that it serve the good of the nation, men will be able to create a culture which will constitute a true heritage of their own in the manner of a true social memory, one which is active and formative of authentic creative personality in the assembly of nations.

VOICELESS INJUSTICES

20) We see in the world a set of injustices which constitute the nucleus of today's problems and whose solution requires the undertaking of tasks and functions in every sector of society, and even on the level of the global society towards which we are speeding in this last quarter of the twentieth century. Therefore we must be prepared to take on new functions and new duties in every sector of human activity and especially in the sector of world society, if justice is really to be put into practice. Our action is to be directed above all at those men and nations which because of various forms of oppression and because of the present character of our society are silent, indeed voiceless, victims of injustice.

21) Take, for example, the case of migrants. They are often· forced to leave their own country to find work, but frequently find the doors closed in their faces because of discriminatory attitudes, or, if they can enter, they are often obliged to lead an insecure life or are treated in an inhuman manner. The same is true of groups that are less well off on the social ladder such as workers and especially farm workers who play a very great part in the process of development.

22) To be especially lamented is the condition of so many

millions of refugees, and of every group or people suffering persecution—sometimes in institutionalized form—for racial or ethnic origin or on tribal grounds. This persecution on tribal grounds can at times take on the characteristics of genocide.

23)   In many areas justice is seriously injured with regard to people who are suffering persecution for their faith, or who are in many ways being ceaselessly subjected by political parties and public authorities to an action of oppressive atheization, or who are deprived of religious liberty either by being kept from honouring God in public worship, or by being prevented from publicly teaching and spreading their faith, or by being prohibited from conducting their temporal affairs according to the principles of their religion.

24)   Justice is also being violated by forms of oppression, both old and new, springing from restriction of the rights of individuals. This is occurring both in the form of repression by the political power and of violence on the part of private reaction, and can reach the extreme of affecting the basic conditions of personal integrity. There are well known cases of torture, especially of political prisoners, who besides are frequently denied due process or who are subjected to arbitrary procedures in their trial. Nor can we pass over the prisoners of war who even after the Geneva Convention are being treated in an inhuman manner.

25)   The fight against legalized abortion and against the imposition of contraceptives and the pressures exerted against war are significant forms of defending the right to life.

26)   Furthermore, contemporary consciousness demands truth in the communications systems, including the right to the image offered by the media and the opportunity to correct its manipulation. It must be stressed that the right, especially that of children and the young, to education and to morally correct conditions of life and communications media is once again being threatened in our days. The

activity of families in social life is rarely and insufficiently recognized by State institutions. Nor should we forget the growing number of persons who are often abandoned by their families and by the community: the old, orphans, the sick and all kinds of people who are rejected.

THE NEED FOR DIALOGUE

27)   To obtain true unity of purpose, as is demanded by the world society of men, a mediatory role is essential to overcome day by day the opposition, obstacles and ingrained privileges which are to be met with in the advance towards a more human society.

28)   But effective mediation involves the creation of a lasting atmosphere of dialogue. A contribution to the progressive realization of this can be made by men unhampered by geo-political, ideological or socioeconomic conditions or by the generation gap. To restore the meaning of life by adherence to authentic values, the participation and witness of the rising generation of youth is as necessary as communication among peoples.

II

THE GOSPEL MESSAGE AND THE MISSION OF THE CHURCH

29)   In the face of the present-day situation of the world, marked as it is by the grave sin of injustice, we recognize both our responsibility and our inability to overcome it by our own strength. Such a situation urges us to listen with a humble and open heart to the word of God, as he shows us new paths towards action in the cause of justice in the world.

THE SAVING JUSTICE OF GOD THROUGH CHRIST

30)   In the Old Testament God reveals himself to us as the liberator of the oppressed and the defender of the poor, demanding from man faith in him and justice towards man's neighbour. It is only in the observance of the duties of justice that God is truly recognized as the liberator of the oppressed.

31)   By his action and teaching Christ united in an indivisible way the relationship of man to God and the relationship of man to other men. Christ lived his life in the world as a total giving of himself to God for the salvation and liberation of men. In his preaching he proclaimed the fatherhood of God towards all men and the intervention of God's justice on behalf of the needy and the oppressed (*Lk* 6:21-23). In this way he identified himself with his "least brethren," as he stated: "As you did it to one of the least of these my brethren, you did it to me" (*Mt* 25:40).

32)   From the beginning the Church has lived and understood the Death and Resurrection of Christ as a call by God to conversion in the faith of Christ and in fraternal love, perfected in mutual help even to the point of a voluntary sharing of material goods.

33)   Faith in Christ, the Son of God and the Redeemer, and love of neighbour constitute a fundamental theme of the writers of the New Testament. According to St. Paul, the whole of the Christian life is summed up in faith effecting that love and service of neighbour which involve the fulfilment of the demands of justice. The Christian lives under the interior law of liberty, which is a permanent call to man to turn away from self-sufficiency to confidence in God and from concern for self to a sincere love of neighbour. Thus takes place his genuine liberation and the gift of himself for the freedom of others.

34)   According to the Christian message, therefore, man's relationship to his neighbour is bound up with his rela-

tionship to God; his response to the love of God, saving us through Christ, is shown to be effective in his love and service of men. Christian love of neighbour and justice cannot be separated. For love implies an absolute demand for justice, namely a recognition of the dignity and rights of one's neighbour. Justice attains its inner fullness only in love. Because every man is truly a visible image of the invisible God and a brother of Christ, the Christian finds in every man God himself and God's absolute demand for justice and love.

35) The present situation of the world, seen in the light of faith, calls us back to the very essence of the Christian message, creating in us a deep awareness of its true meaning and of its urgent demands. The mission of preaching the Gospel dictates at the present time that we should dedicate ourselves to the liberation of man even in his present existence in this world. For unless the Christian message of love and justice shows its effectiveness through action in the cause of justice in the world, it will only with difficulty gain credibility with the men of our times.

THE MISSION OF THE CHURCH, HIERARCHY AND CHRISTIANS

36) The Church has received from Christ the mission of preaching the Gospel message, which contains a call to man to turn away from sin to the love of the Father, universal brotherhood and a consequent demand for justice in the world. This is the reason why the Church has the right, indeed the duty, to proclaim justice on the social, national and international level, and to denounce instances of injustice, when the fundamental rights of man and his very salvation demand it. The Church, ideed, is not alone responsible for justice in the world; however, she has a proper and specific responsibility which is identified with her mission of giving witness before the world of the need for love and justice contained in the Gospel message, a witness

to be carried out in Church institutions themselves and in
the lives of Christians.

37) Of itself it does not belong to the Church, insofar
as she is a religious and hierarchical community, to offer
concrete solutions in the social, economic and political
spheres for justice in the world. Her mission involves defending and promoting the dignity and fundamental rights
of the human person.

38) The members of the Church, as members of society,
have the same right and duty to promote the common good
as do other citizens. Christians ought to fulfil their temporal obligations with fidelity and competence. They should
act as a leaven in the world, in their family, professional,
social, cultural and political life. They must accept their
responsibilities in this entire area under the influence of
the Gospel and the teaching of the Church. In this way
they testify to the power of the Holy Spirit through their
action in the service of men in those things which are de-
cisive for the existence and the future of humanity. While
in such activities they generally act on their own initiative
without involving the responsibility of the ecclesiastical
hierarchy, in a sense they do involve the responsibility of
the Church whose members they are.

III

THE PRACTICE OF JUSTICE

THE CHURCH'S WITNESS

39) Many Christians are drawn to give authentic witness
on behalf of justice by various modes of action for justice,
action inspired by love in accordance with the grace which
they have received from God. For some of them, this action
finds its place in the sphere of social and political conflicts

in which Christians bear witness to the Gospel by pointing out that in history there are sources of progress other than conflict, namely love and right. This priority of love in history draws other Christians to prefer the way of non-violent action and work in the area of public opinion.

40) While the Church is bound to give witness to justice, she recognizes that anyone who ventures to speak to people about justice must first be just in their eyes. Hence we must undertake an examination of the modes of acting and of the possessions and life style found within the Church herself.

41) Within the Church rights must be preserved. No one should be deprived of his ordinary rights because he is associated with the Church in one way or another. Those who serve the Church by their labour, including priests and religious, should receive a sufficient livelihood and enjoy that social security which is customary in their region. Lay people should be given fair wages and a system for promotion. We reiterate the recommendations that lay people should exercise more important functions with regard to Church property and should share in its administration.

42) We also urge that women should have their own share of responsibility and participation in the community life of society and likewise of the Church.

43) We propose that this matter be subjceted to a serious study employing adequate means: for instance, a mixed commission of men and women, religious and lay people, of differing situations and competence.

44) The Church recognizes everyone's right to suitable freedom of expression and thought. This includes the right of everyone to be heard in a spirit of dialogue which preserves a legitimate diversity within the Church.

45) The form of judicial procedure should give the accused the right to know his accusers and also the right to a proper defence. To be complete, justice should include

speed in its procedure. This is especially necessary in marriage cases.

46)   Finally, the members of the Church should have some share in the drawing up of decisions, in accordance with the rules given by the Second Vatican Ecumenical Council and the Holy See, for instance with regard to the setting up of councils at all levels.

47)   In regard to temporal possessions, whatever be their use, it must never happen that the evangelical witness which the Church is required to give becomes ambiguous. The preservation of certain positions of privilege must constantly be submitted to the test of this principle. Although in general it is difficult to draw a line between what is needed for right use and what is demanded by prophetic witness, we must certainly keep firmly to this principle: our faith demands of us a certain sparingness in use, and the Church is obliged to live and administer its own goods in such a way that the Gospel is proclaimed to the poor. If instead the Church appears to be among the rich and the powerful of this world its credibility is diminished.

48)   Our examination of conscience now comes to the life style of all: bishops, priests, religious and lay people. In the case of needy peoples it must be asked whether belonging to the Church places people on a rich island within an ambient of poverty. In societies enjoying a higher level of consumer spending, it must be asked whether our life style exemplifies that sparingness with regard to consumption which we preach to others as necessary in order that so many millions of hungry people throughout the world may be fed.

EDUCATING TO JUSTICE

49)   Christians' specific contribution to justice is the day-to-day life of the individual believer acting like the leaven of the Gospel in his family, his school, his work and his

social and civic life. Included with this are the perspectives
and meaning which the faithful can give to human effort.
Accordingly, educational method must be such as to teach
men to live their lives in its entire reality and in accord
with the evangelical principles of personal and social morality which are expressed in the vital Christian witness of
one's life.

50)   The obstacles to the progress which we wish for ourselves and for mankind are obvious. The method of education very frequently still in use today encourages narrow
individualism. Part of the human family lives immersed in
a mentality which exalts possessions. The school and the
communications media, which are often obstructed by the
established order, allow the formation only of the man desired by that order, that is to say, man in its image, not a
new man but a copy of man as he is.

51)   But education demands a renewal of heart, a renewal
based on the recognition of sin in its individual and social
manifestations. It will also inculcate a truly and entirely
human way of life in justice, love and simplicity. It will
likewise awaken a critical sense, which will lead us to reflect on the society in which we live and on its values; it
will make men ready to renounce these values when they
cease to promote justice for all men. In the developing
countries, the principal aim of this education for justice
consists in an attempt to awaken consciences to a knowledge
of the concrete situation and in a call to secure a total im-
provement; by these means the transformaion of the world
has already begun.

52)   Since this education makes men decidedly more human, it will help them to be no longer the object of manipulation by communications media or political forces. It will
instead enable them to take in hand their own destinies
and bring about communities which are truly human.

Accordingly, this education is deservedly called a continuing education, for it concerns every person and every

age. It is also a practical education: it comes through action, participation and vital contact with the reality of injustice. 54) Education for justice is imparted first in the family. We are well aware that not only Church institutions but also other schools, trade unions and political parties are collaborating in this.

The content of this education necessarily involves respect for the person and for his dignity. Since it is world justice which is in question here, the unity of the human family within which, according to God's plan, a human being is born must first of all be seriously affirmed. Christians find a sign of this solidarity in the fact that all human beings are destined to become in Christ sharers in the divine nature. 56) The basic principles whereby the influence of the Gospel has made itself felt in contemporary social life are to be found in the body of teaching set out in a gradual and timely way from the encyclical *Rerum Novarum* to the letter *Octogesima Adveniens*. As never before, the Church has, through the Second Vatican Council's constitution *Gaudium et Spes,* better understood the situation in the modern world, in which the Christian works out his salvation by deeds of justice. *Pacem in Terris* gave us an authentic charter of human rights. In *Mater et Magistra* international justice begins to take first place; it finds more elaborate expression in *Populorum Progressio,* in the form of a true and suitable treatise on the right to development, and in *Octogesima Adveniens* is found a summary of guidelines for political action.

57) Like the apostle Paul, we insist, welcome or unwelcome, that the word of God should be present in the centre of human situations. Our interventions are intended to be an expression of that faith which is today binding on our lives and on the lives of the faithful. We all desire that these interventions should always be in conformity with circumstances of place and time. Our mission demands that we should courageously denounce injustice, with chari-

ty, prudence and firmness, in sincere dialogue with all parties concerned. We know that our denunciations can secure assent to the extent that they are an expression of our lives and are manifested in continuous action.

58) The liturgy, which we preside over and which is the heart of the Church's life, can greatly serve education for justice. For it is a thanksgiving to the Father in Christ, which through its communitarian form places before our eyes the bonds of our brotherhood and again and again reminds us of the Church's mission. The liturgy of the word, catechesis and the celebration of the sacraments have the power to help us to discover the teaching of the prophets, the Lord and the Apostles on the subject of justice. The preparation for baptism is the beginning of the formation of the Christian conscience. The practice of penance should emphasize the social dimension of sin and of the sacrament. Finally, the Eucharist forms the community and places it at the service of men.

COOPERATION BETWEEN LOCAL CHURCHES

59) That the Church may really be the sign of that solidarity which the family of nations desires, it should show in its own life greater cooperation between the Churches of rich and poor regions through spiritual communion and division of human and material resources. The present generous arrangements for assistance between Churches could be made more effective by real coordination (Sacred Congregation for the Evangelization of Peoples and the Pontifical Council "Cor Unum"), through their overall view in regard to the common administration of the gifts of God, and through fraternal solidarity, which would always encourage autonomy and responsibility on the part of the beneficiaries in the determination of criteria and the choice of concrete programmes and their realization.

60) This planning must in no way be restricted to eco-

nomic programmes; it should instead stimulate activities capable of developing that human and spiritual formation which will serve as the leaven needed for the integral development of the human being.

ECUMENICAL COLLABORATION

61)   Well aware of what has already been done in this field, together with the Second Vatican Ecumenical Council we very highly commend cooperation with our separated Christian brethren for the promotion of justice in the world, for bringing about development of peoples and for establishing peace. This cooperation concerns first and foremost activities for securing human dignity and man's fundamental rights, especially the right to religious liberty. This is the source of our common efforts against discrimination on the grounds of differences of religion, race and colour, culture and the like. Collaboration extends also to the study of the teaching of the Gospel insofar as it is the source of inspiration for all Christian activity. Let the Secretariat for Promoting Christian Unity and the Pontifical Commission for Justice and Peace devote themselves in common counsel to developing effectively this ecumenical collaboration.

62)   In the same spirit we likewise commend collaboration with all believers in God in the fostering of social justice, peace and freedom; indeed we commend collaboration also with those who, even though they do not recognize the Author of the world, nevertheless, in their esteem for human values, seek justice sincerely and by honorable means.

INTERNATIONAL ACTION

63)   Since the Synod is of a universal character, it is dealing with those questions of justice which directly concern the entire human family. Hence, recognizing the importance of international cooperation for social and economic development, we praise above all else the inestimable work which

has been done among the poorer peoples by the local Churches, the missionaries and the organizations supporting them; and we intend to foster those initiatives and institutions which are working for peace, international justice and the development of man. We therefore urge Catholics to consider well the following propositions:

64) Let recognition be given to the fact that international order is rooted in the inalienable rights and dignity of the human being. Let the United Nations Declaration of Human Rights be ratified by all Governments who have not yet adhered to it, and let it be fully observed by all.

65) Let the United Nations—which because of its unique purpose should promote participation by all nations—and international organizations be supported insofar as they are the beginning of a system capable of restraining the armaments race, discouraging trade in weapons, securing disarmament and settling conflicts by peaceful methods of legal action, arbitration and international police action. It is absolutely necessary that international conflicts should not be settled by war, but that other methods better befitting human nature should be found. Let a strategy of nonviolence be fostered also, and let conscientious objection be recognized and regulated by law in each nation.

66) Let the aims of the Second Development Decade be fostered. These include the transfer of a precise percentage of the annual income of the richer countries to the developing nations, fairer prices for raw materials, the opening of the markets of the richer nations and, in some fields, preferential treatment for exports of manufactured goods from the developing nations. These aims represent first guidelines for a graduated taxation of income as well as for an economic and social plan for the entire world. We grieve whenever richer nations turn their backs on this ideal goal of worldwide sharing and responsibility. We hope that no such weakening of international solidarity will take away their force from the trade discussions being prepared by the

United Nations Conference on Trade and Development (UNCTAD).

67)   The concentration of power which consists in almost total domination of economics, research, investment, freight charges, sea transport and securities should be progressively balanced by institutional arrangements for strengthening power and opportunities with regard to responsible decision by the developing nations and by full and equal participation in international organizations concerned with development. Their recent *de facto* exclusion from discussions on world trade and also the monetary arrangements which vitally affect their destiny are an example of lack of power which is inadmissible in a just and responsible world order.

68)   Although we recognize that international agencies can be perfected and strengthened, as can any human instrument, we stress also the importance of the specialized agencies of the United Nations, in particular those directly concerned with the immediate and more acute questions of world poverty in the field of agrarian reform and agricultural development, health, education, employment, housing, and rapidly increasing urbanization. We feel we must point out in a special way the need for some fund to provide sufficient food and protein for the real mental and physical development of children. In the face of the population explosion we repeat the words by which Pope Paul VI defined the functions of public authority in his encyclical *Populorum Progressio*: "There is no doubt that public authorities can intervene, within the limit of their competence, by favouring the availability of appropriate information and by adopting suitable measures, provided that these be in conformity with the moral law and that they absolutely respect the rightful freedom of married couples" (37; *A.A.S.* 59, 1967, p. 276).

69)   Let governments continue with their individual contributions to a development fund, but let them also look for a way whereby most of their endeavours may follow multilateral channels, fully preserving the responsibility of the

developing nations, which must be associated in decision-making concerning priorities and investments.

70) We consider that we must also stress the new world-wide preoccupation which will be dealt with for the first time in the conference on the human environment to be held in Stockholm in June 1972. It is impossible to see what right the richer nations have to keep up their claim to increase their own material demands, if the consequence is either that others remain in misery or that the danger of destroying the very physical foundations of life on earth is precipitated. Those who are already rich are bound to accept a less material way of life, with less waste, in order to avoid the destruction of the heritage which they are obliged by absolute justice to share with all other members of the human race.

71) In order that the right to development may be fulfilled by action:

a) people should not be hindered from attaining development in accordance with their own culture;

b) through mutual cooperation, all peoples should be able to become the principal architects of their own economic and social development;

c) every people, as active and responsible members of human society, should be able to cooperate for the attainment of the common good on an equal footing with other peoples.

RECOMMENDATIONS OF THE SYNOD

72) The examination of conscience which we have made together, regarding the Church's involvement in action for justice, will remain ineffective if it is not given flesh in the life of our local Churches at all their levels. We also ask the episcopal conferences to continue to pursue the perspectives which we have had in view during the days of

this meeting and to put our recommendations into practice, for instance by setting up centres of social and theological research.

73)   We also ask that there be recommended to the Pontifical Commission for Justice and Peace, the Council of the Secretariat of the Synod and to competent authorities, the description, consideration and deeper study of the wishes and desires of our assembly, and that these bodies should bring to a successful conclusion what we have begun.

IV

A WORD OF HOPE

74)   The power of the Spirit, who raised Christ from the dead, is continuously at work in the world. Through the generous sons and daughters of the Church likewise, the People of God is present in the midst of the poor and of those who suffer oppression and persecution; it lives in its own flesh and its own heart the Passion of Christ and bears witness to his resurrection.

75)   The entire creation has been groaning till now in an act of giving birth, as it waits for the glory of the children of God to be revealed (cf. *Rom* 8:22). Let Christians therefore be convinced that they will yet find the fruits of their own nature and effort cleansed of all impurities in the new earth which God is now preparing for them, and in which there will be the kingdom of justice and love, a kingdom which will be fully perfected when the Lord will come himself.

76)   Hope in the coming kingdom is already beginning to take root in the hearts of men. The radical transforma-

tion of the world in the Paschal Mystery of the Lord gives full meaning to the efforts of men, and in particular of the young, to lessen injustice, violence and hatred and to advance all together in justice, freedom, brotherhood and love.

77) At the same time as it proclaims the Gospel of the Lord, its Redeemer and Saviour, the Church calls on all, especially the poor, the oppressed and the afflicted, to co-operate with God to bring about liberation from every sin and to build a world which will reach the fullness of crea-tion only when it becomes the work of man for man.

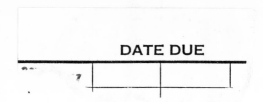

DATE DUE